The New Knowledge Economy of Taiwan

The New Knowledge Economy of Taiwan

Edited by

Tain-Jy Chen

Chung-Hua Institution for Economic Research

Joseph S. Lee

School of Management, National Central University

Edward Elgar

Cheltenham, UK • Northampton, MA, USA

Published by
Edward Elgar Publishing Limited
Glensanda House
Montpellier Parade
Cheltenham
Glos GL50 1UA
UK

Edward Elgar Publishing, Inc.
136 West Street
Suite 202
Northampton
Massachusetts 01060
USA

A catalogue record for this book
is available from the British Library

ISBN 1 84376 763 5

Printed and bound in Great Britain by MPG Books Ltd, Bodmin, Cornwall

Contents

List of Figures

List of Tables

Contributors

Hsi-Huang Chen received his Ph.D. in Agricultural Economics from the University of Georgia in 1974. Upon graduation, he returned to Taiwan to serve in the field of agricultural economics, and in 1982, accepted a professorship at the National Taiwan University. In 1991, in recognition of his contributions on an international scale, he was appointed by the Executive Committee to serve a three-year term on the 30-member board of the International Association of Agricultural Economics.

Shin-Horng Chen received his Ph.D. in economic geography at the Centre for Urban and Regional Development Studies at the University of Newcastle upon Tyne in the UK, and subsequently joined the Chung-Hua Institution for Economic Research (CIER) as an associate research fellow in 1995. He is currently a Research Fellow at the CIER and the Director of the Institution's International Division. His research deals with economic and policy issues on information and communications technologies, science and technology and international economics. His major published works, in English, can be found in the journals, *Research Policy*, *Industry and Innovation* and the *Taiwan Economic Forum*; he has also made a number of contributions to published books.

Tain-Jy Chen is President of the CIER and Professor of Economics at the National Taiwan University. His research interests lie in international trade and economic development, an area in which his works have been published extensively in academic journals. He has also written and edited several books, including *Taiwanese Firms in Southeast Asia: Networking Across Borders*, published by Edward Elgar.

P.K. (Pin-Kung) Chiang is the Vice President of the Legislative Yuan, the Vice Chairman of the Kuomintang (the Nationalist Party) and the Vice Chairman of the National Policy Foundation. He was formerly Chairman of the Council for Economic Planning and Development of the Executive Yuan and the Minister of Economic Affairs (MOEA), both of which are cabinet posts, and has served as the Director-General of the Board of Foreign Trade, the Secretary-General of the China External Trade Development Council, Economic Counselor at the Republic of China Representative Office in South Africa, and Assistant Economic Attaché at the Republic of China Representative Office in Japan. He has produced numerous works in Chinese, English and Japanese on a variety of economic development affairs in Taiwan, including 'A Study of Taiwan's Land Tax Reform' in Japanese, and his biographies, 'P.K. Chiang's Experience of Taiwanese Economic Development', in Chinese, and 'P.K. Chiang's Perception of Japan and Taiwan', in Japanese.

Yun-Peng Chu is a Professor of Economics and the acting Director of the Research Centre on Taiwanese Economic Development at the National Central University. He is also the President of the Asia-Pacific New Economy Association in Taiwan, and is a former Commissioner of the Fair Trade Commission within the Executive Yuan, Director of the Institute for Social Sciences and Philosophy at the Academia Sinica and President of the Jin-Wen Institute of Technology. He has published many articles in various international journals, including the *American Economic Review*, and is editor of many books. His main areas of interest include economic development, income distribution and technological policy.

Chin Chung is the Chairperson of Pacific SOGO Department Stores in Taiwan. She is a former Research Fellow at the CIER, and a Ph.D. candidate in economics at Cornell University. She is also a former Minister within the Executive Yuan and former Director-General of the Government Information Office. Her research interests lie in international economics, finance, technology policy and Chinese economics.

Charles H.C. Kao is the Founder and Chief Executive Officer of Global Views Monthly and the Commonwealth Publishing Company. He is also Chairman of the Board of the Institute of Knowledge Economy and Management. He lectured at the University of Wisconsin at River Falls from 1964 to 1998, and from 1990 onwards, has been an economic adviser to the Executive Yuan. He has published more than ten books on economic policies and issues, and his book, *Taiwan's Investment Experience in Mainland China* (co-authored with Dr. Chu-Chia Steve Lin), a first-hand report, received an award from the *Financial Times* along with the Global Business Book Award (1996) from Booz-Allen and Hamilton.

Chu-Chia Steve Lin is a Professor and former Chairperson of the Department of Economics at National Chengchi University. He was awarded his Ph.D. degree by the Department of Economics at UCLA in 1988 and is a former visiting scholar at the Fairbank Centre for East Asian Research at Harvard University. His major research fields are applied microeconomics, housing economics and economic relations across the Taiwan Strait. He has produced numerous works for international journals and has jointly published several books, including *An Empirical Study of Taiwanese Investment in Mainland China* (with Charles Kao, et al), *Taiwan's Investment Experience in Mainland China* (with Charles Kao, et al), *Managerial Economics* (with I. Png), and *The World of Economics* (with Charles Kao).

Chi Schive is President of the Taiwan Academy of Banking and Finance. He was the Vice Chairman of the Council for Economic Planning and Development within the Executive Yuan and a former Professor of Economics at the National Taiwan University. He is also the former Dean and Director of Management at the Graduate Institute of Industrial Economics at the National Central University, Chairperson of the Department of Economics at the National Taiwan University, and Visiting Professor at the Free University of Berlin. He has received many Research Awards from the National Science Council and produced numerous works, in both Chinese and English, on small and medium enterprises (SMEs), foreign investment and economic development in Taiwan.

Pwu Tsai is an Associate Professor and Chair of the Department of Business Administration at the National Hu-Wei Institute of Technology. He is a Former Vice-director of the Centre for Knowledge-based Economy and Intellectual Property Studies at the CIER. His areas of research cover R&D management, technical value evaluation and aerospace industrial development.

Jiann-Chyuan Wang is a Research Fellow at the CIER, where he also serves as the Director of the Third Division, and an Adjunct Professor in the Department of Business Administration at the National Taiwan Technology University. He is the author of several dozen works in both Chinese and English.

Sze-Yueh Wang is an Associate Research Fellow at the CIER. He graduated from Soochow University in Taiwan with a Masters degree in economics and his main research interests lie in international trade and Chinese economics.

Ho-Mou Wu is a Professor at the Department of International Business and the Department of Economics at the National Taiwan University, and a former Vice President of the CIER. He obtained his Ph.D degree from Stanford University where he subsequently taught as a Visiting Professor. He was the recipient of an Outstanding Scholarship Award from the Foundation for the Advancement of Outstanding Scholarship (FAOS), a Research Award from the National Science Council (NSC), and a Research Excellence Award from the Ministry of Education in Taiwan.

Tzong-Shian Yu is currently the Director of the Chinese Institute of Economics and Business in Taipei, and Academician at Academia Sinica. He received his Ph.D. degree in economics from Indiana University in the US and has previously served as the President of the CIER, Professor of Economics at the National Taiwan University and Director of the Institute of Economics at Academia Sinica. At the last count, he had some seventeen published books to his name and 170 scientific papers (in both Chinese and English) published in a wide range of international journals. His main areas of research are economic development, economic forecasting and foreign trade.

Preface

As well as heralding the beginning of a new millennium, the year 2000 also came as something of a watershed for the previously booming Taiwanese economy. For the first time in the island's history, a new president had been elected from the opposition party, whilst in the subsequent year, Taiwan's economy recorded negative GDP growth, again for the first time in its history. Although some took the opportunity to blame the newly elected and obviously inexperienced government for the demise of the economy, the new government itself pointed to the fallout of the global recession as the cause of Taiwan's economic downturn. Three years on, however, it has become clear that at the turn of the century, Taiwan's economy was in fact entering a new era of development, something which had previously been referred to in the economic literature as the era of the 'knowledge-based economy'. Irrespective of where the blame may lie for Taiwan's economic difficulties, the key point had nevertheless been missed; the fundamental nature of Taiwan's economy had now changed and the performance of the economy must now be judged by different standards. As such, a new policy regime was called for.

Along with other high-performing East Asian economies, Taiwan had seen considerable success in its drive towards industrialisation during the second half of the twentieth century, fuelled mainly by capital accumulation. Nevertheless, around the 1990s, many of the Asian economies found that they had reached a plateau, albeit at very different stages of development. The onset of the Southeast Asian financial crisis in 1997 signalled an end to economic growth driven purely by capital, and also to the dysfunctional economic policies that these economies had somehow managed to manipulate, and quite skillfully enforce, for so long.

Although Taiwan had managed to successfully steer its way through the worst of the ravages of the Southeast Asian financial crisis, the 1990s also brought a virtual landslide of economic reality to the island. Labour productivity growth had begun to slow down and, despite all manner of government incentives to rejuvenate the economy, the rate of capital accumulation still went into decline. Furthermore, in contrast to the relatively low level of capital investment that was now being witnessed in the domestic market, Taiwanese firms were investing heavily in overseas locations, particularly in mainland China. Indeed, the 1990s saw Taiwan developing as a major source of capital imports for both mainland China and many of the neighbouring Southeast Asian economies. Despite all of this, Taiwan was still able to maintain robust economic growth throughout the 1990s (at an average annual GDP growth rate of 6.42 per cent), as well as a low unemployment rate, due largely to its extensive transformation from a manufacturing-based to a service-oriented economy.

The process of industrialisation had essentially come to a halt at the beginning of the 1990s, whilst the service sector, which had long been suppressed as a result of policy distortions which strongly favoured the manufacturing sector, was eventually provided with an opportunity to compete for production resources on a level playing-field. Newly emerging service activities provided numerous job opportunities, which more than offset the loss of jobs from the rapidly migrating manufacturing production lines, but as growth in the service sector returned to normal, many economic problems emerged that exemplified this post-industrialisation period, such as a low economic growth rate and a high unemployment rate.

A knowledge-based economy differs from a material- or capital-based economy in that it recognises knowledge as the fundamental core of national competitiveness, as well as the driving force for long-term economic growth. Unlike the 'old' economy, an economy in which capital was the key to industrialisation and capital accumulation had always been seen as the driving force behind economic expansion, in this 'new' economy, it is clear that knowledge is now seen as the key to competition, with innovation being the springboard for economic growth.

Taiwan's attempts, at the start of the new millennium, to pursue its successful transition from a material-based or capital-based economy to a knowledge-based economy provide the purpose of bringing together this book. Although Taiwan is still at the initial stage of this transition, and there is no telling whether or not the transition will in fact be successful, the experience which Taiwan has so far gained from the process has already provided useful lessons for commentators on economic development. It is common knowledge that it took around a half a century for Taiwan to transform itself from an agricultural economy into an industrialised one; what we may yet come to realise is that it may take even longer to achieve the transition to a knowledge-based economy. If the Taiwanese experience during its process of industrialisation was interesting and revealing, as most scholars seem to agree, then the new challenges in the move towards a knowledge-based economy would appear to be at least equally exciting.

Tain-Jy Chen opens the discussion in Chapter 1 with an examination of the nature of the challenges presented by the knowledge-based economy, describing first of all the changing nature of the global production network and the market structure under a knowledge-based economy, and explaining the reasons why Taiwan's current industrial apparatus may have become obsolete in this 'brave new world'. He points to a number of concrete and daunting challenges that Taiwan now faces, including its outmoded service sector, the inability of its business firms to pursue global production and services, and the lack of capacity to create knowledge and to innovate. Some of these challenges are further addressed in the subsequent chapters.

In Chapter 2, Professor Tzong-Shian Yu takes a broader perspective of the intrinsic constraints on Taiwan in the twenty-first century, pointing out the changing demography in Taiwan, and in particular, the declining fertility rate and ageing population, and their potential impacts on Taiwan's future productivity growth. He also brings our attention to the irreversible trend towards globalisation and the continuing and worrying degradation of the global environment, as well as their implications for Taiwan's policy options.

The role of the state in a knowledge-based economy provides the subject for Dr P.K. Chiang's contribution to this book at Chapter 3. Throughout its history of industrialisation, the role of the state in Taiwan has been widely discussed and largely admired, but the question now arises as to whether the same role can be sustained in a knowledge-based economy. The answer appears to be a resounding 'no', since facilitating capital accumulation for industrialisation is far different from promoting innovation in a knowledge-based economy. In concluding, Dr Chiang suggests that the reengineering of the government in Taiwan will be necessary if the island is to succeed in this new competitive 'game'. The scope of such government reengineering would necessarily include the reorganisation of the bureaucracy, the construction of a set of core competences for the government, and a strong emphasis on human resource development, as opposed to the previous emphasis on physical capital deepening, the refreshing of fiscal discipline in government budgets, the leveraging of social and market resources to offset the weaknesses of the public sector, and so on.

In Chapter 4, Hsi-Huang Chen examines how the agricultural structure of Taiwan can be transformed from its current emphasis on land-based or labour-based production to knowledge-based production. He proposes a number of policy recommendations which include forming strategic alliances in agricultural production, leveraging agricultural production on the industrial strength of Taiwan, combining agriculture with recreation, creating rural commune zones, rebuilding the agricultural environment in order to strengthen biodiversity, and so on. In short, he presents a new vision for Taiwan's declining agricultural sector, a sector whose share of the island's GDP has sunk below 2 per cent in recent years.

The contribution by Yun-Peng Chu, in Chapter 5, presents a number of cases in which Taiwanese manufacturing firms, primarily labour-intensive firms, have successfully transformed themselves through innovation. It is noticeable that, in most cases, innovation did not come in the form of new products, but rather in the form of new services, new business models, or cross-industry alliances. It also becomes apparent from the case study that by anchoring themselves to new technologies, there is ample room for Taiwan's small manufacturing firms to succeed in the knowledge-based economy.

In Chapter 6, Professor Ho-Mou Wu provides a comprehensive examination of the process of globalisation since 1990 in Taiwan's financial markets, dealing with the issues of both institutional development and market integration. He places significant emphasis on the market interactions between Taiwan and the rest of the world subsequent to the gradual opening up of Taiwan's capital account during the 1990s, and points out that the impacts of globalisation have been responsible for complicating the process of liberalisation, an area in which the banking sector and securities markets are highlighted.

Chapter 7 sees Chi Schive and Tain-Jy Chen coming together to provide a balanced discussion on the process of globalisation of Taiwanese business firms. Although small by international standards, these firms are, nonetheless, very active with regard to foreign direct investment (FDI). The authors take a close look at the constraints that Taiwanese firms face in their pursuit of FDI, as well as the measures that they have adopted to overcome such constraints. More importantly, they describe how FDI has changed the role of these firms in the global production network and how it has enabled them to provide new services to their global partners.

The development of the knowledge-based service industries in Taiwan is covered in Chapter 8 by Jiann-Chyuan Wang. Although Taiwan's service sector is generally regarded as being outmoded, the island has nevertheless witnessed the emergence of certain knowledge-intensive services that appear to be extremely competitive on a global scale, particularly those servicing the manufacturing industry, such as IC design companies, logistics management companies, telecommunications companies, R&D contractors, and the like. The chapter concludes by providing recommendations on the policy environment and infrastructure that will be required if further growth in these industries is to be assured.

A joint effort by Chin Chung, Pwu Tsai and Sze-Yueh Wang provides an examination, in Chapter 9, of US semiconductor patents granted to Taiwan, Korea and Japan, pointing to the extraordinary performance of Taiwanese firms and government agencies in obtaining such patents despite the low level of R&D expenditure in Taiwan. It is noted, however, that the patents granted to Taiwan are heavily concentrated in the semiconductor sector and are mostly process-related innovations rather than product innovations. The comparison provided between Taiwan, Japan and Korea reveals the strengths and weaknesses of Taiwan's R&D capabilities.

In Chapter 10, Shin-Horng Chen explores the changes to Taiwan's information industry that are likely to be brought about by the shift towards a knowledge-based economy, particularly in the personal computer and IC sectors. Particular attention is paid to the changing structures of the global production and R&D networks, and the way that Taiwanese IT firms have attempted to cope with the new situation. Interesting discussions are pursued on R&D activities, particularly with regard to the division of labour between Taiwan and mainland China under the influence of multinational companies acting as a flagship in the global production network.

Charles H.C. Kao and Chu-Chia Steve Lin bring this book to its conclusion in Chapter 11, looking at the changing economic relationship between Taiwan and mainland China, with both cross-strait trade and investment relations being examined under the framework of the international division of labour. In light of the accession of both Taiwan and mainland China into the World Trade Organisation (WTO) in 2002, the authors also pursue a discussion on the potential impacts of WTO membership on future cross-strait relationships. They conclude that although both the Taiwanese and Chinese governments are very proactive in directing the evolution of the bilateral trading relationships, it appears that very few of the issues involved will actually come under the direct control of either government.

We would like to express our sincere gratitude to the Chiang Ching-Kuo Foundation for International Scholarly Exchange for providing the funding for this research project. We also offer our very sincere appreciation to Mr George Okrasa for his excellent editorial assistance and tireless efforts in compiling this work to a camera-ready state, whilst thanks also go to our research assistants, Mr Yi-Hui Lin and Miss Chia-Ling Hsu, who have also worked tirelessly to administer the compilation of this book.

Tain-Jy Chen
President
Chung-Hua Institution for Economic Research

Joseph S. Lee
Dean of the School of Management,
National Central University   December 2003

1 The Challenges of the Knowledge-based Economy

Tain-Jy Chen

INTRODUCTION

Throughout the latter half of the twentieth century, Taiwan's economy had demonstrated a level of performance that was nothing short of phenomenal. Between 1960 and 1990, the island experienced GDP expansion at an annual average growth rate of 9.15 per cent, and although a significant slowdown became apparent in the subsequent decade, from 1990 to 2000, the annual growth rate nevertheless remained robust at around 6.42 per cent. In 2001, however, the Taiwanese economy experienced its first-ever period of negative growth, with the unemployment rate simultaneously hitting a high of 5.0 per cent, and this quickly led to a number of suggestions that having steadfastly endured the Asian financial crisis of 1997-1998, Taiwan had nevertheless finally reached its peak, and was now at the start of a new era of slow growth accompanied by high unemployment.

Such a gloomy picture had in fact been painted for the high-flying economies of the East Asian Tigers – Taiwan, Korea, Hong Kong and Singapore – as early as 1994, when Krugman argued that the protracted period of the East Asian miracles, which had been built upon the rapid accumulation of capital, was about to come to an end (Krugman, 1994). Krugman predicted that once global demand was found to be incapable of keeping pace with ever-increasing production capacity levels, diminishing returns would be inevitable. Although Taiwan did manage to survive the Asian financial crisis virtually unscathed (Chen, 2001), the eventual outcome nevertheless seems to attest to the Krugman premonition, as the reality of slowing economic growth is as conspicuous in Taiwan today as in any of the other East Asian economies. However, what was particularly evident in the 1990s was the deceleration in capital formation within the manufacturing sector, which, for the previous forty years, had proven to be the driving force behind Taiwan's economic expansion.

Manifested in the 1990s in the US, the 'new economy' now seems to provide fresh inspiration for Taiwan, with its characteristic combination of high growth rates, and low inflation and unemployment rates. This is a new era which stands in stark contrast to the 'old economy' in which inflation and unemployment were treated as trade-offs. Since knowledge, substituting for the role of capital or labour, is considered to be the core of the new economy, it is also widely referred to as the 'knowledge-based economy' (KBE), a new economic era in which economic growth is driven by knowledge creation, accumulation and extension, issues that are not subject to diminishing returns. Such ideas have clearly been of significant interest to Taiwanese policymakers who had been desperately searching for new recipes to rejuvenate the island's slowing economic engine, and since the term KBE has become a catchphrase in Taiwanese economic policy debate ever since the mid-1990s, in this chapter, we set out to discuss what a knowledge-based economy means to Taiwan, an economy which had been a model of success under the previous 'old' economic conditions.

THE KNOWLEDGE-BASED ECONOMY

A KBE differs from a material or capital-based economy in that it recognises knowledge as being the central element of competitiveness and the driving force behind long-term economic growth. In this new economy, the rules of the game are speed, flexibility and innovation, with those companies that are either new arrivals or achieving rapid growth, almost from their inception finding themselves selling to global markets; thus the well-established companies are now being forced to reinvent their operations in order to remain competitive within this new game.

The KBE has brought about major changes to the organisation of production, market structure, occupational choice, and so on, challenging traditional ideas of national comparative advantage based on the endowment of basic resources of land, capital and labour. In contrast to the old economy where physical capital held sway, the most important forms of capital within the KBE are now human capital and organisational capital, with the evolution of industry now being driven by innovation at a pace previously unimaginable.

Following on from the OECD's (1996) guidelines on the definition of a 'knowledge-based industry' (KBI), Taiwan's Council for Economic Planning and Development (CEPD) calculated that in 1996, the share of the KBI in Taiwan's economy was 40.6 per cent. Based on the new guidelines for a KBI – recalculated by the OECD in 2001, and setting a much higher standard – the revised share of the KBI in Taiwan's economy for 1996 was put at 31.6 per cent. In 2001, under the new standard, Taiwan's KBE accounted for a 36.1 per cent share of industry as a whole (see Table 1.1). By either standard, Taiwan's knowledge-based industry is growing over time, but as a proportion of the entire economy, the figure for Taiwan is substantially lower than the average for all OECD countries.

Table 1.1   Knowledge-based industry growth in Taiwan

Unit: % of GDP

Year	Knowledge-based Industries		
	All Industries	Manufacturing [a]	Services [b]
1991	37.7	6.1	31.7
1994	39.2	5.7	33.5
1996	40.6	6.8	33.7
1996 [c]	31.6	12.3	19.3
2001 [c]	36.1	12.8	23.3

Notes:
[a]   The knowledge-based manufacturing industries include aerospace, computer and data processing equipment, pharmaceuticals, telecommunications, semiconductors, scientific instruments, automobiles, electrical equipment, chemical products, machinery and other transport equipment.
[b]   The knowledge-based service industries include transport and storage, communication services, finance, insurance and real estate, commercial services, social and personal services.
[c]   Figures are based on the new definition of knowledge-based industries revised by the OECD (2001).

Source: Figures are based on the Input-Output Tables for 1991-6 and 2001 provided by the Council for Economic Planning and Development.

The challenges brought about by the KBE have enormous impacts on the role of the government; as opposed to managing business cycles, the policy focus of the government has necessarily shifted to a role of fostering innovation. Thus, the crucial infrastructure for today's industrial competition no longer comprises of roads, ports and public utilities, but instead, 'information super-highways' which are capable of facilitating the rapid transmission of precious knowledge.

Clearly, therefore, the adequacy of public infrastructure is no longer measured by highway and rail coverage, but instead by the penetration of broadband networks, and the like. Technological advances in personal computers, telecommunications and the Internet have in fact already laid the foundations for this level of infrastructure; no longer are indicators such as television or automobile ownership an appropriate measure of the state of economic development. Indeed, figures on Internet access are now probably more suited to that purpose. Moreover, the software infrastructure, such as laws and institutions, which support sustainable knowledge enhancement are now just as important, if not more so, than the hardware infrastructure.

The East Asian economies have been very successful in accelerating their level of investment – with particular emphasis on physical capital – in order to achieve attractive economic growth rates, and Taiwan is of course included in such success stories. Various government policies have been adopted to achieve this particular goal, including forced saving, credit rationing and direct government investment (Chen and Ku, 1999). With the resultant rapid accumulation of capital, these economies were subsequently able to switch the mode of production within their industries from labour-intensive to capital-intensive. The switch then allowed these economies to maintain their course towards high economic growth once they had been able to make use of the previously underutilised labour force, a phenomenon which typically exists within the rural sector of an economy during the early stages of economic growth (Fei and Ranis, 1964). Thereafter, the various governments resorted to taxation policies, financial controls, and other measures designed to support the accumulation of physical capital.

Within a KBE, however, although human capital is the key to success, this form of capital is both intangible and difficult to control or allocate. Output is expanded not through any increase in inputs, but through the adoption of different production methods, or different ways of organising existing production methods. Government intervention in the production process, or in the allocation of inputs, becomes irrelevant, and sometimes even counter-productive, which presents an enormous challenge to the pursuit of further economic development, since this depends so much on correcting market failures so as to create opportunities for growth (Wade 1990; Rodrik 1995). Within a KBE, the market for intangible capital may not yet even exist, thus the question of controlling or allocating such capital also becomes irrelevant. The challenge for a government is therefore to determine ways of creating and accumulating such intangible assets in the event that there is no source from which these assets can be purchased or borrowed.

In the old economy, a country could easily borrow assets from abroad in order to fill the investment-saving gap, and even in a KBE, a country can still obtain human resources from abroad equipped with certain talents, but such borrowing will not yield good results unless appropriate human resources are available domestically to complement this imported foreign talent. Indeed, as Amsden (2001) argued, the economies of East Asia have been more successful than their Latin American counterparts at sustaining their economic growth rates because they were prepared to spend substantial sums on the development of domestic human resources and national proprietary skills, whilst the Latin American countries depended heavily on borrowed skills. Knowledge pertinent to product innovation, marketing, the organisation of production, and the like, can only be learned and accumulated within a society, and there may be a need for society to reach critical mass before any positive learning and accumulation process can effectively take place. On this basis, it also becomes difficult to model economic policies based upon those of other economies. Outside experts can persuade a country to adopt certain policies, but optimal effectiveness of the policies will only be achieved if policymakers are actively involved in the process of adapting and shaping these policies to suit the domestic economy (Stiglitz, 1999).

THE RESTRUCTURING OF GLOBAL PRODUCTION SYSTEMS

The greatest impact of the KBE has been its effects on the reorganisation of global production. Within a KBE, a firm is seen as a producer, repository and user of knowledge, producing or acquiring knowledge by whatever means are available to the firm, and putting it to use in the most efficient way. Thus, a firm's stock of knowledge is directly correlated to its competitive advantage, and all firms are therefore likely to be heterogeneous because they possess idiosyncratic knowledge. Firms engage in production activities in areas in which the knowledge they possess provides them with a competitive advantage, and any transactions in these products imply that there is some form of exchange of knowledge.

As compared to the rather rare and uneven distribution of knowledge, non-knowledge inputs to production, which include both labour and capital, are now available to all firms almost on equal terms, and as capital markets have become much more globalised, such non-knowledge inputs may even have lost the country-specific characteristics that they once possessed. And although wage differentials remain, cheap labour is accessible to all through foreign direct investment (FDI); thus, a firm's sustainable competitive advantage has to be built on its possession of knowledge rather than on the primary inputs to which it has access. Indeed, it has already been noted that because of the external economies, knowledge-based industries now tend to concentrate geographically, with these industrial clusters having succeeded in attracting the congregation of both local and multinational firms (Almeida and Kogut, 1999).

Within a KBE, the total partitioning of innovation and production activities becomes the norm, but this does in fact make sense because the correlation between innovating and producing is, at best, only marginal. Although the knowledge used in inventing a product can be useful in the manufacturing process, and vice versa, it would not generally be prudent for innovators to invest in manufacturing capacity unless they were unable to realise the full value of their innovations through outsourcing. Indeed, contract manufacturers can invariably perform the production function at much lower cost than the innovators themselves because of their ability to exploit economies of scale through the sharing of their manufacturing capacity with more than one client.

In order to produce a perfect product, innovators usually need to share some of the product knowledge with manufacturers and, conversely, some of the knowledge gleaned from the manufacturers can often help in subsequent product innovation; however, the sharing of knowledge is best arranged in a cooperative relationship, because knowledge is intangible and knowledge sharing entails organisational learning. Therefore, alliances are clearly set to become an important form of business organisation within a KBE, and also an important source of learning and innovation (Powell et al., 1996).

The sharing of knowledge with others may well be more efficient than the internal accumulation of such knowledge because of the 'non-rivalry' nature of knowledge, which allows the one who partakes of the knowledge to pay only a small marginal cost to compensate the owner for the transfer of the knowledge. The acquisition of knowledge through exchanges or alliances would also seem to be more efficient than setting out to acquire the firm that owns the knowledge because, when acquiring the firm, one also acquires other non-essential assets. In short, a KBE is characterised by alliance capitalism, and as a result, the international production networks within a KBE are integrated systems of activity nodes that take advantage of specialised technology, skills and know-how at each node (Borrus et al., 2000).

Product innovation entails an assortment of different areas of knowledge which have relevance in the various stages of production. The knowledge that is applied to the manufacturing, marketing and customer service processes is complementary to the knowledge used in product innovation; however, vertical integration in the value chain is only justified if the internalisation of such activities is the most effective way of acquiring the relevant knowledge, which is often not the case. As product innovation caters to the needs of customers, the knowledge obtained from interactions with customers, i.e., marketing, is clearly of the greatest value to product innovation.

A combination of product innovation and marketing may therefore be the optimal mix of services to be offered by firms within a KBE. Merchandisers such as Nike, Reebok and Calvin Klein are typical examples of an innovator-marketer combination in the traditional footwear and apparel industries. Even in the high-tech industries, we can observe a trend towards promoting innovation and marketing functions as the new core functions of the firm. Within the information industry, integrated device manufacturers (IDMs), such as Apple, Compaq, Dell and Motorola, have each separated their organisations from the manufacturing process and have now delegated such activities to dedicated contract manufacturers. Even within the semiconductor industry, 'fabless' designers have been the driving force behind product innovation, working closely with the providers of foundry services.

Within this overall process of the modern metamorphosis of production, in addition to the actual manufacturing and delivery of products, we are increasingly observing a requirement for contract manufacturers to perform customer service functions. So-called 'global logistics' has prevailed in the KBE mainly because the production knowledge that exists within the organisation is also useful in the arrangement of shipping and warehousing, and the knowledge of product manufacturing is also useful in the repair of products. Therefore, we can identify a new division of labour in the KBE where firms endowed with heterogeneous knowledge are performing production activities in line with the knowledge-content of production, and country-specific advantages become secondary factors in the determination of the production process. As a manifestation of this argument, it is clear that in the US, there has been a resurgence of manufacturing activities taking the form of consigned production (Sturgeon, 2000). Contract manufacturers that choose to retain their global production facilities, such as Solectron and Flextronics, invariably divide the labour within the firm in line with their location-specific advantages, whilst their R&D is also similarly globalised (Pearce, 1997).

Foreign investment has become an increasingly important source of innovation (Zander, 1999), and the new division of labour has enhanced the role of contract manufacturers. Within the electronics industry, for example, revenues at the world's largest twenty contract manufacturers grew at an annual rate of 30.7 per cent from 1988 to 1992, and at an even higher annual rate of 46.4 per cent between 1992 and 1995 (Sturgeon, 2000). Since Taiwanese firms have traditionally served as main subcontractors for many of the Western multinationals, the emergence of these contract manufacturers therefore poses an enormous challenge to manufacturers in Taiwan. Their response to this challenge must be that in addition to manufacturing, they also need to offer integrated knowledge-intensive manufacturing services, including product design (Chen and Liu, 2003).

MARKET STRUCTURE IN A KNOWLEDGE-BASED ECONOMY

As early as 1942, Schumpeter observed that increases in productivity in the US economy were largely attributable to innovation delivered by the R&D laboratories of large US firms in an environment characterised by high barriers to market entry. Schumpeter argued that large firms which enjoy stable profits in an oligopolistic market structure have the financial resources to build up the 'knowledge base' required to apply scientific principles to ever more complex innovations. This argument implies that 'a market structure involving large firms with a considerable degree of market power is the price that a society must pay for rapid technological advancement' (Nelson and Winter, 1982).

However, two of the major building blocks of the Schumpeter argument have ultimately been broken down by the new economy. First of all, the financial resources necessary for supporting product innovations do not have to come from the innovators themselves, given that the new developments in financing, such as venture capital, can now provide a mechanism for the full support of innovative activities. Secondly, market power is not necessarily correlated with firm size, especially if a firm's size is measured by its scale of production. Instead, it is knowledge that now forms the cornerstone of market power. In fact, it can often be observed that small new enterprises can provide more fertile ground for innovation than their larger, well-established counterparts (Stiglitz, 1999).

The breakdown of the Schumpeter hypothesis manifests itself in the increasingly important role being played in product innovation by small firms. These days, a start-up company with good innovative ideas has the capacity to attract both financial and human resources, and thereby, has the opportunity to become a large company within a very short period of time. In fact, in modern times, even the monopoly power created by innovation is often short-lived because it can soon be nullified by further new innovations. There is, therefore, no effective way for a monopoly firm to erect entry barriers without the assistance of the government, and market power can only be sustained through continuous innovation, as exemplified in the case of the central processing units (CPU) of personal computers.

On the other hand, there does seem to be growing concentration on the manufacturing stage of production. One explanation for this phenomenon may be that large manufacturing firms enjoy economies of scale, scope and speed in the application of the available knowledge, whereas such benefits do not exist at the innovation stage. The knowledge required within the manufacturing process includes product engineering, process technologies, tooling, quality control, the organisation of production, and so on. This kind of knowledge can be reapplied to the same product with different designs, and across different production locations; therefore, a contract manufacturer can now work for multiple designers, and produce similar products, from various locations around the world.

For manufacturers, the advantage of being large increases with the knowledge content of manufacturing; thus, knowledge can be thought of as a sunk fixed cost. The more costly this knowledge is, the greater the advantage that can be gained from a larger production scale. Therefore, the process of manufacturing involved in the newly-innovated products will tend to be more concentrated than the manufacturing process for mature products. Small firms that do not possess the requisite knowledge endowment that might otherwise enable them to engage in the production of innovative products are therefore limited to participating in only the mature product markets; but even there, the prospects for small firms remain bleak within a KBE, because large firms still enjoy economies of scope in the application of their superior knowledge. Small firms can therefore only retreat to those niche markets that are immune to the dominance of their larger counterparts through their economies of scale and scope. These large firms also enjoy the benefits of globalised production stemming from the common governance of knowledge application in various locations, and from being able to deliver products to consumers much more rapidly than small firms, who do not have the means to engage in multinational production.

Speed is increasingly gaining greater importance than cost in global competition; indeed, within a KBE, speed is the essence of competition. The increasing accessibility of knowledge and the increasing speed of knowledge diffusion have resulted in innovations accelerating at a more rapid pace than ever before; however, such a rapid pace of innovation shortens product life cycles and makes inventory an unbearable burden within the overall production process. In order to cope with the competition based on speed, firms have to find ways of cutting the time to market in every element of the production process. Hence, the other previously neglected elements of production, particularly logistic services, now take centre stage in the competition. Taking personal computers (PCs) as an example, the product life cycle for each generation of PCs, which stood at around one year throughout the 1980s, has today been reduced to around four months.

In such time-based competition, firms have to organise themselves in a global logistics network, such that components and parts can be procured and assembled efficiently, and such that final products can be assembled rapidly and immediately delivered to the market. Modernisation of the shipping and storage system has therefore become another crucial factor in national competitiveness. From air cargo to containers, to bark-commodity shipping, the providers of all kinds of transportation methods have to concentrate on finding ways of speeding up the overall shipment process, whilst there is also a clear need for the lowering of barriers to shipping, such as customs procedures. Of even greater importance is the necessary upgrading of mechanisms for the transmission and exchange of information in order to facilitate the efficient organisation of production and prompt decision-making. Therefore, within this new era of global competition, both traditional and modern means of communication are now taking centre stage. As a direct result of its Asia-Pacific Regional Operations Centre (APROC) plan, Taiwan now operates a 24-hour customs clearing service for air cargo at its international airport, and is currently working on introducing a paperless customs documentation procedure. The final touch for the APROC plan, which was unveiled in August 2000, was the reduction of overall shipping and handling costs to a maximum of 10.0 or 11.0 per cent of GDP (from the current 13.1 per cent level), to be achieved through the overall enhancement of transportation facilities and electronic-based transactions (CEPD, 2000).

THE IMPORTANCE OF INFORMATION TECHNOLOGY IN A KNOWLEDGE-BASED ECONOMY

Information technology (IT) has of course become the major driving force behind a KBE, with an appropriate example of this being provided by Jorgenson et al (2002), who pointed out that in the US, between 1995 and 2000, overall investment in IT (including computer hardware, software and telecommunications equipment) contributed more to labour productivity growth than any other assets. Such investment is clearly resulting in rapid advances in the ability to access, exchange and process information through digital devices, and these are developments that will undoubtedly have serious consequences.

As regards information flow, the world is now networked, and any country which lags behind the rest of the world, in terms of information access, exchange and processing, runs a high risk of being left out of the global production network. All that will be left for these economies will be to retreat to the production of standard products, such as agricultural products or common-purpose materials, requiring little coordination with the rest of the world with respect to the acquisition of the necessary inputs or the sale of the final products. With their inherent inability to keep pace with the non-standardised product cycles, they will become isolated from the diffusion of new technologies, and will hence be unable to enjoy the growth in productivity stemming from these new technologies. If they are to have any hope of seeing growth in their domestic per-capita income levels, then this will have to come from capital accumulation, which will only be possible through FDI, since indigenous firms will be unable to penetrate the export markets to capture sufficient demand to support their investment expansion. The old view of dependence economics and the extreme pessimism directed towards the model of export-driven growth will probably regain popularity in the KBE.

Since superiority in information technology allows multinational companies to play an ever-expanding role in the allocation of production, it may well become a 'necessary evil' for developing countries if they are to benefit from the externalities of new knowledge. Production is increasingly disintegrated within a KBE, but the room for horizontal division of labour seems to have been squeezed. This is because the information-processing capability of a firm allows it to enjoy economies of scope through its ability to offer multiple products. Such product differentiation can be achieved through the variation of parts and designs at certain stages of production without making any sacrifice in terms of scale economies, with the practice of 'configure-to- order' (CTO) in the PC industry being a typical example of the economies of scope that can come into play, allowing little room for horizontal differentiation of the product between firms.

Firms' so-called market niches are already becoming increasingly difficult to protect, unless they are sufficiently well guarded by some proprietary knowledge; nevertheless, within a KBE, even proprietary knowledge may have to be shared with collaborators in a vertically-disintegrated production chain in order to be able to offer a competitive product to the market. In the end, the fact is that the product itself does not actually represent a niche any more, but instead, just one part of a whole range of differentiated products offered by a group of producers working collaboratively. The resultant shrinkage of the space for horizontal division of labour will make market entry increasingly difficult for IT-backward countries, and what we will observe is an increasing concentration on the manufacturing of certain products, in certain countries, all of which will be organised by just a few multinational corporations.

Although Taiwan has been a major producer of IT hardware for some time, it has not been a major consumer of IT hardware and services. In 2000, for example, Taiwan produced US$22,157 million worth of IT hardware which, on a global scale of IT output, ranked it fifth, behind only the US, Japan, Singapore and China. Standing in stark contrast to this achievement, the total number of PCs owned in Taiwan is relatively small, estimated at around 224.65 pieces per thousand people. This figure is overshadowed by the 344.52 per thousand in Australia and indeed, dwarfed by the 483.11 per thousand in Singapore. Overall expenditure on IT also accounts for a very small proportion of Taiwan's GDP. In 2002, for example, only 1.47 per cent of the island's GDP was spent on IT hardware, software and related services, much lower than the proportions of other IT-producing countries, such as the US, where 4.56 per cent of the country's GDP was allocated to IT spending in 2002 (Chen, 2003).

With the increasing availability of information, there will be an inevitable reduction in the value of such information. Within a KBE, simply knowing something is not sufficient to secure a competitive edge; rather, it is the ability to respond more rapidly than one's competitors to any influx of new information that will create a competitive edge. This therefore implies that in order to excel in the KBE, the structure of an organisation has to be configured in such a way that the response to new information is sufficiently flexible and nimble; therefore, the traditional hierarchical organisation, with centralised control, is now facing tremendous challenges in this whole new ball game.

Alliance capitalism will become prevalent in the KBE, with firms combining and recombining themselves to respond to ever-changing market demands. Constant exchange of information between the alliance members will become a prerequisite, whilst the development of routine practices for processing such information will form the core strength of the alliance. The types of information technologies sourced and installed will dictate whether a group of collaborative firms can act together as an efficient processor of information; this will require something beyond tangible facilities, such as the electronic networks that tie firms together, since such groups will need to develop the capability to respond to new information rapidly and effectively if they are to beat the growing competition. Such strengths will naturally entail product design capability, manufacturing capacity and marketing channels. Once all of these capabilities have been successfully developed, which will take considerable amounts of time and money, the network itself will then represent an entry barrier to other firms, thereby becoming a foundation for competitive advantage. Networking, therefore, is clearly a key word in a KBE, and information technologies serve as the backbone of networking.

CONCLUSIONS

The New Challenges for Taiwan

The knowledge-based economy (KBE) presents a number of significant challenges to Taiwan, an island whose government had traditionally placed great emphasis on its manufacturing capability with much less emphasis being put on either services or R&D. Since both producer and consumer services have now become important factors in international competition, Taiwan must learn how to effectively provide such services.

Producer services, in the form of telecommunications, shipping and warehousing, are particularly crucial components of time-based competition. The costs of shipping and handling goods can determine the overall competitiveness of manufacturers, whilst telecommunication services and other electronic-based information exchange mechanisms are important tools in every aspect of the organisation of production, such as supply chain management. Indeed, information technology may enhance the productivity of the service sector more significantly than it does the manufacturing sector.

The ability to provide effective services to consumers also takes centre stage in the new era of competition. Providing better services to consumers is an effective way of enhancing the value of a firm's products, even for specialised manufacturers, such as those in Taiwan. Indeed, this issue has not gone unnoticed at the higher echelons of global production, since many of the world's leading manufacturers, such as IBM and Hewlett Packard, have gone on to become active service providers. Taiwan also has to recognise that the KBE gives rise to the need for internationalisation. Taiwan's economy is dominated by small and medium enterprises (SMEs) which lack the capacity to operate globally; however, within a KBE, the major advantage of multinationals lies in their ability to access local knowledge through multiple locations (Almeida, 1996). Lacking such ability may well preclude the participation of Taiwanese firms in the global production networks.

A further challenge presented by the KBE is that of knowledge creation. Although Taiwanese firms have shown themselves to be very good at tapping into external knowledge through their various alliances, they have nevertheless proved unwilling to undertake any significant investment in innovation. Their global reputation for emulating, and indeed, copying the products designed or invented by others, has caused serious damage to their image as potential technology partners. Thus, as knowledge becomes the core of competition, it is becoming increasingly difficult for Taiwanese firms to acquire the required knowledge from external sources.

These three areas of specific challenges to Taiwan stand as lessons that Taiwan has to learn in order to survive in the KBE, and provide the conclusions to this opening chapter.

The Modernisation of Taiwan's Service Sector

The Taiwanese government has in fact been implementing the Asia-Pacific Regional Operation Centre (APROC) plan since 1996 in its efforts to modernise the service sector. At the core of this plan are the attempts to liberalise the telecommunications industry and promote electronic commerce (e-commerce).

The government's first efforts towards the overall liberalisation of the telecommunications market came in 1996, when it attempted to induce greater competition within an industry that had previously been monopolised for some considerable time by a state agency. The government agency that had been operating the sole telephone system in Taiwan was converted into a state-owned corporation, Chunghwa Telecom (CHT); the government agency, which was then left without any other operational responsibilities, subsequently became the regulatory agency for the telecommunications market. Licences for private cellular-phone service providers were issued in 1997, with a total of eight licences being granted; however, market consolidation has reduced the number of operators to four today. The opening up of the competition has led to lower service provision charges, contributing to a boom in the cellular-phone subscription rate. Today, the combined share of the private cellular-phone operators exceeds that of CHT by a significant margin.

Following the liberalisation of the cellular-phone market, the government further allowed the establishment of four private fixed-line operators in March 2000, so as to compete with CHT in the provision of fixed-line services, including voice and data communications. The government had planned to privatise CHT by the end of 2001 but the pace of privatisation was slowed by the shrinking stock-market trading volume at that time, and, as a result, the target date has been delayed.

Along with the liberalisation of the telecommunications market, the Taiwanese government has also initiated several programs aimed at promoting e-commerce. The government effort began in 1999 with the launch of the Industrial Automation and Electronic Business (iAeB) program, with tax incentives being provided to private enterprises for investment in computerisation, and also for investment in related technological development and personnel training to accommodate such computerisation. In accordance with the provisions of the *Statute for Industrial Upgrading*, a certain proportion of this expenditure can be taken as a tax credit, just as in the case of R&D expenditure. By December 2000, tax credits had been granted to 36,293 cases of e-commerce-related investment, amounting to a total investment of NT$795.5 billion (around US$24 billion).

In addition to tax incentives, the Industrial Development Bureau (IDB) also took on initiatives to construct 'model' electronic-based exchange systems in the PC industry, with the emphasis being on supply-chain management. The aim was to link PC system producers to their suppliers for the purpose of coordinating the functions of ordering, production, warehousing, transportation, delivery and sales, with the model program being divided into A and B projects. A projects take an international system producer as the core firm around which the exchanges are to be clustered; whilst B projects take an indigenous producer as the core firm. Although the model systems are heavily subsidised by the government, the technologies accumulated during the process of developing such systems are nevertheless made available to other firms which intend to emulate them. After reviewing the tenders submitted by the industry, the IDB chose IBM, Compaq and HP to run the A projects, and 15 indigenous PC makers, including Acer, Mitac and Asustek, to run the B projects.

Globalisation

The second challenge to Taiwan within a KBE is that of globalisation. In order to be a world-class competitor, a manufacturer needs to build up the capability to offer products and services on a global scale, which clearly indicates that globalised production is a prerequisite to engaging in worldwide competition. Hampered by their size constraints and lack of managerial resources, both of which inhibit their ability to run truly global operations, Taiwanese firms consequently have only a limited capacity for internationalisation. They have, however, sought to enhance their globalisation capabilities through engaging in alliances which have both prompted, and facilitated, overseas investment by Taiwanese firms.

As contract manufacturers for multinational companies offering worldwide services, Taiwanese firms were themselves forced to provide global production and logistics capabilities. For example, by 2000, Delta Electronics, the world's largest producer of switching power supply (used in personal computers) had established factories in China, Thailand, Mexico and Taiwan, and was operating 27 warehouses around the globe. The products for its major clients – which include the world's top-ten PC producers and top-five cellular telephone handset producers – are shipped from Delta's nearby warehouses to their assembly lines twice a day in typical 'just in time' (JIT) fashion.

The overseas investments undertaken by Taiwanese manufacturers, such as Delta, have been occurring en bloc since the mid-1980s. Traditionally, FDI is envisaged as an extension of the ownership of foreign resources, which are brought under the command and control of the internal hierarchy which, in turn, governs the division of labour. Clearly, however, an investor has to command a very strong 'ownership' advantage in order to engage in such rent-generating activities (Dunning, 1991). Nevertheless, FDI can also be seen as an extension of the 'connection' to foreign-based resources without owning them. This is conveniently referred to as 'alliance capitalism'.

The FDI which is engaged in by Taiwanese manufacturers comes largely under the category of 'alliance capitalism', with Taiwanese firms taking advantage of their valuable relationships with multinational companies, first of all, as a means of reducing the risks involved in overseas investment; secondly, in order to leverage the external resources for globalisation; and finally, as a means of accumulating important knowledge so as to enhance their position vis-à-vis the multinationals, which often act as their clients. With the appropriate IT support, Taiwanese subcontractors have built up digital information networks to create appropriate linkages with their clients in the coordination of the supply chains, inventory control, production and shipping management. These digital information networks allow a shorter lead-time to market, more flexible production scheduling and reduced inventory levels, and eventually form entry barriers that will effectively protect the position of the Taiwanese firms (Chen, 2003).

There are, however, important limitations to alliance capitalism within a knowledge economy. Alliances can create conflicting incentives for competition and cooperation, but ideally, the knowledge to be shared between partners is that which is complementary to each other's business. Clearly, knowledge cannot be partitioned in such a way that only a permitted portion of such knowledge is transferred to the partner. It is also difficult for alliances to offer the kind of richness and flexibility within their mechanisms that will ensure an effective transfer of knowledge, especially in the case of cross-border transfers (Almeida et al., 2002).

Knowledge Creation

Although Taiwanese industry has demonstrated particular competency in the application of knowledge, this is not the case with regard to knowledge creation. Taiwan has thus far been highly dependent on the social network that exists between its own specialists and those within the innovation centres as an effective means of acquiring and diffusing technology. However, it will undoubtedly become increasingly difficult for such a mechanism to function in the future because knowledge will become more and more intensely guarded. As knowledge becomes more dispersed and disintegrated, it is important for firms to possess some specific knowledge of their own to trade or to share with others. Clearly, therefore, knowledge creation is an important leverage in terms of acquiring new knowledge.

As regards its overall expenditure on such knowledge creation, Taiwan spent just 1.66 per cent of the island's GDP on R&D in 1990, with the proportion rising only slightly, to 2.05 per cent, in 2000. In 1990, the public sector accounted for 45.8 per cent of overall R&D expenditure with the private sector accounting for the remaining 54.2 per cent, although by 2000, there had been an encouraging increase in the private share of R&D, to 62.5 per cent (NSC, 2001).

Greater incentives for R&D expenditure are demonstrated by Taiwanese manufacturers for two reasons, the first of which is competitive pressure. Taiwanese manufacturers need to compete through lower costs, which are in turn achieved through the payment of lower wages; thus, as domestic wages rose significantly, their competitive edge was eroded. Innovation therefore became an obvious option if manufacturers were to regain their former competitive edge. Although some Taiwanese firms invested abroad, taking advantage of the lower wages there in an effort to regain their cost advantage, they soon found that this advantage was unsustainable; this was because the cost advantage based on the employment of foreign workers could easily be imitated, as exemplified by the

US-based electronic manufacturing service (EMS) companies who built factories worldwide to serve as contract manufacturers, just like the Taiwanese firms. In an attempt to outcompete these EMS companies, Taiwanese firms then began offering both manufacturing services and product design as a means of holding on to their clients. Referring to themselves as original designer-manufacturers (ODM), Taiwanese PC makers, in particular, have defended their market shares quite well, despite the challenges from the much larger and financially stronger EMS companies that emerged in the 1990s.

The second motivating factor behind the rise in the level of R&D expenditure is a strategic one. Within the knowledge economy, intellectual property (IP) becomes the key barrier to entry, substituting for capital and the other scarce resources of the past. Low-cost producers may not have any chance of participating within the industry if they cannot gain permission to access the relevant IPs, whereas technologically-advanced countries can effectively use IP as a barrier to block the attempts by latecomers to enter new industries that are presumably more lucrative but not yet subject to cost competition. Taiwanese firms that aspire to upgrade their product lines are inevitably faced with these IP barriers and the only way to overcome this problem is to possess IP of their own, which can then create opportunities for cross-licensing. A few Taiwanese semiconductor firms are leading recipients of US patents although their business revenues are relatively small as compared to other recipients of the same class. This indicates their strategic move towards building up IP inventory in order to secure a favourable position in the field of technology competition.

REFERENCES

Almeida, P. (1996), 'Knowledge Sourcing by Foreign Multinationals: Patent Citation Analysis in the United States Semiconductor Industry', *Strategic Management Journal*, **7**: 55-165.

Almeida, P. and B. Kogut (1999), 'The Location of Knowledge and the Mobility of Engineers in Regional Networks', *Management Science*, **45**(7): 905-17.

Almeida, P., J. Song and R. Grant (2002), 'Are Firms Superior to Alliances and Markets? An Empirical Test of Cross-Border Knowledge Building', *Organisational Science*, **13**(2): 147-61.

Amsden, A. and W.-W. Chiu (2002), *The Rise of the Rest: Challenges to the West from Late-Industrializing Economies*, New York: Oxford University Press.

Borrus, M., D. Ernst and S. Haggard (2000), *International Production Networks in Asia: Rivalry or Riches?*, London: Routledge.

CEPD (2000), 'E-commerce Added to Global Logistics Center Plan', APROC Newsletter No.38 (August), Taipei: Council for Economic Planning and Development.

Chen, S.-H. and M.-C. Liu (2003), 'Taiwan's Transition from an Industrializing Economy to a Knowledge-Based Economy', in S. Maguyama and D. Vandenbrink (eds.), *Towards a Knowledge-Based Economy*, Singapore: Institute of Southeast Asian Studies, and Tokyo: Nomura Research Institute.

Chen, T.-J. and Y.-H. Ku (1999), 'Second-Stage Import Substitution: The Taiwan Experience', in G. Ranis, S.-C. Hu and Y.-P. Chu (eds.), *The Political Economy of Taiwan's Development into the 21st Century*, Cheltenham, UK: Edward Elgar.

Chen, T.-J. (2001), 'Weathering the Asian Financial Crisis', in A. Chowdhury and I. Islam (eds.), *Beyond the Asian Crisis*, Cheltenham, UK: Edward Elgar.

Chen, T.-J. (2003), 'The Globalisation of E-Commerce: Environment and Policy in Taiwan', Department of Economics, National Taiwan University, unpublished manuscript.

Dunning, J. (1991), *The Nature of the Transnational Firm*, London: Routledge.

Fei, J. and G. Ranis (1964), *Development of the Labor Surplus Economy*, Homewood, Ill.: Richard D. Irwin.

Jorgenson, D., M. Ho and K. Stiroh (2002), 'Projecting Productivity Growth: Lessons from the US Growth Resurgence', *Economic Review* (Federal Reserve Bank of Atlanta) Third Quarter, **87**(3): 1-13.

Krugman, P. (1994), 'The Myth of Asia's Miracle', *Foreign Affairs*, **73**: 62-78.

Nelson, R. and S. Winter (1982), 'The Schumpeterian Tradeoff Revisited', *American Economic Review*, **72**(1): 114-32.

NSC (2001), *Science and Technology Statistics 2001*, Taipei: National Science Council.

OECD (2001), *OECD Science, Technology and Industry Scoreboard: Towards a Knowledge-based Economy*, Paris: Organisation for Economic Cooperation and Development.

Pearce, R. (1997), 'The Implications for Host-country and Home-country Competitiveness from the Internationalisation of R&D Innovation', in R. Pearce (ed.), *Global Competitiveness and Technology: Essays in the Creation and Application of Knowledge by Multinationals*, New York: St. Martin's Press.

Powell, W., K. Koput and L. Smith-Doerr (1996), 'Inter-organisational Collaboration and the Laws of Innovation: Networks of Learning in Biotechnology', *Administrative Science Quarterly*, **41**(1): 116-45.

Rodrik, D. (1995), 'Getting Interventions Right: How South Korea and Taiwan Got Rich', *Economic Policy*, **20**: 53-107.

Stiglitz, J. (1999), 'Public Policy for a Knowledge Economy', speech presented at the Department of Trade and Industry and Centre for Economic Policy Research, UK, at http://www.worldbank.org/html/extdr/extme/jssp012799a.htm.

Sturgeon, T. (2000), 'Turnkey Production Networks: A New American Model of Industrial Organisation', *Industrial Performance Centre Working Paper*, Massachusetts Institute of Technology.

Wade, R. (1990), *Governing the Market*, Princeton, NJ: Princeton University Press.

Zander, I. (1999), 'How Do You Mean Global?: An Empirical Investigation of Innovation Networks in the Multinational Corporation', *Research Policy*, **28**(2-3): 195-213.

2 Taiwan's Responses to the Challenges of the Twenty-first Century

Tzong-Shian Yu

INTRODUCTION

Although we clearly have a great understanding about the events of the past, there is enormous uncertainty surrounding potential events of the future. Indeed, throughout the history of mankind, prophets have invariably remained ignorant of their own destiny; looking back to the early twentieth century, no economists at that time had predicted the onset of the great depression of the 1930s, and at the turn of the century, none had foreseen the bursting of the US bubble economy early in 2001. What seems somewhat ironic is that there are many distinguished economists, including Nobel laureates, who are lauded for their familiarity with past trends in economics rather than the future patterns of irregular and potentially dramatic fluctuations.

This is not to suggest, however, that we know nothing of the future, since we can judge the likelihood of changes, and their potential direction, from an examination of certain important and influential events. As we begin to recognise the development of an influential event that is gradually influencing human behaviour, we can of course analyse the nature of the event, along with its developmental trend. Take, for example, population problems and economic growth; as a country manages to achieve successive growth leading to substantial improvements in the well-being of its people, population growth will tend to slow down. The problem is, once such a declining population trend becomes firmly established, it is extremely difficult to reverse its direction in the short run.

The aim of this chapter is to try to determine those events that are set to substantially influence the behaviour of human beings and to bring about further changes in the general structure of economics. This chapter therefore focuses on two particular areas of interest, the first of which involves those events which, although taking place in one country or region, have the ability to rapidly spread across borders, through trade flows or mass media contagion, to affect many different countries or regions. The second area of interest is the potential future introduction of essential technological innovations capable of substantially shortening working hours, reducing operating costs and thus, raising productivity levels.

In light of these two criteria, a number of events are selected that will increasingly influence people's behaviour whilst having a significant impact on the shaping of the economic structure of the twenty-first century. These are: (i) the gradual decline of the younger population; (ii) global warming and environmental catastrophes; (iii) the various impacts of globalisation; (iv) financial internationalisation/bubble economies; (v) the prevalence of the knowledge-based economy; (vi) the formation of the economy of Greater China; and (vii) the widening gap between rich and poor.

These seven events, which constitute the most influential challenges to society, will continue to affect economic life, production processes and social relationships, and based upon our analysis of these events, we can argue that there is an unquestionable need to adopt effective measures aimed at achieving sustainable development in order to respond to these enormous challenges.

THE CHALLENGES OF THE TWENTY-FIRST CENTURY

We should begin the main section of this chapter with an examination of some of the events that took place during the last century; particularly those which have tended to draw considerable public attention. We ignore such events at our peril, since it seems reasonable to assume that they will continue to create challenges to our future way of life and to our future economic structure.

The Gradual Decline of the Younger Population

It is generally observed that 'the poorer a country, the higher the fertility rate', a phenomenon which can be readily observed in many African, South American and South Asian countries. However, as a developing country sets out on its gradual transformation into a newly-developed country, there is a tendency for its fertility rate to decline, whilst at the same time, the country will often find itself faced with the problem of a rapidly ageing society.

Taiwan stands out as a general example of this phenomenon. The birth rate and the rate of natural increase have both been in decline in Taiwan since 1976, which means that the younger population of Taiwan will be the first group to display a marked declining trend. Examining the population change by age group, we can see the natural progression of a decline in the 0-4 year-old group in 1982; a fall in the 5-9 group in 1985; a decline in the 10-14 group in 1990; and a subsequent fall in the 15-19 group in 1998. We can very simply extrapolate from this that in forty-five years from now, the senior population in Taiwan (aged 65 or over) will also start to decline (Table 2.1).

The current changes in Taiwan's population provide a clear indication of an eventual decline in the available labour force (16-64 year olds), with a corresponding increase in the ageing population. If technological progress remains unchanged, the former is not good for the development and growth of economic activities, whilst the latter is an essential condition for, and worrying element of, a nation's increasing healthcare burden. It may prove beneficial therefore to attempt to determine here which factors have contributed to the declining trend of the younger population and to try to determine whether it is possible to reverse this trend.

Thirty years ago, a time when the birth rate and the rate of natural increase in Taiwan were both rather high, the government decided to initiate a family planning program, encouraging people to adopt birth control measures, so as to avoid the plunge into a vicious cycle of poverty.[1] In order to achieve this goal, the government encouraged all government employees, including civil servants, military forces and schoolteachers, to restrict their families to no more than two children. From 1976 onwards, the birth rate demonstrated a declining trend, moving from 2.55 per cent growth in 1976, to 1.29 per cent growth in 1999, whilst the rate of natural increase also went into decline from 2.12 per cent in 1976, to 0.81 per cent in 2000.

The declining trend in the birth rate can be attributed to two important factors: the rise in educational levels, and the formation of the core family. Alongside the rapid growth of the Taiwanese economy, average family income levels also increased significantly, which provided considerable help with regard to the level of financial support required by parents to enable their children to attend colleges or universities. Thereafter, once these students graduate, they have a strong desire to look for jobs and set out on their own chosen career path, with females in particular showing a marked trend towards seeking work outside of the home, as opposed to working within the home as housewives.

There is a growing tendency for the number of larger families in Taiwan to dwindle, with instead, considerable growth in the number of 'core' families. Within many of these core families, where both the husband and the wife are in gainful employment, neither may have any desire to give up their work in order to maintain the family home; hence there has been a growing tendency towards birth control and a resultant decline in the island's birth rate.

Table 2.1 Taiwan's changing population, by age group

Unit: x 1,000

Year	No. of under 5s (1)	Change (2)	No. of 5-9 year olds (3)	Change (4)	Sub-total (5) = (2) + (4)	No. of 10-14 year olds (6)	Change (7)	Sub-total (8) = (5) + (7)	No. of 15-19 year olds (9)	Change (10)	Sub-total (11) = (8) + (10)
1982	2,000	-	-	-	-	-	-	-	-	-	-
1983	1,982	-18	-	-	-	-	-	-	-	-	-
1984	1,923	-59	-	-	-	-	-	-	-	-	-
1985	1,861	-62	-	-	-	-	-	-	-	-	-
1986	1,772	-89	-	-	-	-	-	-	-	-	-
1987	1,679	-93	2,024	-	-	-	-	-	-	-	-
1988	1,639	-40	1,999	-25	-65	-	-	-	-	-	-
1989	1,602	-37	1,950	-49	-86	-	-	-	-	-	-
1990	1,609	7	1,888	-62	-55	-	-	-	-	-	-
1991	1,619	10	1,789	-99	-89	-	-	-	-	-	-
1992	1,626	7	1,704	-85	-98	2,017	-	-	-	-	-
1993	1,611	-15	1,665	-39	-54	1,990	-27	-81	-	-	-
1994	1,598	-13	1,611	-54	-67	1,947	-43	-110	-	-	-
1995	1,587	-11	1,597	-14	-25	1,878	-69	-94	-	-	-
1996	1,587	-	1,611	14	14	1,771	-107	-93	-	-	-
1997	1,595	8	1,623	12	20	1,683	-88	-68	2,006	-	-
1998	1,542	-53	1,610	-13	-66	1,651	-32	-98	1,983	-23	-121
1999	1,504	-38	1,621	11	-27	1,597	-54	-81	1,935	-48	-129
2000	1,485	-19	1,611	-10	-29	1,594	-3	-32	1,870	-55	-87

Source: CEPD (2001).

Furthermore, since the 1990s, more liberal attitudes have prevailed, with many young people choosing to cohabit with their partners in preference to formalising the relationship through marriage. Even if these couples eventually decide to marry, many are choosing not to have children, which further exacerbates the problem of the declining younger population.[2]

This phenomenon is now also discernible in mainland China where, for many years, there was considerable concern over the rapid rate of growth of the population. More recently, however, it is clear that in many metropolitan areas, although the government has adopted a strict policy of 'one-child' birth control in order to reduce the population growth rate, many younger families have nevertheless become opposed to having any children at all, leading to a rapid decline in the birth rate of these metropolitan areas.[3]

The reversal of past trends, towards a rapidly declining younger population, poses a serious challenge not only to educators but also to public policymakers. Educators must take into consideration the decline in numbers of students along with related problems, such as the overall capacity of the education system, educational equipment, and so on, whilst public policymakers have to consider the change in infrastructure supply, the construction of school buildings, as well as the simultaneous concerns of the ageing population and necessary social welfare programs.

Global Warming and Environmental Catastrophes

Many scientists argue that today, not only is the atmosphere becoming much warmer, but the current rate of warming is accelerating, and that consequently, temperature change will become increasingly disruptive. As the oceans become warmer, glaciers will begin to melt, causing sea levels to rise and salt water to inundate many low-lying coastal settlements. Weather patterns will also become more erratic and storms more severe.[4] Such an increase in global warming will lead to greater amounts of precipitation and more rapid evaporation of water, with these weather changes leading to greater frequency of extremes of wet and dry conditions. Of even greater concern is that climate change is likely to have the greatest impact on natural ecosystems. A draft document produced by the US Global Change Research Program (USGCRP) suggested that precipitation could raise sea levels, causing further loss of wetlands in some coastal areas and water shortages in others. The frequency of excessive heat conditions is also likely to increase, causing a variety of changes in day-to-day life. The Alpine Meadows of the Rocky Mountains may disappear altogether whilst the forests of the Southeast could be overtaken by Savannah and grassland.

Global warming can also present a profound threat to the well-being of humans, as evidenced by the frequency and intensity of floods and droughts causing substantial damage and destruction to people and property in many regions. Global warming can impact upon human health in many different ways; most directly, it can generate stronger, fiercer heatwaves, which will become particularly treacherous if the evenings fail to bring the necessary cooling effect. In some regions, it is currently being projected that the number of deaths related to heatwaves will double by 2020. In addition, prolonged heat can enhance the production of smog and the dispersal of allergens producing further hazards to health.

It is readily apparent that as the atmosphere has warmed over the past century, droughts in arid areas have persisted for much longer, whilst sudden massive bursts of precipitation have become more common. Climate change is expected to increase the number of undernourished people in the developing world and aside from deaths caused by starvation and drowning, such disasters will also promote the emergence or resurgence and spread of infectious diseases by various means. Heavy rains and higher temperatures favour the proliferation of disease-carrying mosquitoes, allowing them also to thrive at higher altitudes, and higher temperatures, heavier rainfalls and changes in climate variability will encourage these insect carriers of infectious diseases to multiply and move further afield.

According to Epstein (2001), floods and droughts associated with global climate change will also undermine health in other ways; they can damage crops, making them increasingly vulnerable to infection and infestations by pests and choking weeds, and thereby reducing food supplies and contributing to potential malnutrition levels.[5] Furthermore, the worsening freshwater shortage in some countries could lead to global peril, threatening to reduce the global food supply. These shortages would lead to hunger, with the potential for civil unrest and even wars over water resources. It should be noted that 40 per cent of the world's food comes from irrigated croplands; however, water tables are dropping steadily in several major food-producing regions as groundwater is being pumped out faster than nature's ability to replenish it. Without any significant increase in water resources and productivity enhancements to irrigation, these major food-producing regions will be left with insufficient water to sustain future crop production.

Environmental catastrophes have recently become very serious in many areas of the world, with two closely related factors being responsible for their occurrence. The first of these is the rapid growth of heavier polluting industries, whilst the second is the rapid growth in population density in cities around the world.

The rapid growth of heavier polluting industries

Prior to the 1970s, many of the developed nations had placed considerable emphasis on the development of their industries whilst ignoring the polluting effects on water and air. For some considerable period of time, such water pollution was not only damaging crops, but it had also been the cause of many diseases amongst livestock, fish and even human beings. At the same time, air pollution has given rise to the so-called 'greenhouse gas effect', which has, in turn, resulted in global warming.

Since the 1970s, many of the developing countries have also been engaging in industrial development, whilst ignoring the problem of environmental protection, with many of their industries being active producers of pollutants. Doubtless, their industrial development has added to the serious nature of global pollution whilst also exacerbating global warming.

The effects of population density

Virtually all of the developing countries have experienced alarming growth in the concentration of the population of their major cities, leading to the rapid expansion of these cities; however, given the lack of the necessary infrastructure to support such rapid expansion, these larger cities simply go on to produce greater levels of pollution. Rapid population growth in Asia, coupled with government inaction and weak institutions, is pushing the region to the brink of environmental catastrophe.

The Asian Development Bank has indicated that environmental degradation in Asia is all-pervasive, accelerating and unabated. As for Africa, the situation is much worse; however, in Asia, the rapid population growth has contributed to additional pressures on scarce land resources, with the result that land resource needs in Asia have become the most severe in the world. Almost 30 per cent of the region's land area has suffered from some form of degradation as a result of population expansion.[6]

The Impacts of Globalisation

Along with the spread of economic liberalisation and enhancements to international communication, the general trend towards globalisation has become increasingly prevalent throughout the world. Although there are still some voices from minority groups against globalisation, it has nevertheless become an inevitable and irreversible process. Globalisation, considered as a system, is an approximate set of rules by which to conduct life, and since it is a new and powerful force erasing national borders and linking the world in an unprecedented web of trade and investment, a generally held belief is that it can also eliminate conflicts and bring about world peace. Many opponents of globalisation, on the other hand, see it as nothing but a device employed by rich countries to conquer poor countries, not only through their social values but also through their socioeconomic systems.

International trade has traditionally been the starting point for the move towards globalisation. Where such trade exists with either high tariff or non-tariff barriers, it actually hinders the promotion of globalisation, but where international trade has shifted from unilateral to multilateral trade, and from heavy tariff to non-tariff barriers, and from non-tariff barriers to no barriers at all, these shifts undoubtedly represent an important step towards globalisation. As an international trade organisation, the World Trade Organisation (WTO) has made a significant contribution to the promotion of trade liberalisation with those pursuing membership being required to reduce, or remove altogether, such barriers to trade.

Foreign direct investment (FDI) is clearly another channel facilitating the move towards globalisation. In an effort to make use of the comparative advantage of lower production costs, including cheap labour, low land costs and preferential treatment in the form of tax reductions and exemptions, the direction of most FDI in the early stages tends to come from the developed countries to developing countries. FDI also takes place between different developed countries as a means of introducing managerial skills and specific 'know-how'. Thereafter, once the developing countries have succeeded in effectively upgrading themselves to become newly developed economies, there is also a tendency for these countries to pursue FDI in other developing countries. It should be noted, however, that because of their shortage of foreign reserves and the severe effects that sudden capital outflows can have on their economies, capital movement is invariably subject to strict controls imposed by the developing, or even newly developed countries.[7]

International business in its various forms is also supportive of the development of globalisation; for example: (i) multinational corporations, the structure of which is based upon utilising each country's comparative advantage, including its natural resources and its market capacity; (ii) multi-channel television, which has spawned not only global networks but also countless small community stations; (iii) business alliances, which have extended to foreign as well as local companies; (iv) enterprise mergers, which take place not only within a country but also across borders; (v) e-mail, which has made it relatively easy for individuals and enterprises in different countries to deal with issues at any time of the day or night; (vi) the Internet, which has become an effective instrument for communication between one business and another, between businesses and consumers, and between individuals. This instrument is also a highly effective tool for assisting with high design efficiency.

Globalisation refers to the spread of free-market capitalism in every country of the world, with the driving force being the notion of the free market. In other words, globalisation ensures that borders become more porous for the two-way transmission of goods, ideas, capital and people.

However, the system of globalisation is built around a set of balances that overlap and intimately impact upon each other, the traditional balance between countries, the balance between countries and 'super' markets, and the balance between countries and 'super-empowered' individuals.[8] Indeed, there are actually three driving forces behind globalisation: technology, the capital market and management, each of which is sufficiently powerful in its own right.[9]

Technology

New technology makes it easier to move capital to relatively obscure places; technology gives entrepreneurs the freedom to challenge giant companies and to break up their concentration of power. Technology also provides people with the power to weave connections all over the world, allowing them to escape from the tyranny of place, computers and telephones, and it is arguable that the more mundane innovations have had the greatest effects.

The capital market

The liberalisation of the capital market is a relatively recent process, which is, as yet, incomplete. During the twentieth century, all national economies were linked together by trade in commodities, with capital flows being limited to those transactions necessary to finance such trade; however, many governments found it necessary to undertake financial reform in the aftermath of the 1997-1998 Asian financial crisis. Capital now moves around the world much more easily than ever before, particularly since the entry into the market of electronic financing means. Although there are still some barriers, or even regulatory chasms, which may succeed either in restricting or slowing down its movement, the areas it can permeate have clearly increased.

Management

Management is used to link the world together. It is arguably just another form of technological know-how produced by the pressure on companies to adopt such processes as their connection to the capital market. The spread of common management methods, the growth of the management industry of consultants and business schools, and the development of a new multinational cadre of professional managers, have each transformed those companies that were able to organise themselves better than their rivals, to quickly expand beyond their national borders.

Financial Internationalisation and Bubble Economies

Since the late twentieth century, financial internationalisation has been gradually permeating throughout the newly developed world with the spread of the idea of financial liberalisation, which lies mainly in the development of general economic liberalisation. In other words, the financial liberalisation of a country is a concrete expression of its general economic liberalisation. Many would argue that Taiwan's economy has been transformed from an industrial to a financial economy, whilst the financial economy has gradually evolved from a constrained into a liberalised economy. However, with the spread of financial liberalisation, the financial economy dominates the mainstream of current economic thinking.

The financial economy is characterised by high dynamics and a particularly high degree of uncertainty. Its high dynamics lie in the rapid development and evolution of the financial markets, whilst the high degree of uncertainty comes as a result of the rapid formation of international funds and the collapse of barriers between countries. Capital flows are still subject to political instability and speculative activities; indeed, in many developing countries, if capital was able to flow freely, the political stability stemming from such a process might well induce the instantaneous flow of capital.

The forces that can substantially influence markets and institutions are technological progress and financial innovation. The former provides the instruments for financial transactions and their increased efficiency, whilst the latter provides derived financial commodities and various reform measures used for supervision and management. A combination of these two forces can raise the financial capacity of a nation to meet its people's demands.

Technological progress
Information technology includes the Internet, the world-wide web, e-mail, voice mail, cell phones, pagers, personal computers, palm devices, co-axial and fibre optic cables, communications satellites, and so on. All of these are the fruits of technological progress and constitute essential elements of the communications and information technology revolution that has truly enriched and changed our lives.

Clearly, technological progress has been extremely far-reaching. Major advances in telecommunications and data processing are accelerating the pace of geographical expansion and strengthening the links between national and international financial markets. Technology has closely connected global markets and it may well be creating greater economies of scale and scope that could drive consolidation within the financial service industry.[10] Through the advances made in information technology, we can communicate and process information much more quickly and cheaply than ever before; for instance, it is now possible to create a direct and effective link between buyers and sellers by way of 'e-markets'.

Financial innovation

Technological innovation has played an important role in facilitating financial innovation, which has meant lower costs, greater flexibility for users, increased liquidity and better risk allocation. Consumers now have many financial products from which to choose, such as floating rate bonds, interest only and principal-only call options, caps, floors, collars, income warrants, dual currency bonds, commodity-linked bonds, yield-curve notes, interest swaps, currency swaps, equity swaps, floor-ceiling swaps, ratio swaps, spread locks, wedding bands, 'swaptions', labour-squared turbo swaps, and so on. However, the advent of financial innovation also brings about new dimensions of credit risk.[11] These new types of credit risk require the sophisticated skills of both bank managers and regulators alike, to develop measurement techniques for the estimation of loss distribution probabilities, their efforts on capital adequacy and standards, and ultimately, the performance of the financial system. However, the complexity of many of these financial products has left many regulators perplexed.

It should be noted here that globalisation has also been an important force in the transformation of the financial system. Global financial competition promises enormous benefits for consumers in the form of better, more varied and less expensive services; however, if a financial system is not sufficiently sound and the financial markets are fairly speculative in nature, globalisation can also introduce speculators into local financial markets. Such speculation usually involves the investment of significant funds, which subsequently gives rise to a bubble economy; as many countries throughout the region found during the period of the Southeast Asian financial crisis, such speculation can lead to problems of horrendous proportions once these bubble economies burst. Another example is the effect of the downturn in the US economy in 2001. Following the sharp fall in the NASDAQ on the New York Stock Exchange, corresponding and immediate declines were also suffered by the high-tech share indices of many other countries.

It is clear, therefore, that in addition to providing many opportunities, the increasing spread of globalisation also carries with it many risks. Financial services today are operating in an enormous and increasingly unpredictable market. As financial markets become even more integrated and globalised, there is the clear potential for the emergence of new challenges to systemic stability.

The Prevalence of the Knowledge-based Economy

The benefits and implications of an economy based upon knowledge have actually existed for some considerable time, and indeed, throughout world history, the influence of a 'knowledge-based economy' has basically changed the world economy many times over. The fact is that no one ever actually dubbed it a 'knowledge-based economy'. However, following the issue of various OECD publications in 1996, the idea of a knowledge-based economy started to draw considerable attention on a global scale.[12] The US, in particular, maintained a high economic growth rate with a lower unemployment rate for eight years, and without inflation, a phenomenon which has been dubbed the 'New Economy' and considered to be attributable to the basing of its economy on knowledge. Furthermore, the notion of a knowledge-based economy has become a hot issue in many developed and newly developing countries in Asia. Many governments within the region have become so enthusiastic as to base their entire new economic planning on knowledge economy thinking.

Thus far, there has been no generally recognised definition of what constitutes a knowledge-based economy; however, from the various explanations proposed, we may draw several fundamental requirements of such an economy. A knowledge-based economy is described by the World Bank Annual Report 2001 as an economy characterised by creation, learning and diffusion of knowledge; or a firm, institution, individual or community making effective use of knowledge to lead its economy and society towards more advanced development.[13] A mid-1990s OECD report on the knowledge-based economy considered that it had become the driving force for raising productivity and economic growth, and that it was destined to change the pattern of development of the global economy. Thus, we can postulate that the knowledge-based economy is an economy that directly sets up the stimulation, diffusion and application of knowledge and information.

Based on this explanation, we can roughly classify the two main ingredients of a knowledge-based economy as 'knowledge' and 'information technology'. The importance of knowledge lies in the fact that it not only raises the efficiency of production, but can also improve our general quality of life. For instance, major inventions such as paper, the steam engine, independently powered vehicles, electricity, airplanes, and so on, which have substantially raised the efficiency of production, have also had notable effects on the quality of life.

Knowledge can be dissected into various categories of 'know-what', 'know-who', 'know-why' and 'know-how'. In other words, there is information knowledge, talent knowledge, research knowledge and skills knowledge. 'Know-what' and 'know-why' can be referred to as *codified* knowledge, whilst 'know-how' and 'know-who' may be classified as *tacit* knowledge which cannot be codified. As for information technology, this is mainly concerned with the diffusion and application of knowledge. Its affiliations include the Internet, and the digital and information economy. All of these are simply parts of the knowledge economy; in other words, they assist in raising the functions of the knowledge-based economy.

The major differences between traditional and knowledge-based economies are the factors of production. In a traditional economy, these production factors are land, natural resources, capital and the labour force, which are of course physical resources, whilst in a knowledge-based economy, non-physical and non-embodied knowledge are the main resources of wealth creation. Although still of enormous significance, the other resources are of lesser importance than knowledge; one reason for this is that physical resources are subject to the law of diminishing returns whilst knowledge-based resources are not.

The achievement of the development of a knowledge-based economy can be verified by the 'new economy' of the US, as already referred to. It is also evidenced by the economic performance of Northern Europe. The OECD was also much improved in the 1990s, as compared to the 1980s, because of the development of economic policies based upon knowledge.

Knowledge-based industries are classified by the OECD as those involving either knowledge-based manufacturing or knowledge-based services. Within industry as a whole, knowledge industry output has increased annually, from 45 per cent in 1985, to 50 per cent in 1996; unsurprisingly, those countries where the knowledge-based industry plays a leading role are the developed countries, such as Germany (58.6 per cent), the US (55.3 per cent) and Japan (53.0 per cent). It should also be noted, however, that although information technology can accelerate productivity, a knowledge-based economy cannot completely shield itself against recessionary pressures. Indeed, as already noted, the US economy has found itself mired in deep recession since the second quarter of 2001.

The Formation of the Economy of Greater China

The overall economy of Greater China comprises of mainland China, Taiwan, Hong Kong and Macao. Hong Kong became an integral part of China in 1997, as did Macao in 1999; only Taiwan remains independent of the sovereignty of mainland China in a political sense, despite Taiwan's economy being closely aligned with that of the mainland. In view of the recent developments in terms of economic exchanges across the two sides of the Taiwan strait, many commentators on both sides have become confident of the ability of these four economies to combine forces in the future. Their confidence is based on the following considerations:

No ideological economic conflict
Through the implementation of more than twenty years of economic reform and open-door policies, the Marxist and Leninist doctrines no longer prevail amongst farmers, businessmen and even young officials in mainland China.

Most people there have learned of the market economy and the emphasis on entrepreneurship. More importantly, Chinese people are now allowed to own their own properties, which is clearly inconsistent with Marxist doctrine. The unification of the market economy is an essential step in promoting the political unification of the two sides, and so far, at least in terms of economic ideology, there are no salient issues of conflict between the economies of the two sides of the strait.

Direct investment in mainland China by Taiwanese companies

In 1987, when the government of Taiwan first decided to allow Taiwanese citizens to visit their relatives in the mainland, many businessmen took advantage of this opportunity to seek out business opportunities and undertake FDI there using Hong Kong, Singapore or the US as gateways, and thereby effectively avoiding government interference. Between 1987 and 2000, there was at least US$30 billion invested in the mainland by Taiwanese enterprises with more than 10,000 firms being established (see Table 2.2).[14] In the Dongkuan, Kungdong province alone, for example, more than 4,000 factories were set up by Taiwanese entrepreneurs, and indeed, there are more than 300,000 Taiwanese citizens residing in Kuenshan, Shanghai.

Table 2.2   Taiwanese direct investment in mainland China

Year	Agreed Amount			Actual Realised Amount			(3) = (2)/(1) (%)
	Amount US$m (1)	Rate of Change (%)	Proportion of Total [a] (%)	Amount US$m (2)	Rate of Change (%)	Proportion of Total [b] (%)	
1991[a]	2,783	-	-	844	-	-	30.33
1992	5,543	-	7.99	1,050	-	5.49	18.94
1993	9,963	79.78	8.94	3,139	198.67	11.41	31.50
1994	5,393	-45.87	6.53	3,391	8.03	10.04	62.85
1995	5,777	7.08	6.33	3,162	-6.75	8.43	54.73
1996	5,141	-11.01	7.02	3,475	9.90	8.33	67.59
1997	2,814	-45.26	5.44	3,289	-5.36	7.26	116.88
1998	2,982	5.97	5.72	2,915	-11.38	6.41	97.75
1999	3,374	13.14	8.19	2,599	-10.85	6.45	77.01
2000	4,042	19.80	6.48	2,296	-11.66	5.64	56.81
Totals	47,816		7.07	26,160		7.51	54.71

Notes:
[a]   Figures for 1991 represent the accumulated total prior to 1991.
[b]   Indicates the percentage of the total amount of foreign investment

Source: PRC Foreign Trade and Economic Cooperation; and Mainland Commission, *Monthly Report of Economic Statistics for Mainland China and Taiwan.*

Even in the most remote areas of the northeast and the western frontier, there are many factories and stores currently being run by Taiwanese businessmen, and along with mainland Chinese businessmen, they have formed very close relationships through unilateral FDI. The recent trend amongst many Taiwanese enterprises has been a growing preference for undertaking direct investment in the mainland and within all of the ASEAN countries, simply because Taiwanese people are not handicapped in terms of their language or living habits

Now that the two sides have both gained accession to the WTO, and once 'the opening of the three links' is actually realised, we can clearly expect that these events will assist in the development of bilateral direct investment. From an economic perspective, such an approach will also lead to a much closer relationship between the two sides.

Taiwan's increasing dependence on trade with the mainland

Prior to 1990, bilateral trade between the two sides of the Taiwan strait was barely of any significance because of the prohibitions put in place by the Taiwanese government; however, since then, bilateral trade between the two sides has increased rapidly, and indeed, by 2000 the mainland had become the second largest market for Taiwanese exports. In view of the growing trend for Taiwanese exports into the mainland, it is readily apparent that the mainland could quickly become the largest market for Taiwanese exports. In other words, Taiwan is likely to become increasingly dependent upon the mainland market. As Table 2.3 indicates, exports from Taiwan to the mainland amounted to US$6,928.3 million in 1991, increasing to US$26,144 in 2000, an average growth rate of 21.71 per cent. Clearly, as a result of the two sides' accession into the WTO, their mutual trade will undoubtedly be strengthened, and under such conditions, Taiwan will no longer have any reason to restrict imports from the mainland.

The Widening Gap between Rich and Poor

Immediately after the Second World War, a time when the communist powers had expanded rapidly and were demonstrating their clear intention of conquering the free world, many of the world's market economies had to adopt social welfare programs or social security systems in order to discourage the penetration of communist doctrine. These systems have been of considerable help in improving income distribution and erecting systems of social justice within the developed nations, achievements that inspired many developing countries to adopt similar measures once their economies had taken off; Taiwan may provide a good example here. From the very beginning of Taiwan's economic development, the government emphasised the importance of taking special care of the poor. The island's land reform policies, for example, have been helpful in improving the income distribution of farmers, whilst the encouragement of SME development has not only created more employment opportunities but also increased the income levels of the island's poorer citizens. The requirement for general levels of education, and the continued raising of this general level, has also proved to be an effective approach to improving the well-being of poorer families, whilst the implementation of progressive income tax policies has been demonstrably helpful in improving income distribution.

Table 2.3   Bilateral trade between mainland China and Taiwan

Year	Indirect exports from Taiwan to mainland China		Indirect imports into mainland China from Taiwan		Trade Balance (3) = (1)-(2)
	Amount (US$m) (1)	Rate of Change (%)	Amount (US$m) (2)	Rate of Change (%)	
1991	6,928.3	66.1	1,126.0	47.1	5,802.3
1992	9,696.8	40.0	1,119.0	-0.6	8,577.8
1993	12,727.8	31.3	1,015.5	-9.3	11,712.3
1994	14,653.0	15.1	1,858.7	83.0	12,794.3
1995	17,898.2	22.1	3,091.3	66.3	14,806.9
1996	19,148.3	7.0	3,059.8	-1.0	16,088.5
1997	20,518.0	7.2	3,915.3	28.0	16,602.7
1998	18,380.1	-10.4	4,110.5	5.0	14,269.6
1999	21,221.3	15.5	4,526.3	10.1	16,695.0
2000	26,144.0	23.2	6,223.3	37.5	19,920.7

Source: Straits Exchange Foundation (2001), *Straits Business Monthly* (September), No.117: 10.

All of these strategies and measures have provided useful input to the improvements seen in Taiwan's poorer communities and to the overall distribution of income throughout the island. Since the 1980s, however, it has become a commonplace argument in many developed countries that it may not ultimately prove to be the best policy for a country to continually strive to maintain equal income distribution, since this has resulted in unfavourable feedback. Progressive income tax measures, for example, do not stimulate entrepreneurship or encourage either innovation or a hard-working spirit. Any country that is devoid of innovation and technological progress will find it impossible to raise its productivity levels and, in the absence of any growth in productivity, it is extremely easy for a country to lose its competitiveness in the world markets. This explains why the government in Taiwan has reduced the extent of its progressive income tax policies over recent decades.

We can expect that, in the new century, the knowledge-based economy will dominate the world economy and that electronics and information industries will become the driving forces in promoting economic growth. Those groups that are involved in any form of industrial development connected with electronics and information industries will have greater potential for higher levels of income than those dealing in traditional industries, such as textiles, steel, shipbuilding, and so on. Indeed, it can be shown that most of the one hundred richest people in the world today started out in the electronics and information industries. Prior to the 1980s, the majority of this illustrious group came from businesses such as petroleum, steel mills, vehicle manufacturing, and the like. However, after the 1980s, those people dealing in computing and software very quickly became millionaires, or, as in the case of Microsoft, billionaires!

Such developments have given rise to concerns amongst many people. Their arguments are based on considerations such as: (i) those enterprises dealing in the electronics and information industries can earn massive amounts of money in a very short period of time, merely because their share prices can multiply several-fold overnight;[15] (ii) the high speed of information technology, such as the Internet, creates higher productivity which can ultimately result in reducing labour costs significantly. Under these conditions, a failure to create more job opportunities will result in growing numbers of unemployed people; (iii) regardless of which country we examine, those people who have become very well educated in the field of information technology tend to enjoy much higher salary levels, whilst those with lower levels of information technology education may well find themselves with no job at all; and (iv) in the era of the knowledge-based economy, the discrepancy between income levels in the developed and developing countries will continue to grow.

RESPONDING TO THE CHALLENGES

Faced with so many challenges, one has to consider how to respond to them, since there is, of course, no way that they can simply be ignored. These challenges have actually existed for some considerable time already and seem to form and develop increasingly severe impacts on our economic structures and on our way of life. There is, therefore, no alternative but to face up to them boldly and deal with them effectively.

The Response to the Gradual Decline in the Younger Population

Once a declining trend becomes embedded in the fertility rate, it is extremely difficult to reverse its direction. First of all, there is a need to adjust educational facilities, transportation, housing and other infrastructure in order to cope with this trend. If the declining trend is particularly strong, we may then be faced with a demographic trough, and finding a cure for this is of paramount importance. The corresponding problem of an ageing population also becomes a very serious issue as there will be insufficient numbers of younger people to replace those leaving the labour force. As a result, they, in turn, will themselves become part of this ageing population problem. It is therefore necessary for us to consider ways of encouraging people to raise the fertility rate whilst also looking at effective measures for ensuring that the growing elderly population is cared for. These two questions are closely interrelated. If the first issue cannot be resolved, then there can be no solution to the second.

The current family planning programs in Taiwan are no longer aimed at restricting the number of children born to each family; however, the removal of such policies alone cannot serve to encourage young couples to have more children. Measures which would be more effective in raising the fertility rate would be to greatly reduce the total cost of raising and educating a child, from birth to 15 years of age (including longer holidays for the gestation period, subsidised baby foods and housing, and subsidised tuition for a child's schooling). Given the needs of the current situation, the more children a family could raise, the lower the costs should be that such a family should have to bear. If such a principle cannot be effectively realised, then the government will clearly have to adopt an open-door policy in terms of immigration. Immigrants can nevertheless be very helpful in assuming caring roles for the aged; in addition, they usually demonstrate a preference for raising more children of their own.

The Response to Global Warming and Environmental Catastrophes

The issue of global warming is a global problem and in order to solve it, all individuals have to become responsible for reducing their input into this phenomenon. It is well known that the main cause of global warming stems from the emission of CO_2 gases. Finding effective ways of eliminating the production of CO_2 gases requires the cooperation and support of enterprises. In this regard, the government should also play a leading role in the supervision of those industries producing CO_2 gases.

In October 1997, the leaders of many countries gathered in Kyoto to reach agreement on the 'Kyoto Protocol', with the common aim of finding ways of reducing CO_2 emissions. In accordance with the agreement reached at that meeting, every government was to enforce the implementation of the Kyoto Protocol. Unfortunately, the US government has shown itself increasingly reluctant to stick to the Protocol, continuing instead to produce excessive amounts of CO_2 gases, a stance criticised by many countries.

Nevertheless, it should be especially emphasised that the elimination of the production of CO_2 emissions should be the responsibility of every country and every individual. We also need to pursue simultaneously rational arrangements for the constrained use of fossil fuels (coal and oil) and to find alternative sources of energy.

Environmental catastrophes, such as floods, land subsidence, mud slides and so on, have become much more serious in recent years, causing increasingly serious damage and growing numbers of deaths or casualties. If we continue to ignore issues of environmental protection and go on destroying ecological conditions, we will lose the opportunity to live comfortably in the world. We clearly need to go to great lengths in order to protect the world's rivers, mountains and woods, and effectively reduce such environmental catastrophes.

The Response to Globalisation

Despite the proliferation of anti-globalisation groups across the world, globalisation has nevertheless become a prevailing phenomenon and there is precious little time left for us to ignore its development and its effects. In order to cope with the growing trend towards globalisation, we have to equip ourselves with necessary measures and actions. Clearly, it is possible that globalisation may result in the 'survival of the fittest'. Thus, in order to cope with the possible consequences the best approach for a country would be to enhance its competitiveness. Competitiveness comes from innovation, efficiency and cooperation. Innovation provides the driving force for promoting growth and efficiency comes from the rationalisation of management, whilst the cooperation of enterprises can create comparative advantages and also help to achieve economies of scale.

The Response to Financial Internationalisation and Bubble Economies

As a direct result of financial internationalisation, effective 'firewalls' no longer exist between countries. If a financial crisis breaks out in one country, or region, its contagion to other countries or regions will be virtually unstoppable. In view of such a possibility, it becomes necessary for all developing countries to undertake financial reform through measures which should include: (i) the merger of small financial institutions into larger institutions in order to achieve economies of scale; (ii) the establishment of an effective system of banking supervision; (iii) raising risk management skills in order to reduce the penetration of potential speculators; (iv) controlling the issuing of loans with collateral based on shares issued by enterprises; and (v) discouraging the use of short-term debt to finance long-term investment. Furthermore, all of the state-owned financial institutions should be completely privatised and the government should take a 'hands-off' position in order to avoid the problem of 'moral hazard', a major cause of the financial crisis in the late 1990s throughout the East Asian countries.

The Response to the Knowledge-Based Economy

No one country can be isolated from the rest of the world. Once the knowledge-based economy has become the mainstream of the world economy, we must be prepared to meet the basic requirements for the total development of the knowledge-based economy. We must simultaneously awaken ourselves to the fact that when we stress the development of information technology, we should not ignore the importance of upgrading our culture; without the upgrading of culture, human beings will become slaves to technology.

We have so far found that the use of the Internet has contributed significantly to the raising of efficiency in design, production, transportation, marketing, collection of information, and so on, but we have also found that the Internet has become an effective instrument for cheating, stealing, causing chaos, undermining national security, and the like. Therefore, although it is necessary for us to strengthen the development of information in order to raise efficiency, it is equally important to pay attention to the raising of cultural standards.

The Response to the Formation of the Economy of Greater China

In the wake of the Cold War and East-West conflicts, political conflict will gradually give way to regional cooperation, which is set to become the mainstream of international political economics. In 1992, the European Economic Community (EEC) demonstrated such cooperation by forming a single market for Europe, the European Union (EU). Similar efforts were undertaken by APEC and NAFTA, which were respectively established in 1989 and 1994. Such regional cooperation indicates that the whole world is moving towards greater regionalism, although amongst these three regions, only the EU and NAFTA have the integrated power to carry out real economic measures.[16] The nature of regionalised economies is that they have sufficient liberalisation within all of the member states, and some degree of protection between the region and other regions or individual countries.

If a country belongs to one of the two giant regional economies, it usually has greater bargaining power than any of its trading partners, particularly those that are not a part of any regional economic community.

Both Taiwan and mainland China have had such bitter experiences over the past decade. Based upon this consideration, many scholars and experts have proposed that mainland China, Taiwan and Hong Kong (Macao included) should organise themselves into a so-called 'Greater Chinese Economy' in order to counter the strength of other regional economies. This proposition has, however, been echoed only by private enterprises, not by the respective governments, because the governments of the two sides of the Taiwan strait remain extremely cautious in expressing their view on such a proposition, one way or the other.

In the closing decade of the twentieth century, despite their individual GDP levels being relatively small, as compared to other regional economies, the overall economy of the 'Greater China' area has consistently achieved the highest economic growth rates. Although Japan has held the number two position in world trade volume for a considerable period of time, second only to the US, total exports from the Greater Chinese economic area have exceeded those from Japan since 1996, whilst its total imports have exceeded Japan's since 1992 (Table 2.4). In addition, the Greater Chinese economic area has the largest volume of foreign reserves in the world, amounting to US$407.7 billion in June 2001.

This region also houses the world's largest population, and thus, the world's largest available labour force. A census of the total population revealed an estimated 1,283.8 million people living in the 'Greater Chinese Economy' area in 1999, with an available labour force of 733.2 million. If all of these people were to receive higher levels of education, their potential productivity contribution would be immeasurable, and if this whole area could be gradually formalised, it would provide a market of gigantic proportions for trading with the rest of the world, whilst also being in a position to play a stabilising role in the global economy.[17]

Since we can reasonably expect that mainland China will become an economic power of much greater significance in the twenty-first century, if Taiwan persists in its efforts to secure independence from 'China', the island will undoubtedly find itself engaged in long-running chaos and crisis.[18] Once an economy loses its stability, it becomes impossible to achieve steady economic growth; a prime example of this comes from the experiences over the past two decades of the former leading regional economy of the Philippines. Therefore, we must hope, with all sincerity, that both sides of the Taiwan strait can leave behind their conventional ideologies, accepting instead the notion that ultimately, only close cooperation between the two sides will prove beneficial to both economies. As such, the formation of the economy of Greater China should be the common goal. Nevertheless, there has so far been no real difficulty or lack of opportunity for both individuals and enterprises to have further exchanges, coordination and cooperation.

Table 2.4   Main economic indicators for mainland China, Taiwan and Hong Kong

		1991	1992	1993	1994	1995	1996	1997	1998	1999	2000
Economic Growth Rate in real terms (%)	China	9.19	14.27	13.54	12.83	10.54	9.58	8.84	7.77	7.10	8.20
	Taiwan	7.55	7.49	7.01	7.11	6.42	6.10	6.68	4.57	5.42	6.50
	Hong Kong	5.06	6.26	6.13	5.40	3.89	4.49	4.97	-5.14	2.91	10.00
GDP (US$ billion)	China	406	483	601	543	700	816	898	946	989	1,074
	Taiwan	179	212	224	244	265	280	290	267	288	325
	Hong Kong	86	101	116	131	139	154	171	164	159	167
	Total	671	796	941	918	1,104	1,250	1,359	1,377	1,436	1,566
Average GDP Growth Rate (%)		(19.3)	(20.9)	(21.5)	(17.1)	(29.9)	(26.6)	(31.5)	(34.9)	(31.9)	(33.0)
Commodity exports (US$ billion)	China	72	85	92	121	149	151	183	184	195	243
	Taiwan	76	81	85	93	111	116	121	110	121	139
	Hong Kong	99	120	135	151	174	181	188	175	174	205
	Total	233	286	312	365	434	448	492	469	959	587
Commodity Imports (US$ billion)	China	64	81	104	116	132	139	142	140	166	194
	Taiwan	63	72	77	85	104	103	114	105	111	140
	Hong Kong	104	127	141	166	196	201	213	187	181	218
	Total	231	280	322	367	432	443	469	432	458	552
Population	China	1,151	1,165	1,178	1,192	1,205	1,218	1,230	1,242	1,255	1,267
	Taiwan	20.6	20.8	20.9	21.1	21.3	21.5	21.7	21.9	22.0	22.2
	Hong Kong	5.7	5.8	5.9	6.0	6.2	6.3	6.5	6.7	6.8	7.0
	Total	1,177.3	1,191.6	1,204.8	1,219.1	1,232.5	1,246.1	1,258.2	1,270.6	1,283.8	1,296.2
Labour force	China	654	662	670	679	687	697	706	714	720	-
	Taiwan	8.6	8.8	8.9	9.1	9.2	9.3	9.4	9.5	9.7	9.8
	Hong Kong	2.8	2.8	2.9	2.9	3.0	3.1	3.2	3.4	3.5	3.4
	Total	665.4	665.6	681.8	691.0	690.2	709.4	718.6	726.9	733.2	-

Source: INSEAD (2001).

These various agents should make use of their intangible power as a means of influencing policymakers on both sides of the strait to recognise the trends of the times and to enhance the overall level of cooperation. If capital, manpower and information can be allowed to move freely on both sides, then the formation of the economy of Greater China could indeed become a reality in the very near future.

Responses to the Widening Gap between Rich and Poor

The gap between rich and poor is becoming increasingly obvious because it is widening at an extremely rapid pace. The simple and most effective approach to narrowing this gap relies upon nothing but education, which can ultimately increase the competitive abilities of individuals. It is, of course, unrealistic to ever hope to achieve the equalisation of all citizens, but the divide between rich and poor can be maintained at tolerable levels, provided that the discrepancy in income distribution is not so great that the poor do not have enough food to eat, no home in which to live, or sufficient means to support their children in striving to complete their elementary school education. There are two necessary and effective measures for reducing this gap, the first of which is to put in place an effective educational system which ensures that everyone with the ability receives professional or higher education, whilst the other is to adopt appropriate social work programs aimed at providing help for the disabled, the poor and ageing population, in order to help them lead a normal life.

CONCLUSIONS

The future is of course full of uncertainties and it is extremely difficult for anyone to make accurate predictions. Throughout the history of mankind, it has been regularly confirmed that whilst we may know a great deal about the past, we are totally ignorant of the future. What we have dealt with in this chapter is based mainly on consideration of the economic phenomena of our past experiences, since these events can assist in the formulation of strong trends for further development. These events have an enormous influence on the economic structures under which we operate, whilst changing significantly the way in which we live our lives. Faced with the challenges that are born of these events, we must not ignore their underlying development and their potential impacts. We should try our utmost to eliminate unfortunate impacts by all means possible. What we must do today is to study these events and equip ourselves with the necessary means of meeting similar challenges in the future.

NOTES

[1]   The birth rate was in excess of 4 per cent in the 1950s, with the natural growth
       rate standing at more than 3.6 per cent, whilst in 2000, the former was 1.38 per
       cent and the latter 0.81 per cent (see CEPD, 2001).

[2]   The change in the figures can help to explain the reason for the decline in the
       younger population. For instance, in 1990, one-member and two-member
       households accounted respectively for 13.4 per cent and 12.7 per cent of all
       households; ten years later, the former accounted for 21.6 per cent, and the latter
       for 17.4 per cent. Within these two household groups there may be either no
       children at all, or only one child.

[3]   After 22 years of economic reform, mainland China has achieved an
       exceptionally high growth rate with the younger generation enjoying the fruits of
       economic growth under the protection of their parents and grandparents; however,
       they appear increasingly reluctant to assume the burden of family.

[4]   Coastal settlements in the Gulf of Guinea, Senegal, Gambia and Egypt, as well as
       those along the Southeast African coast, would all be adversely affected by a rise
       in the sea level through inundation (flooding) and coastal erosion (refer to United
       Nations Environment Program, Press Release on 'Global Warming', website:
       http//www.unep.ch/ipccl).

[5]   See: Epstein (2001).

[6]   Air pollution levels in Asian cities are already amongst the highest in the world.
       For instance, air pollution in cities in India, Pakistan and Bangladesh is reported
       to be the cause of 100,000 premature deaths each year. In Taiwan, due to the
       island's limited land and population density, many river banks and sloping
       mountain lands have been over-exploited, resulting in recent cases of large-scale
       mudslides which have mixed with rocks to cause terrible catastrophes, killing
       many people and swallowing up many buildings.

[7]   In developing countries, there is usually some measure of political instability,
       which can result in capital outflow. Governments are inclined to take strict
       control over capital outflows in such cases, whilst capital inflow is always
       welcomed.

[8]   See: Friedman (2000).

[9]   See: Micklethwaite and Wooldridge (2000).

[10]   See: Spillenkothen (1999).

[11]   See: Carnell (1999).

[12]   See: OECD (1996).

[13]   See: Lee (2001).

[14]   The amount of investment may be underestimated. In order to avoid government
       interference, many enterprises would often set up paper offices in Hong Kong
       and then undertake direct investment in the mainland, which was not actually
       counted by the government of either side of the strait.

15   This is not always true. For instance, the NASDAQ index began to fall from the winter of 2000, eventually declining from 5,000 points to 1,600 points in the summer of 2001. Many people who held such shares have lost considerable amounts and have now entered the ranks of the 'former rich'.

16   There are, in fact, many economic regions in the world, even in Latin America and Africa; however, they are just entities in name, with no concrete activities. In Asia, the ASEAN, established for more than two decades, has expanded from five to ten countries, but this remains a very loose organisation. Even APEC has no integrated powers which it can exert within the region.

17   The labour forces of both Taiwan and Hong Kong are characterised by higher levels of professional education, whilst the level of professional education in the mainland is rather low because of the long-running political disruption prior to the 1980s.

18   The use of the term 'China' here does not refer solely to the 'PRC' or to the 'ROC', but indicates a free, democratic and prosperous China, which, it is hoped, will eventually be built by the two sides of the Taiwan strait.

REFERENCES

Carnell, R.S. (1999), 'Dead Weight and a Distant Shore', in D.B. Papadimitriou, (ed.) (1999), *Modernizing Financial Systems,* New York: St. Martin's Press, pp.18-25.

CEPD (2001), *Taiwan Statistical Data Book, 2001,* Taipei: Council for Economic Planning and Development, Ministry of Economic Affairs.

Dilenschneider, R.L. (2000), 'The Coming Age of Content and Critical Thinking', speech delivered in Atlanta, Georgia (December).

Economist, the (2001), 'Is Globalisation Doomed?' (29 September 2001), p.13.

Epstein, P.P. (2001), 'Is Global Warming Harmful to Health?', *Scientific American* (August): 50-57.

Friedman, T.L. 'A Manifesto for the Fast World', in Sjursen, K. (ed.) (2000), *Globalisation,* New York: H.W. Wilson & Co., p.8.

Halal, W.E. and K.B. Taylor (1999), *Twenty-First Century Economics: Perspectives of Socioeconomics for a Changing World,* New York: St. Martin's Press.

INSEAD (2001), *East Asian Economic Perspectives: Recent Trends and Prospects for Major Asian Economics,* Kitakyushu, Japan: International Centre for the Study of East Asian Development.

Jorgenson, D.W. (2001), 'Information Technology and the US Economy', *American Economic Review,* **91**(1): 1-32.

Lee, J.C. (2001), 'What is a Knowledge-based Economy?', in J.C. Lee (ed.) (2001), *The Myth and Thinking behind the Knowledge-based Economy,* Taipei: Commonwealth Publishing Co., pp.3-4 (in Chinese).

Lin, W.-L. and P. Lin (2001), 'Emergence of the Greater China Circle Economies: Cooperation vs. Competition', *Journal of Contemporary China*, **10**(29): 695-710.

Micklethwaite, J. and A. Wooldridge (2000), *A Future Perfect: The Challenge and Hidden Promise of Globalisation*, New York: Crown Business Press, pp.29-77.

OECD (1996), *The Knowledge-based Economy*, Paris: Organisation for Economic Cooperation and Development.

OECD (1999), *The Future of the Global Economy: Towards a Long Boom?*, Paris: Organisation for Economic Cooperation and Development.

Sjursen, K. (2000), *Globalisation*, New York: H.W. Wilson & Co.

Spar, D. (2001), 'The New Economy and Global Governance Issues', paper presented at the 43rd Annual Conference International Institute for Strategic Studies, UK.

Spillenkothen R.S. (1999), 'Innovation in the Supervision of Financial Institutions', in D.B. Papadimitriou, (ed.) (1999), *Modernizing Financial Systems*, New York: St. Thomas' Press, pp.37-53.

Stiglitz, J. (1999), 'Public Policy for a Knowledge Economy', World Bank, at website: http://www.worldbank.org/html/extdr/etme/jsp012799a.htm.2001.

United Nations Environment Program, Press release, Global warming, at website: http://www.unep.ch/ipccl.

World Bank (2001), *Global Poverty Report*, World Bank updates.

3 The Role of the Government in a Knowledge-based Economy

P.K. Chiang

INTRODUCTION

To the citizens of Taiwan, the island's economy represents not only the means of their survival, but also a source of considerable pride. Ever since the sixties, under the strategic planning and management of the Taiwanese government, the island has witnessed the sequential implementation of policies for 'the incubation of industry with agriculture' (and vice versa), 'pushing growth with trade' (and vice versa), 'adjustment of the economic structure and advancement of industrial upgrading' and latterly, 'the acceleration of industrial upgrading and the development of strategic industries'. These policies have been largely responsible for the successful transformation of Taiwan from an agricultural economy into a newly industrialising economy, and have led to the island making significant headway towards becoming a developed economy.

Not only has the government of Taiwan been responsible through the years for a whole range of economic achievements, but it has also used political forces to great effect to generate economic forces, and in turn, used economic forces to forge social and cultural forces, all of which have improved the living standards of the island's population. By leading the pluralist development of society and political reform towards full democratisation, the government has helped to create the 'Taiwanese miracle', a term which has become familiar to most of the developed and developing countries around the world. The creation of this 'miracle' provides a concrete example of omnipotent government which, although heavily dependent on the efforts of the island's people, was also built on the premise that the government had significant foresight and a comprehensive set of ideas for effective governance and appropriate economic policies, along with the capability to govern the island within appropriate rules and systems.

All of this has contributed to the outstanding results that have thus far been achieved in Taiwan (Figure 3.1). However, in light of the era of liberalisation and the rapidly developing phenomenon of globalisation, both the government of Taiwan and the island's huge number of enterprises are now faced with two serious issues. The first of these is the need to determine their position in the international division of labour, whilst the second involves seeking out effective competitive strategies aimed at broadening the available niches for survival.

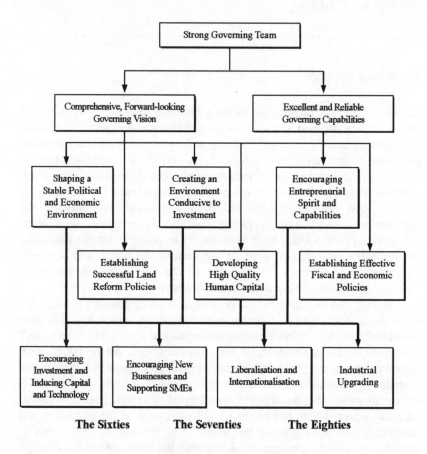

Figure 3.1   Analytical diagram of the Taiwanese 'economic miracle'

As a result of their respective high economic growth rates, as well as their economic strengths in various areas, Taiwan, Hong Kong and Singapore came to be regarded as three of the 'Four Little Tigers' (the fourth being

South Korea). Throughout the history of the global survey on national competitiveness (conducted by the IMD in Lausanne, Switzerland), Singapore has always ranked second, whilst Hong Kong has remained in the top ten, with the exception of the year 2000 when it fell to fourteenth; Taiwan's position, on the other hand, has fluctuated wildly between 1996 and 2001 (IMD, 1996-2001).

The Asian financial crisis, which emerged in Thailand in 1997, caused serious damage to Hong Kong, placing its economic system in real danger. However, Hong Kong has recently become a *de facto* international financial, trade, service, telecommunications and transportation centre, largely as a result of the steady state of equilibrium that exists in the management environment in Hong Kong, along with its stable tax system, lower tax rates, independent judicial authorities, cheaper costs of information access and its special relationship with mainland China, all of which have been created, shaped, institutionalised and maintained by the Hong Kong government. The fact that foreign investment grew throughout 2000 and the first quarter of 2001 suggests that Hong Kong has successfully reestablished its dominant position as a gateway for European and American companies into the markets of mainland China.

It is also worth examining the determination of, and the results obtained by, the promotion of electronic government in Singapore. In June 1997, Singapore embarked on an ambitious project to develop the world's first national multimedia and broadband network (Singapore One) and in June 2000, the government announced that over the subsequent three years, over US$1 billion would be spent on developing Singapore as the world's finest example of electronic government. A report released in March 2001 by the American firm, Accenture, noted that Singapore was only just behind the United States with regard to innovation leadership.[1] Furthermore, it is clear that the Singaporean government has tried its utmost to attract transnational corporations as a means of helping it to rapidly transform the economic structure of the city state, and to develop it as a site for transnational corporations to establish their operational headquarters. This was made possible by Singapore's political and social stability, its flexible economic development policies, its integrated and capable bureaucracy, universal education, preferential policies for the encouragement of investment, and its open environment based upon a very strong international flavour.

Since Taiwan has always been an 'export-oriented' economy, it is extremely sensitive to political and economic situations on an international scale, and within the mechanism of globalisation, huge numbers of Taiwanese businesses have been forced to move their production bases to other countries where costs are lower, for the sole purpose of maintaining or boosting their current level of competitiveness. However, this situation is further exacerbated by a number of issues, including political instability, complicated and outdated laws and regulations, extremely rigid and restrictive policies on cross-strait trading and investment, government inefficiency, and other such debilitating traits, which have led to the steady worsening of the investment environment in Taiwan, causing even more businesses to relocate overseas, and resulting in significant capital flight. The combined effects of all of this are the catastrophic changes that are now being triggered in the domestic market and in the island's overall economic structure, with Taiwan's politics, its economy and society in general, showing serious and alarming reactions to the global economic recession. There are now even some serious concerns as to whether Taiwan will actually be able to regain its former impressive rate of economic development, or indeed catch up with the relative stability and healthy performance of the neighbouring newly industrialising economies.[2]

It would clearly be preferable for the progress of a country to be based on the balanced development of its politics, economy and society, which would include a wide range of issues, such as political democratisation, economic liberalisation, social openness and cultural pluralism. However, since consideration is given to specific situations in Taiwan, the government's strategies for development have tended to focus almost exclusively on strengthening economic forces, to the detriment of other areas, with the expectation that such policies would stimulate the development of these other areas; the result is that the island's economy has become the sole and vital organ of Taiwan's future development.

Nevertheless, having stepped into the twenty-first century, Taiwan, like other countries, is facing extreme tests of governance, which are placing unprecedented obstacles on the road to Taiwan's continuing economic development. There is no doubt that the government's primary role is still the preservation of continuous development and prosperity; however, giving equal weight to issues such as environmental sustainability, in-depth cultivation of a humanistic spirit and the establishment of social equality, are constantly running into conflicting missions of maintaining the economic achievements of the past and of balancing various aspects of development, which are also heavily dependent on constructing new visions and the reengineering of the government's functions and administrative systems.

Ever since the eighties, the leading economies of the world have been faced with dilemmas involving serious fiscal deficits, the incessant rise in the demands of the population and rising administrative inefficiency, regarded by some scholars as the main ingredients of 'ungovernability' (Crozier et al.,1975), or referred to by some as a 'catch-22 situation' (Lin and Chiang, 1997, p.219). Indeed, Kirkpatrick and Lucio (1999) held out a warning for contemporary governments, proposing that: 'modern states will fall into the contradictory and tense relationships of being a social welfare provider and a leading steersman of stable economic growth'.

In order, therefore, to cope with such difficult situations, the leading economies of the world have sought to implement various reform measures, all of which seem to be along similar lines. In the UK, for example, when the Conservative Party became the ruling party in 1979, a series of 'New Right' ideas and policies for governing were put into effect under the successive leadership of Margaret Thatcher and John Major; these included 'Efficiency Units', 'Next Steps' (Ranson and Stewart, 1994), 'The Citizens' Charter' (Lovell, 1992), and the introduction of 'Financial Management Initiatives (FMI)'. In New Zealand, when the Labour Party became the ruling party in 1984, the government withdrew its insistence on socialism, adopted a line of total liberalism, reevaluated and reengineered procedures within the public sector, repealed inadequate or inappropriate regulations, and actively promoted privatisation of government functions and the implementation of performance management systems.

The Australian example is provided by the ruling Labour Party from 1983 onwards, with the government emphasising free competition and the market mechanism, actively seeking ways of reducing costs, improving the overall quality of government service and strengthening performance management. In the US, the Clinton administration established the National Performance Review (NPR) system and implemented a whole basket of policies for the reengineering of government (Kettl and Dilulio, 1995), most of which were essentially measures aimed at downsizing, strengthening process reengineering, abolishing over-regulation, encouraging community participation, adopting the widespread use of information technology (although still emphasising customer-orientation and employee empowerment) and exploiting the market mechanism. The main aim behind all of this was to seek to build a system of 'entrepreneurial government'.

The common denominator behind many of the reform measures adopted by the countries described above has been the right-wing notion of 'small government'. The general perspective of governance has been transformed from top-down hierarchical control by governments to the utmost respect for the operation of the market mechanism and the spread, by governments, of external and parallel network relationships. This clearly spells out the end for 'great government' and the imminent arrival of the era of 'small but beautiful' and 'small but capable' government. The reform measures proposed and adopted by various Premiers in Taiwan (notably, Lien Chan, Vincent Siew and Chang-Chun Hsiung) have in fact followed roughly the same reform lines as those of the right-wing movement. Generally speaking, a market-oriented mode of governance seems to stand out as the most familiar and most effective measure to be adopted by governments when faced with fiscal difficulties and any radical shift in the needs and expectations of society; however, it is worth noting that government policies are essentially based upon more contextual considerations. For example, do governments ever seriously consider the actual needs of local governance when resolutely insisting on forging ahead with reform policies that adhere rigidly to the line of small government?

It was proposed, over twenty years ago, that in terms of their value differences, governments fall into three main types (Hood, 1991), and these categories seem to have stood the test of time. First of all, governments are regarded as being lean and purposeful; therefore, efficiency, efficacy, austerity and performance are their inherent values. Secondly, honesty and equity are seen as the essential guiding principles; from such a standpoint, the major value of governments lies in their desire and ability to uphold values of honesty and fairness, achieving social equity, justice and legitimacy, as well as taking responsibility in an appropriate manner.

The third example proposes governance based upon robustness and resilient domination; governments must be forceful, self-confident, reliable, adaptable and safe, and equipped with the capabilities to deal with change in a calm and efficient manner. The first type is an example of the all too familiar 'small government' mode, whilst the second is an example of a 'great government' which treasures social equality and justice; however, the third example demonstrates the willingness to withdraw from the controversial arguments of government size, emphasising instead values of 'high capabilities', 'high performance' and 'high adaptation'. The inherent ability to construct this type of government is extremely important for governments in transition.

Take Taiwan as an example. Most of the economic achievements of the past were made under the guidance, planning and promotion of the government and the island's system of bureaucracy. Although such policies and guidance were an appropriate means of achieving the government's mission during that particular era, there should now be some serious consideration given to reducing both the size and the functions of the government in Taiwan, and some real concern over the issues now being faced by the island's economy, such as management of the economic and trade relationships across the Strait, dealing with the transformation of the economic structure brought about by globalisation and WTO accession, as well as the continuing enhancement and development of politics, society and culture in Taiwan, all of which are in urgent need of a robust style of government and appropriately robust administrative systems. In other words, when assuming a standpoint of developmental administration, a strong governing team is still an important prerequisite for Taiwan's future development.

THE CONDITIONS AND LIMITATIONS OF TAIWAN'S ECONOMIC DEVELOPMENT

In the changing 'new world', democratisation, globalisation and the amassing of knowledge have become the three major prerequisites of economic development. As a result, governments in economies all around the world are now finding themselves drawn into a transitional period of democratisation, albeit at different rates of progress. Despite this phenomenon clearly being generated domestically, growing international competition – which became apparent in the 'post-cold war' period – has now turned towards a greater emphasis on mutual cooperation and coordination, and rewriting the rules on trading, as well as environmental conservation and protection. The ubiquitous and instantaneous nature of information has placed the entire globe into a scenario of high tension, within which there is now a constant race against time and everyone is competing head-to-head with technology. Clearly, however, the transient nature of technology and information ensures that any efforts to monopolise these assets are futile. In order to revitalise the island's life force and establish an attractive international stage for the twenty-first century, the government in Taiwan has to discard outmoded ways of thinking and adopt a whole new outlook, searching for appropriate short-term, medium-term and long-term goals and directions, whilst making the most of the foundations that have thus far been put into place, taking heed of international trends, and relying upon Taiwan's local characteristics. Only then will Taiwan have any hope of once again taking up a leading role in future global trade and industry.

Whilst the governments of Hong Kong and Singapore have been actively pursuing ways of becoming regional business, financial and technological centres, the Taiwanese government has been doggedly pushing projects such as the 'Asia Pacific Regional Operations Centre' and the 'Green Silicon Island', developing 'global logistics' and a 'knowledge-based economy', all of which demonstrate the determination of the government to strengthen the island's competitive capabilities. However, under the enormous competitive pressure from other countries and the worsening political and economic situation at home, if the Taiwanese government has any desire to extend the past experience of the island's 'miracle', the time seems right for it to adopt a 'New Managerialism' stance, holding on to the goal of building an 'entrepreneurial state' in which reform can be accomplished, whilst devoting its energy to precluding obstacles to trade and economic development, and actively promoting internationalisation, so that the island may be better placed to cope with the global pressures of the twenty-first century. With such dramatic and ongoing changes in both internal and external contexts, the Taiwanese government is now undergoing a variety of tests which can be examined from a number of different aspects.

Economic Aspects

International economic recession

At around the end of 2000, signs of a significant slowdown in the global economic climate started to become apparent; such a slowdown stood in stark contrast to the robust recovery that had been generally displayed in the aftermath of the Asian financial crisis. The general malaise, which was becoming apparent on a global scale, was essentially due to negative influences from the slowdown in economic growth in many of the European countries and in the Americas, along with sky-high oil prices and the general anticipation of inflationary pressures. The '911' terrorist attacks on the twin towers of the World Trade Center in New York on 11 September 2001 further stalled the expected recovery of the US economy and led to those countries whose economies were heavily reliant upon the US market experiencing significant losses.

The 'World Economic Situation and Prospects' released by the UN on 10 October 2001 indicated that the 911 tragedy would lead to a 1.0 per cent decline in the global economy, which converts into an actual output loss of US$350 billion. The UN's release also adjusted the estimation of the global economic growth rate down to 1.4 per cent, its lowest value in ten years, and forecasted a 'near-zero' growth rate for international trade, with suggestions that Hong Kong, Malaysia, Singapore, South Korea and Taiwan would be faced with the most serious impacts. The figures subsequently released by the IMF on 18 December 2001, in a document entitled 'Global and Regional Economic Prospects', also proposed a downward adjustment of the global growth rate for 2001, from 2.6 per cent to 2.4 per cent.[3] The IMF report considered that 'the current outlook remains subject to considerable uncertainty . . . but we observe that a number of factors should help to support recovery in 2002' (IMF, 2001).

Domestic economic degradation

Taiwan's economy has started to show signs of recession as a result of the pressures of the global economy and international political instability. The Council for Economic Planning and Development (CEPD) has continued to announce the presence of signals of severe recession with the economic growth rate in Taiwan experiencing a steady decline, whilst the Taiwan stock market index, the TAIEX, fell by 40 per cent, with the total market value of listed companies dropping NT$68 billion (United Daily News, 2001). Other indicators, such as the incessant rise in the unemployment rate, the increasing number of business closures, and the alarming growth in the bad loans ratio amongst many of Taiwan's banks, also pointed to domestic economic woes. Furthermore, the 911 terrorist attacks on the US clearly represented the last straw, as the ripple effects stemming from the attacks were starting to be felt. Given the island's current politico-economic conditions, Taiwan's capacity to absorb the risks of economic recession have become severely limited and if the government should do anything unwise in an effort to artificially lift the economy out of recession, this could have profound implications on the island's economic future and on its population.

Sluggish participation in regional economic integration

Globalisation has become the mainstream argument for advancement amongst international society, and global governance has gradually come to represent the framework through which public issues are managed, and policies are formulated. Although matters of politics, environmental protection and human rights are the main issues within the debate on globalisation, the demand for 'economic' integration may still represent the most important mechanism for the more rapid attainment of globalisation. Society has been living in a world characterised by high interdependence and the need for global cooperation, with a number of issues having now transcended national boundaries, such that any country, in isolation, no longer has the ability to fully control the knowledge and information that are important for dealing with the issues at hand. For example, any country, organisation, or group now has sufficient legitimacy to demand the sharing of power on the basis that the overall aim is to resolve public issues, a development which suggests that national sovereignty is increasingly being overshadowed by national participation in international matters.

Within the whole process of economic globalisation, the promotion of regional trade cooperation – or trade agreements – has become a primary strategy for the enhancement of national competitiveness on a global scale. Indeed, according to the WTO Secretariat, by July 2000, 220 such cooperative trade agreements had been declared. Some of the major incentives prompting countries to pursue such regional economic integration have been the lifting of trade barriers, the establishment of dispute settlement mechanisms and the mutual authentication of standards; other incentives include the economic advantages stemming from the deepening of industrial specialisation amongst member countries, enhancements to the efficient exploitation of resources, the widening of markets and creation of scale economies, the minimalisation of uncertainty, the facilitation of free-flowing production factors and a general reduction in unemployment levels (METI, 2000).

Taiwan's participation in regional economic integration in the past has been passive, indeed sluggish, and regularly interrupted by political forces. In the future, Taiwan will have to participate in all forms of regional economic integration, following the trends of economic globalisation and using methods that are forward-looking, proactive and creative.

Insufficient globalisation and internationalisation

Globalisation involves a series of processes characterised by complex, interdependent and mutually related changes. These processes will, on the one hand, lead to the enhancement, deepening and acceleration of the complex interrelationships that exist between global politics, economies, societies, cultures, environments and diplomatic interactions, whilst, on the other, they will also have the simultaneous effect of leading to individuals, groups and countries from every corner of the world being influenced by the events that are occurring, and the decisions that are being taken, in other areas of the world (Kim, 1999).

The wave that is created by globalisation diminishes national boundaries whilst propelling the mobility of technology, real capital and human capital to reach levels far higher than those previously set. Therefore, since these important economic resources are being concentrated in low-cost and highly profitable areas, governments need to be sufficiently astute in their efforts to implement business and industrial policies that are inherently more attractive than those of their major competitors. In order to ensure that they can maintain their competitive edge within the globalising environment, the government needs to shape a competitive environment with greater equity, to build incentive structures with greater emphasis on the market mechanism, to incubate valuable human capital and to establish much more efficient administrative systems.

Taiwan's real problem, at the present time, lies in the fact that the pace of globalisation and internationalisation is too slow, and remains extremely dependent on the mainland market. According to the mainland government's official statistics, when the flow of investment via third countries is taken into consideration, Taiwan currently holds second place in overall mainland China investment (Hsu, 2001, pp.134-6). Indeed, as a result of the economic recession at home, Taiwan has seen a spate of high-tech businesses selecting the mainland market as their first choice for overseas investment. Taiwan's efforts towards joining a whole range of international organisations have also been continually interrupted by a number of political factors, thus preventing the government from gaining the support of the international community and from playing an active part within it.

Despite the excellent achievements of the past, Taiwan's competitive edge has suffered continual diminution in the face of the highly competitive international environment – with particular reference to the newly rising Southeast Asian and mainland Chinese economies – and the island's economy is now facing a number of daunting challenges resulting from the necessary transformation of both the internal and external economic structure. In view of such a changing economic situation, it has become necessary to reexamine and reevaluate the role of the government.

The challenge of WTO accession

Taiwan's recent accession into the WTO was brought about as the result of sixteen years of negotiations, which eventually gained the recognition of the WTO multilateral working group, and which finally resulted in Taiwan's acceptance into the global trading body, as a full member, at the beginning of 2002. With the total number of WTO members now amounting to more than 140, the WTO might well be labelled 'The United Nations of Economy and Trade'. Consequently, having gained accession into such an important body, Taiwan should now find itself in a position to enhance its economic competitiveness, raise its overall visibility and integrate itself into the global community. Nevertheless, it is clear that the impacts on the Taiwanese economy brought about as a result of WTO accession must not be underestimated.

First of all, Taiwan's traditional industries will be severely hit as a result of the challenges posed by other member countries, particularly those whose labour costs are considerably lower. Therefore, it is now incumbent upon Taiwan's traditional industries to engage in significant transformation if they are to stand any chance of strengthening their current competitiveness. Secondly, in view of the WTO's regulations on non-discrimination, Taiwan's economy will have to become more open to mainland China, which will undoubtedly pose a number of direct challenges to the government's existing mainland China policies. Thirdly, as a result of the accession of both China and Taiwan into the WTO, economic competition between the two sides of the Taiwan strait is also set to become much more intense. What clearly stands out as a task of paramount importance is the need to adjust the whole structure of industry without any delay, in order to quickly determine the optimal models for the division of labour and complementarity which will allow Taiwan to exploit the effects of economic integration and transcend the 'zero-sum' position.

The whole issue of cross-strait interaction has been characterised by feelings of animosity and uncertainty for a significant period of time, with the two sides demonstrating a frustrating inability to construct institutional communication channels to deal with issues of free trade, direct air and maritime transportation links, criminal activities and various matters relating to the WTO. This is a source of continuing worry, since the economic and trading relationship across the strait, a relationship which should now be developing as a result of the accession of both sides into the WTO, clearly needs to be dealt with on the basis of normal member country relationships, or privileged relationships, as opposed to mutually exclusive ones (Tsai, 2001). Taiwan must also be aware that it has to face up to a number of additional challenges stemming from WTO accession, a few examples of which are identified below.

The impacts on agriculture. In general, being a member of the WTO will have more positive influences than negative ones, but there will undoubtedly be certain individual sectors that will feel the shocks to a far greater degree. Taiwan's agricultural sector is a case in point; as a result of the higher production costs and weaker capabilities, in terms of market competitiveness, the sector is set to lose around NT$20 billion to 30 billion within the first two years of WTO membership, whilst the number of unemployed persons in both the agricultural and fisheries sectors is likely to demonstrate a year-on-year rising trend (Chang, 2001). There is therefore a clear and urgent need for the government to formulate plans which take into consideration all of the options for dealing with the rising number of employees.

The impacts on environmental policies. Environmental protection has become a universally accepted goal and as such, those engaging in international trade must abide by the environmental regulations of importing nations, such as the ISO14000 series which has now prevailed for some considerable time. Taiwan's accession into the WTO will bring the island ever deeper into the international economic and trading system, which clearly suggests the importance that it must now place upon examining issues such as the quality of its regulations, and whether these are compatible with the spirit of green consumption. The issue of whether the current environmental regulations have rendered Taiwan's industries more competitive, and thus, whether they have achieved environmental worth, must also be determined.

The impacts on higher education. During the early stages of Taiwan's WTO accession, the opening up of the island's domestic education market will permit foreigners to establish higher education institutions, to set up short-term cram schools, and indeed, to provide cross-border 'tele-education' and offer intermediary services for overseas study. As compared to the advanced countries, the history, standards and norms of Taiwan's higher education are rather weak, and once the market protectionism that currently exists begins to disintegrate under the tide of global competition, with some of the more renowned universities finding their way into Taiwan, the absorption effects on the current 'black hole' will come into play.

Under the principles of 'mutual recognition' and 'academic accreditation', the Taiwanese government will also have to start recognising diplomas issued by the mainland Chinese authorities. Clearly, in order to offset the difficulties arising from WTO accession, an extremely pressing task for the government in Taiwan is to urge the island's domestic schools and higher education institutions to strengthen their academic research capabilities and thereby, their international competitiveness.

Political Aspects

Incessant cross-strait tension

Apart from the inherent and enduring differences in the fundamental ideologies of Taiwan and mainland China, which are themselves extremely problematic, there have been a number of serious issues that have arisen on regular occasions, caused in part by incidents such as the 1996 missile crisis and the recurrent claims of 'two countries' and 'two governments'. Nevertheless, the lack of clarity in the Taiwanese government's policies on the mainland, its rigid and restrictive policies under the stated principle of 'no haste, be patient', and indeed, the continuing inconsistency of the government's position, have put the existing relationship across the Strait under considerable strain.

According to a recent survey undertaken by the Department of Statistics and Information Science at Fu-jen University in Taiwan, the issue of cross-strait instability and uncertainty is seen as the most damaging factor affecting the island's continuing economic development, trade and investment (Table 3.1) and has been generally detrimental to national development.

Table 3.1   Survey responses - factors causing Taiwan's current economic recession

Unit: %

Factor	Contribution to Taiwan's recession
Cross-strait instability and uncertainty	14.8
Global Economic Recession	12.2
Minority of seats held by the ruling party	11.8
Improper or inappropriate decision-making	11.4
Capital flight and overseas investment	10.5
Other	8.59
Non-cooperation by minority party legislators	6.2
Extensive boycotting by the Legislative Yuan	2.7
Overabundance of guest workers	2.1
Serious unemployment	1.2

Source: Department of Statistics and Information Science (2001).

The primary task for the government must now be to determine how to ease the political conflict across the Strait, strengthen the basis of confidence which will undoubtedly be beneficial to the interaction between the two sides, and transcend the current zero-sum game with the aim of constructing a win-win situation for both sides.

Government inefficiency

According to the IMD's 2000 competitiveness report, Taiwan has now slipped to fourteenth position in the global competitiveness rating. This serious decline has been attributed to areas such as chaotic government organisations, the lack of clarity in the power base of central and local government, as well as blurred areas of roles and responsibilities, rigid personnel and budgetary systems, policies that fail to provide any emphasis on generating productivity, but instead concentrate on preventing corruption, opaque decision-making processes, excessive bureaucracy and unnecessary regulations, all of which have lowered the general administrative efficiency of the island and prevented the public authorities from exercising legitimate power. The inefficiency within the law-making system in Taiwan, in conjunction with the imbalance between the legislative and executive branches, has had a severely negative impact on the overall efficiency of governance in Taiwan, preventing the government from pursuing national construction and administration and, most importantly, preventing it from taking overall political responsibility.

Lack of knowledge and reflection on globalisation

Without doubt, the greatest impact for governments in the twenty-first century is the current era of expanding globalisation. Globalisation does not resort to political or military force, but to soft power, in the form of economic trade and culture (Held and McGrew, 1999, pp.483-96). From a perspective of institutional economics, globalisation promotes international economic convergence, cuts out negotiation costs and transaction costs between nations, and increases the possibility of effectively implementing global governance (North, 1990). Clearly, these are consequences that can be very beneficial to the advanced capitalist economies, in terms of promoting international capital flows and cutting down on economic costs; therefore, what the government in Taiwan must consider, is how to gain a complete understanding of the whole process of globalisation, and its influences on Taiwan, in order to develop and implement appropriate strategies to deal with these influences.

When seeking to follow the globalisation trend, the government in Taiwan must recognise the need to challenge outdated modes of governance. It must, for example, begin to bring into play non-traditional resources to deal with the global paradox characterised by increasing economic integration and resultant political decentralisation. An entrepreneurial government should be able to deal with cross-border issues in a more flexible way by using a strategy of cooperation between industry and government, or academia and government. Moreover, given the current rigid nature of government agencies, non-governmental organisations (NGOs) could provide assistance to these agencies in the handling of public or international affairs. As liberty and democracy become the mainstream values of the international society, the operations of government administration must correspond to market patterns, since the boundaries between the public and private sectors will become obscured as a result of accelerating privatisation and liberalisation (Song, 2001). However, it is worth noting that in their efforts to develop new modes of governance, a number of advanced capitalist economies have established 'governance paradigms' from which the developing countries could learn a great deal. These paradigms are referred to in various ways, such as 'public governance' (Kickert, 1997), 'good governance' (IBRD, 1994; OECD/DAC, 1996), 'sound governance' (UNDP, 1996) or 'democratic governance' (UNESCO, 2002). The characteristics of these modes of governance include a democratic and liberal society, healthy capitalist economic institutions, sound legal systems, open international policies, highly effective administrative systems and total insistence on justice and equality. The influence of such 'governance paradigms' has already begun to spread alongside the mechanism of globalisation, with the most important driving force being the efforts of such international financial institutions or international organisations as the World Bank, Asian Development Bank, OECD and the IMF.

In the eighties, crises had emerged in the area of social security which had a significant influence on OECD members, with the huge pressure of public debts forcing the governments of the OECD countries to do better with fewer resources and to try to learn better methods of management from their domestic enterprises. However, a number of countries are now facing fiscal deficits in the post-cold war era, as real problems associated with ineffective social security policies have emerged. Many of these countries have begun to push large-scale privatisation having regarded the spread of neo-liberalism as being based on the poor performance of Latin American and African 'developmentalism', characterised largely by the unreasonable operations of the state, corruption, general inability, and high levels of debt. Furthermore, with the support of advanced economic power, the IMF and the World Bank have followed extreme liberalist lines, hastily promoting a variety of structural adjustment projects as a means of helping the developing countries to implement such neo-liberal economic policies. Following suit, many international financial institutions have urged those countries that asked for their assistance to implement such neo-liberal economic policies, using 'proper governance' as the basis for their 'legitimate' demands (Smouts, 1998, p.81).

In summary, given the trend towards globalisation, structures of 'proper governance' have begun to represent the standards by which a country's economy is judged, and indeed, the adherence to such 'proper governance' is inevitable for any country which is involved in the international economic competitive system; the result is that the era of the 'governance of globalisation' is approaching at an increasingly rapid pace. The government in Taiwan now has to consider its position, and rather than blindly following the trend towards globalisation, it has to discard the current subjectivity that is causing the incessant disintegration of the economy within the globalisation mechanism. Since there are also many negative consequences of globalisation, the alternative is to lose ground in its pursuit of sustainable development, with a reduction, or total loss, of national sovereignty, constraints on democracy and the disappearance of communities.

Whilst conceding that democracy has fulfilled its mission to become part of Taiwan's history, with the island experiencing the various stages of authoritarian rule, government transformation and initial democratic consolidation, there nevertheless remain many problems that need to be tackled, such as the necessary repositioning of the island's economic subsystems and the restructuring of Taiwanese society and culture. In its efforts to face the challenges of the new century, the government must consider adjusting its pace and its thinking, and explore the various directions available in its efforts to place appropriate focus on the various economic, political, social and cultural dimensions.

Economic Aspects of Government Reengineering

Accelerating globalisation and internationalisation

Since it is clearly impossible to bring globalisation to a halt, in addition to rescinding a wide range of unnecessary statutes and removing current trade barriers, Taiwan needs to strengthen its economy through the creation of an environment conducive to business investment, speeding up the mobility of international capital and human capital, and attempting to participate vigorously in international economic and trading organisations. The overall aim must be to enhance the island's national competitive capabilities and to totally integrate with international society. Taiwan's recent accession into the WTO demands that the Taiwanese government, and the island's people, now place a great deal more effort into dealing with the pertinent issues.

Shaping visions of economic policies

Taiwan's industrial structure has endured various stages of transformation from agricultural production to industrial production, and has since demonstrated success in the development of its high-tech industries. This has been a great source of pride to the Taiwanese people. Nevertheless, faced with the epoch of the so-called 'knowledge-based economy', which also represents the island's uncertain future, in conjunction with the maintenance and further development of the high-tech industries, the primary focus must be on the ways in which Taiwan can promote the next stage of the structural transformation of its industry. It is therefore necessary for the government to hold on to a vision with greater clarity and to design policies with greater precision.

Clarifying the government's role in the market

There has been a recent slump in confidence in the Taiwanese government, largely as a result of the worsening domestic financial situation, and unstable fiscal and economic government policies. It is therefore important for the government to clarify its role, and to become a free market builder and regulator, in order to avoid committing the grave error of simultaneously being a player and an umpire, since this clearly represents inappropriate intervention in the market mechanism. With the regime of 'directing democracy' having now come to an end, the government's current focus should be on enhancing the resource allocation function of the market mechanism.

Political Aspects of Government Reengineering

Reviewing the policy on cross-strait relationships

The ambiguous relationship that currently exists between the two sides of the Taiwan strait, and the hesitant nature of the Taiwanese government's policy with regard to the mainland, has raised the level of uncertainty for Taiwanese firms, which has, in turn, raised their investment costs. The government must therefore establish a set of clear, comprehensive and enduring guidelines, accompanied by a set of concrete measures showing greater tolerance and aiming to maximise enterprise benefits, so that businesses and people will be totally aware of how to proceed. Whilst the principle set forward by the Chen Shui-Bian government, for 'active opening and effectual management' is clearly the appropriate direction, details of the practical operation of such a policy will stand as the real test for his government.

Respecting the constitution

The constitution has been revised six times without deference to constitutional conventions or constitutionalism; indeed, the constitution seems to have increasingly become the vehicle used by politicians to achieve their personal goals. This tendency to push forward revisions without systematic thinking can lead to the destruction of constitutional institutions and faltering national foundations. If Taiwan is to continue to develop under stable constitutional order, it is important that the government accepts its responsibility for guarding the life and security of its people, on the one hand, whilst, on the other, respecting the structure of the constitution and maintaining its integrity.

Improving government interaction

The quality of the interaction between the Legislative Yuan and the Executive Yuan has been less than satisfactory, largely because of the immaturity of Taiwan's democracy and its primitive laws. However, the interaction between these two important arms of government has become even worse since the changeover of power from the Kuomintang (KMT) to the Democratic Progressive Party (DPP). As a result of the ideological leadership exercised by the ruling party, and the lack of trust in its exercise of power, the coherence of the government's policies has been seriously undermined, with the result that its policies are unstable, administrative and legislative efficiency has been negatively affected, the influence of checks and balances has dwindled and the island's constitutional framework is now facing even greater challenges. The fundamental means of solving these problems would be to seek to rebuild mutual trust and to reconstruct effective patterns of interaction.

Increasing administrative efficiency

The vast array of bureaucratic and complicated regulations in Taiwan has long been a target for criticism. Such never-ending paperwork, the seal culture and the rigidity of the regulations not only generate complaints, but also make it difficult for Taiwan to respond promptly and effectively to the social needs of a post-industrial society. The government should do everything in its power to seek out ways of enhancing administrative efficiency using a range of innovative measures.

The background to the extensive range of laws and regulations developed in the past is that they were put in place to deal with particular contexts. However, with the passage of time, despite the basis of the support for these laws and regulations having long disappeared, many of them linger on and now serve only to hamper the efficacy of the administrative actions of civil servants. This type of 'appendix process' needs to be curtailed through government reengineering, and as soon as practicably possible (Hammer and Champy, 1994). The Clinton government in the US set an admirable precedent by abandoning its earlier personnel regulations and restructuring codes, institutions and processes. The end result was that a total of around ten million pages of administrative orders, rules and regulations were totally discarded.

Social and Cultural Aspects of Government Reengineering

Rising new forces in Taiwan's pluralised social and cultural structure

The interaction and mutual impacts of traditional Chinese culture and foreign cultures in Taiwan (prime examples being the widespread acceptance of US and Japanese cultures) have created heterogeneity, resulting in cultural innovation and dilemmas for infusion. Because of the changes brought about by political and economic circumstances, social interests and structures of influence have been significantly transformed. The consequences of population redistribution are the creation of interest games with more animosity and vehemence, rising social fragmentation and the creation of difficulties in the area of social integration.

Significant changes in the social psychological structure

There is now a rapid rise in 'rights awareness' in Taiwan. Along with the spread of democratically guided education, Taiwan's political culture has started to shift away from the traditional form of 'subordinate culture' and there is now a gradual strengthening of 'citizenship consciousness'. Such dynamics are characterised by a rise in rights awareness and escalating inputs into the political system, resulting in increasing demands on the government and the need for guaranteed protection of Taiwanese citizenship underpinned by the constitution.

As the Taiwanese economy has developed, the universal standard by which many of Taiwan's citizens judge the issues around them has become increasingly utilitarian. Such subjective thinking makes it extremely difficult for 'citizenship consciousness' to take root and to thrive, and has led to a general loss of humanistic spirit, resulting in serious estrangement in interpersonal relationships, as well as preventing the formation of civil society. However, with Taiwanese citizens having begun to turn their backs on the erstwhile culture of subordination, they have consequently begun to obtain increasingly greater political efficacy, which is reflected in their growing willingness to participate in political debate and the growing number of grassroots political movements, demonstrating a desire amongst Taiwanese citizens to become their own masters.

Diversifying ideas and expectations

Following the opening up of Taiwanese society, the people's ideas, values and interests are becoming increasingly diversified. Nevertheless, although this can provide a growing number of opportunities for society, it will also result in Taiwan having to face a whole range of extremely complicated chain reactions. This will represent a real test for the government with regard to its inherent ability to transcend various group or individual interests. However, the people's demands of the government will be aimed not only at quantitative increases, but also at qualitative enhancements. The painstakingly slow pace of government functions is currently failing to keep pace with social expectations, and this will require the government to examine exactly what it is aiming to achieve, and in what sort of time-frame. Such an examination should lead to adjustment of the pace of its general governance and, ultimately, lead to more radical reengineering.

It is also important for the government to take notice of the impact of foreign cultures on Taiwanese culture. Foreign popular cultures from the US, Japan and Korea have recently gained a strong foothold in Taiwan by various means, especially through the various communications media that are now so widespread, and it seems that local culture is unable to resist this onslaught, with the end result being a weakening of the subjectivity of Taiwanese culture. When faced with the totality of globalisation, a great challenge for the government will be its ability to protect traditional culture, reinforce native cultural values and promote extended cultural infusion and creativity.

REENGINEERING GOVERNMENT CAPABILITIES

To summarise the above analysis, since the onset of the latest stage of economic transformation, which began about a decade ago, Taiwan has been ignoring the importance of convergence with globalisation. Furthermore, given that the strategies and the essential core of the new era of economic development have not yet been established, the government is now facing a growing number of challenges. It has seen a worsening of the investment environment, political paralysis, and struggles within the system that are gravely damaging the island's constitutional institutions and its essence, a social psychological structure that is becoming increasingly unhealthy, and cultural development that is steering a somewhat abnormal course. In light of these issues, the government must demonstrate an ability to envisage the rapid changes that will come about as a result of the internal and external environments and begin to radically transform its functions in response to its ever changing role. Only then can Taiwan hope to determine its new competitive advantages and embark upon another Taiwanese 'miracle', stepping towards full participation in the twenty-first century, a century characterised by liberalisation and internationalisation.

The influence that government organisations will have on socio-economic and political development in the twenty-first century, and on technological change, will undoubtedly become progressively momentous as time goes by. Therefore, not only is the focus of global competition set to shift from 'enterprise level' to 'national level', but it will also experience a shift from a basis of 'force' to one of 'capabilities'. It is clear that the traditional definition of national government functions was transformed from a principle of 'the less, the better' (a system upheld by the liberalism of the sixteenth and seventeenth centuries), into that of providing a more active and supportive role (giving rise to the welfare-state era of the nineteenth and twentieth centuries, within which the role of national governments was to solve the problems of income disparity). In the twenty-first century, however, under the newly emerged system of liberalisation and internationalisation, governments must now take into account the rising political consciousness of its citizenry, and the increasing demands of social welfare. The role of government must now include many other areas such as national defence, regulations, services, assistance, development and emerging needs resulting from the arrival of new technologies, each on a scale sufficient to meet the needs of its people.

Nevertheless, whilst the functions of the government will have to be redefined, this process must be carried out within the boundaries of both public pressure and fiscal austerity. In a pluralist society, we can expect to see a constant increase in the range of conflicting demands, which will necessitate additional roles for the government as arbitrator of social struggles, leader of national development and integrator of social forces (i.e., the integration of humanities and technologies, of government and society, and of civil servants and ministers), all this in addition to fulfilling its traditional functions. Moreover, governments should aim to assist in the strengthening of the capabilities of both citizens and local governments, for the overall purpose of promoting self-reliance and self-governance. These individuals and government bodies can thereby learn to take responsibility and actively assist in building an environment beneficial to national and social development.

Government organisations have traditionally been based on Weberian principles, with their bureaucracies characterised by a pyramid, and emphasising hierarchical control and comprehensive codes and laws. By the turn of the century, such limited organisations had become ill equipped to cope with the rapidly changing economic environment. Indeed, they had proved themselves particularly inept at providing civil servants with sufficient motivation to produce creative work or at stimulating any desire to enhance levels of efficiency. It therefore became necessary for governments to transform their constitutions and ways of operation, to engage in large-scale reengineering, which included external organisational structures and internal organisational cultures, and to discard the rigid, traditional forms of hierarchical control. Since the nineties, however, many of the world's leading economies have been engaged in large-scale government reengineering, attempting to infuse entrepreneurial spirit into government agencies and emphasising a model of 'market-based governance' (Peters, 1996).

Following the mainstream ideas of competition, privatisation, contracting-out and the decentralisation of power, many countries successfully readjusted their government organisations and their organisational cultures, leading to improvements in the overall efficacy of government operations and the realisation of a governance ideal of 'small but beautiful' and high efficiency.

The governments concerned pushed forward measures for the reform of public services, such as the abovementioned 'efficiency units' in the UK, the 'National Performance Review' (NPR) of the US and the 'Commonwealth Ombudsman' of New Zealand, each of which were based on the principle of changing the previous 'government to people (i.e., customer) relationships' and of renewing notions and techniques.

The Implications of Reengineering Government Capabilities

Governance in the twenty-first century will be based largely on the market, and under such circumstances, the Taiwanese government must seek to adjust its own functions, following the directions proposed in Figure 3.2 and described thereafter.

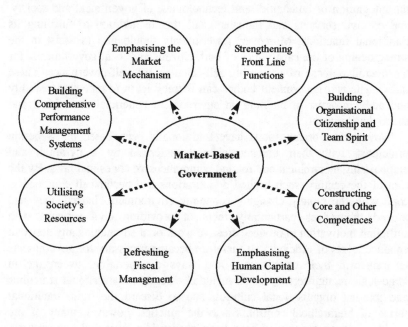

Figure 3.2   Reengineering Taiwan's government capabilities

Emphasising the market mechanism

'Market-based' governments are those that favour the use of 'market efficiency' as the appropriate apparatus for resource allocation. The appropriate adoption of the market mechanism can enhance the economic rationality of both civil servants and civil society, with the result that public services provided by the government are rendered more competitive. Concrete measures of such adoption include the establishment of flexible remuneration systems within the public sector, stressing the focus on internal competition, privatisation and outsourcing, and a service culture which is totally customer-oriented.

Strengthening front line functions

In order to support their emphasis on the market mechanism, 'market-based' governments also try to accentuate the decentralisation of policymaking and implementation, and attempt to dismantle the monopolistic power created by centralisation. In this era of enhanced customer orientation, front line workers need to be given sufficient power to deal with the questions and demands of consumers, whilst local governments must also be equipped with greater decision-making power to become independent units capable of solving such consumer problems and issues, thus reinforcing the functions of the front line. As stated by Dr. Sun Yat-Sen, many years ago, 'local self-governance is the foundation of a nation, and a nation would not be able to sustain itself without a consolidated foundation'; those words clearly demonstrated the importance of strengthening foundations at that time, and are of equal, if not greater, relevance today.

Building organisational citizenship and team spirit

In order to secure multiple effects and synergies, the administrative sector must seek to forge an internal *esprit de corps*, in an effort to help shape the organisational citizenship (Hult and Walcott, 1990) that will be a model for Taiwan's future, and also to effectively reduce the alienation felt by public servants, so that they can begin to feel 'a part' of their organisations. These public servants can then develop an awareness of their rights vis-à-vis their organisations and can also begin to recognise the need to treasure their promises and obligations to their organisations (the true spirit of organisational citizenship), integrating themselves with the internal planning and policymaking of the organisation, and reinforcing the efficiency of bureaucracy. Such efforts will serve as the foundation of respect for the market mechanism and healthy finances. The neutrality of civil servants can only be secured by respect for their professional abilities; this is the only way of preventing inappropriate political interference from disrupting the administrative functions of civil servants.

Constructing core and other competences

Professional capabilities and the efficient use of such capabilities are the cornerstones to the successful achievement of government functions. As noted above, expertise serves as the basis for the neutrality of civil servants, but given that political forces have an inherent lack of respect for professional abilities, they will tend to cut through such neutrality. The strengthening of levels of efficiency and professional capabilities is therefore essential to the acceptance of the market mechanism and the maintenance of financial health. Along with such strengths, civil servants should also be loyal to their nation (as is admirably demonstrated in the British notion of civil service loyalty); they should be concerned about society, devoted to the government and to serving the people, and responsible for their actions. Any profession must generally include both 'techniques' and 'ethics', which means that in addition to grounded expertise, civil servants should also be equipped with the civil service ethics of administrative neutrality and democratic administration, in order to build an effective professional reputation and appropriate social status.

Emphasising human capital development

Human capital is the fundamental strategic resource through which organisations are able to achieve their goals. Living in this era of enhanced human capital value, any organisation that is actively able to attract, employ, develop and retain capable people will stand out as an organisation with enduring competitive capabilities. 'Market-based' governments must recognise the importance of human capital, viewing human resource costs in accordance with the performance capabilities of these resources. They must avoid making any strong links between downsizing and the lowering of human resource costs, whilst adjusting incentive structures and reward systems. This will encourage civil servants to become involved in innovative activities aimed at enhancing government efficiency and service quality. For example, given higher levels of personal empowerment and autonomy, civil servants could begin to exploit their own capabilities, deciding where they should concentrate their efforts for the benefit of the organisation.

Refreshing fiscal management

Fiscal management is the mother of all administrative affairs, since a good fiscal system will allow a national economy to move forward without the constant need to keep looking back. Expenditure priorities therefore need to be examined from a short-run perspective, in order to avoid long-term policy chaos; that is, short-term budget arrangements, projects and programs should be prioritised in accordance with their importance, but should also be tempered with rationality. Since tax systems are intimately related to social justice, in order to achieve the goal of tax equality in the long run, and to bridge the gap between the rich and the poor, governments should re-examine their current tax systems and relevant laws with the overall aim of pursuing the development of an 'ideal' system of tax equality on a comprehensive scale.

In their pursuit of such an ideal, governments need to be adamant and insistent. Goals such as healthy finances and the promotion of national economic development can be achieved by governments at a single stroke, but will only be made possible through the construction of comprehensive tax structures. The principles of fiscal reform implemented by 'market-based' governments aim to separate buyers, providers and creators in the domestic market. In addition, the demand for fiscal management within democratic societies is reflected in the emphasis on the 'auditing' function, which revolves around the values of three Es, economy, efficiency and efficacy, and focuses on enhancing the overall effectiveness of government reforms.

Utilising society's resources

Governments should recognise that instead of having one overall role, as the remote director of operations, they need to take in-depth responsibility for multiple roles as policymakers, arbitrators and supervisors, and make efforts to speed up the pace of privatisation, the rate of outsourcing of government affairs and the level of participation in public construction by civil society. Market-based governments rely heavily on the assistance of civil society to extend government relationship networks, to strengthen the functions of government services, to learn innovative, risk-taking and responsible behavior from private businesses, and to introduce mature management techniques – developed by such enterprises – into their administrative processes. Through strategic measures such as subcontracting and outsourcing, civil society could also be encouraged to join in the ranks of government service, which would also help to incubate 'citizenship awareness'. What's more, the important work carried out by volunteers and non-profit organisations must not be ignored; the participation and contribution made by these massive forces can have a significant impact on the structure of government service functions.

Building comprehensive performance management systems

It is important for systems to be constructed that are based on encouragement and performance. This should be accompanied by the introduction of competitive and innovative mechanisms, with any projects involving the management of civil service human resources being based upon the idea of strategic and systematic planning. The government needs to conform to the demands of environmental changes, whilst accommodating the governance goals of agencies, building reasonable training performance indicators and enhancing the efficacy of training resource allocation in order to realise overall government visions. They must also construct appropriate performance management mechanisms, ensuring that civil servants begin to recognise that they are totally responsible for their actions, their behaviour, and the eventual outcomes. By means of such mechanisms, the proper functions of punishment and reward can be achieved, the service functions of civil service systems reinvigorated, and legitimacy and righteousness reconstructed.

This era of globalisation and knowledge will not stand still and wait for those who are content to hesitantly watch and wait as the development of information technology accelerates beyond their reach. Government roles must be reconsidered with the aim of determining the adverse impacts of traditional government functions and how new ways of thinking can be put into place. There is clearly a need for the adoption of appropriate strategic and 'market-based' principles and the thorough transformation of organisational structures and cultures; the government can then ensure that its organisations become highly flexible public organisations that dare to pursue innovation, and only then will it become possible to strengthen competitive capabilities and cope with the challenges of both the internal and external environment.

By adopting as their basis 'new public services', through a pattern of public-private collaboration characterised by 'socialisation of public management' and the 'grass-rooting of public services', governments can significantly raise administrative efficiency and governing efficacy. This would include the strengthening of organisational citizenship and team spirit, the effective stimulation of grassroots forces, replacing leadership with assistance, and the construction of appropriate core capabilities, all systematically linked to the market mechanism.

THE ROLE OF THE GOVERNMENT IN THE TWENTY-FIRST CENTURY

In facing the challenges of the twenty-first century, the Taiwanese government has to carefully determine a completely new blueprint for governance, one that is capable of portraying achievable visions which underline aspects of domestic politics, the economy, society and its culture. These represent the government's most important functions, since they are based upon the fundamental principles of securing the lives and livelihood of society, as well as improving communal welfare. In order to achieve this, the government will have to deal with twelve difficult missions, as illustrated in Figure 3.3.

Each of these missions is further described in accordance with the construction of an appropriate vision, active development and reinforcement of the foundations and the environment (Figure 3.4).

Figure 3.3 *The challenging areas for the Taiwanese government in the twenty-first century*

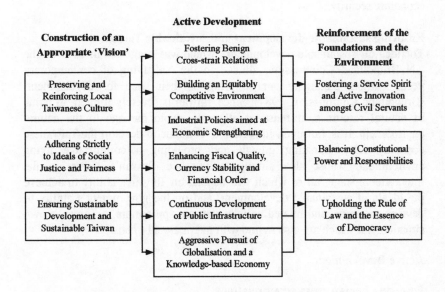

Figure 3.4 *The role of the government in the twenty-first century*

Construction of an Appropriate Vision

Preserving and reinforcing local Taiwanese culture

Although dominant cultures from abroad are now impinging on the local culture, supported largely by the mechanism of globalisation, it is clear that these multifarious foreign cultures could help to stimulate local culture, creating the effects of cultural innovation and open cultural vision. Therefore, in its efforts to provide support for the maintenance of local cultures and values, in addition to regulating businesses, the government should be more aggressively trying to assist businesses to re-examine the strengths and weaknesses of the local culture, so as to retain the former and discard the latter; only then can they raise the level of competitiveness, and thereby, the level of exports.

Adhering strictly to ideals of social justice and fairness

The government is now faced with 'social injustice' brought about by market competition, such as the increasing gap between the rich and poor, and the growing gap that is becoming evident in terms of the level of knowledge possession. Whilst clearly demonstrating its devotion to the continued development of the economy, the government in Taiwan should not, however, ignore the necessary planning and implementation of social welfare policies, so as to ensure that Taiwanese citizens can continue to enjoy social and economic security.

Ensuring sustainable development and sustainable Taiwan

The idea of 'sustainable development', which was suggested in 1987 by the UN Brundtland Commission, alluded to the 'satisfying of contemporary needs without damaging our offspring or their need for development' (Brundtland Commission, 1987). Since Taiwan is severely limited, in terms of natural resources, it must, at all costs, avoid damage to the natural environment. It is, however, important to continue to develop the Taiwanese economy fully, pursuing growth and providing a comfortable living environment, whilst also aiming to improve Taiwan's status on the international stage, all of which will depend on Taiwan's ability to achieve the ideals of sustainable development, and on the government's ability to develop measures and related policies that are appropriate to Taiwan's own situation, but which are also in line with international trends.

Active Development

Fostering benign cross-strait relations

It is inevitable that the discordant cross-strait relationship currently existing between mainland China and Taiwan will eventually be transformed into a relationship of peaceful coexistence, and this will clearly be in the interests of Taiwan in particular. Therefore, in order to advance the current level of exchange between the two sides of the strait, the Taiwanese government has to ponder the appropriate model for future governance in this new century, dealing carefully with the relationship in the early stages of its transformation, and shaping the inevitable moment of peaceful coexistence through the pursuit of innovative integration, and through an active and positive attitude. Clearly, the future relationship between the two sides of the strait should be developed on a new principle of 'less politics and more culture and economy'.

Building an equitably competitive environment

There is no necessity for governments to be omnipotent; indeed, the twenty-first century is set to become an era of 'small government and big society', an era in which the engines of national development will arise more from civil society, particularly the private sector and the newly emerging non-profit organisations. Within this new era, the focus of the government will necessarily be placed upon the establishment of a new set of rules for social and economic competition, emphasising the formulation of standards (as opposed to prescribed means of their implementation), reducing market intervention, stressing more navigation than 'hands on' paddling, and constructing a pluralist model of communication and negotiations. Not only will there be a need for the reexamination and revision of outmoded laws and regulations, but there should also be an emphasis on regular administrative reforms, where necessary, so that the administrative sector can also play an active role in energising the economic forces of civil society.

Industrial policies aimed at strengthening Taiwan's economy

In this era of globalisation characterised by 'countrylessness', as the Taiwanese economy continues to develop, the government must avoid any excessive role-playing as industrial regulator, and instead aim to follow the trends of globalisation, defining Taiwan's industrial development policies for the future and determining its competitive industrial niche, whilst establishing its appropriate position in the international division of labour and building a quality economic environment suited to industrial investment. Only then will it be possible for Taiwan to attract the necessary capital, in terms of human resources, materials and technology.

Taiwan must also make a leap of faith to rid itself of the old style of thinking, with its focus on national boundaries, and reposition itself in the global industrial division of labour, seeking to continuously strengthen its technological capabilities and construct competitive advantages that will lead to growth in productivity, driven by knowledge and technology. Taiwan can thereby distance itself from the tangible competition, formerly characterised by 'sweat-shop' profits, and can move away from the miserable days of 'OEM imprisonment', creating autonomous brands and striding forward in this new century of knowledge creation and competition based on intangible assets.

Enhancing fiscal quality, currency stability and financial order

The Taiwanese government has played the roles of both lawmaker and market participant in the past, thereby ignoring issues of equality and neutrality. There will clearly be a need to refocus its roles in this new century, with the emphasis being on building an environment for fair competition, accentuating the fulfilment of public power and prestige and encouraging private businesses to build on their knowledge base whilst utilising the wisdom that they already possess. The government can achieve this by means of liberal economic rationality whilst also making appropriate adjustments at the macro level and appropriate controls at the micro level. In essence, the stability of fiscal and financial order is similar to the blood of a human body, with the government's fiscal policy being akin to the human heart, the provider of the life-giving flow.

Continuous development of public infrastructure

Continuing national development must be based on complete infrastructures. Taiwan's overall infrastructure has, in the past, proved to be woefully insufficient, and the government must now place a great deal of effort into catching up; however, the requirement is not based solely on the strengthening of hardware infrastructures, such as roads, sewage, airports and ports, but also on software infrastructures, including education and welfare. The government must push for the comprehensive construction of electronic and networking infrastructures, and accelerate the shift towards optical-fibre and broadband networks, so that Taiwan's infrastructure is adequately prepared for the new challenges of the twenty-first century.

Aggressive pursuit of globalisation and a knowledge-based economy

Having achieved WTO accession, the government must now actively push for membership of other international organisations, such as the IMF and the World Bank, as well as regional organisations, such as the East Asian Free Trade Area. It must also seek to achieve the basic ideals of a 'knowledge-based economy', developing Taiwan's organisational capabilities based upon the knowledge gained from its prior experience in participating in free trade areas, establishing global and local economic forums, and exercising influence by playing 'non-governmental roles' using established NGOs and transnational or multinational corporations.

Reinforcement of the Foundations and the Environment

Fostering a service spirit and active innovation amongst civil servants

Traditionally, most of the codes and institutions established for civil servants in Taiwan were based on 'passivity' and 'abuse-proof' thinking. The Civil Service Law, for example, is full of 'must not' directives, terms which naturally breed alienation amongst civil servants and a mindset characterised by 'more action, more blame . . . no action, no blame'. In contrast, active promises abound in the oath of the public service sector in Singapore, which Taiwan may wish to reflect upon:

> We want to give you quality services and we will be polite and unbiased; we will try our best to provide assistance; we are proud of what we do; we want to improve incessantly; your feedback points out the things we could do better; and your suggestions help us reform; your praise helps us work with a smile on our face; we need your trust, support and cooperation, and only then will it be possible to build an excellent public service sector.

In this new century, it is clear that the spirit is shifting from 'passivity' and 'abuse-proof' measures into 'active participation' and 'benefit-creation'. Taiwan's codes pertaining to civil servants must therefore be relaxed, so that civil servants will not be under pressure to help others to gain benefits in what is, essentially, an illegal manner. Such reforms will energise their capabilities, shape the positive minds of potential winners and create overall benefits for the people.

Balancing constitutional power and responsibilities

One of the fundamental principles of democracy is that the majority rules, and since the revision of the constitution in Taiwan the central government process has developed towards a system characterised by twin administrative leaders. However, as a result of the differences in political cultures, and the inadequacies of the current level of democratic sophistication, this new, experimental system has so far proved to be less than successful. The most serious problem is the imbalance of power and responsibilities, which contravenes the fundamental essence of the constitution.

According to the basic principles of organisational operation, it is normal for those who take on the greatest responsibilities to be equipped with greater power, and one assumes, therefore, that those who are given such power must take on even greater responsibility. The Taiwanese government should be totally committed to defending the spirit of the constitution, ensuring that the state operates under its constitutional framework, and devoting effort to rationalising the constitutional framework and its governing structure.

Upholding the rule of law and the essence of democracy

There are three salient features of a quality democratic system: (i) full reflection of public opinion; (ii) a democratic culture which emphasises political morality; and (iii) the pursuit of highly efficacious government. The rule of law and the essence of democracy are the cornerstones of democratic and liberal nations. Therefore, respect for the constitution, the protection of human rights and governance in accordance with the law are the fundamental standards by which democratic and lawful countries work. The behaviour of all people should therefore be in accordance with the law, as opposed to following the will of a few individuals.

In addition to exercising democratic administration, the Taiwanese government has to establish the rule of law; this is the only way that it can construct a quality environment that will ensure the island's permanent and peaceful existence, whilst being beneficial and acceptable to the population, to their lives, and to their continued development. Democracy is not simply an institution based on written statutes, but must also be based on the sincere promise of democratic operation made by those who control power, and on ensuring that such attitudes are internalised throughout the entire government.

CONCLUSIONS

The dawning of the era of the knowledge-based economy is essentially underlined by professional capabilities, the pursuit of facts, and depoliticisation, and although small government has become the mainstream of government reengineering in the academic world and in administrative practices, many countries, such as Japan, are still characterised by big government, with the development of the nation continuing to be led by administrative bureaucracy. However, as Peter Drucker once noted:

> We need a government that is able to govern, not one for implementing and executing; that is, a government that navigates, rather than paddles.

The Taiwanese government is currently finding itself faced with severe problems of fiscal deficits, severe resource limitations and the demands of its citizens for much more comprehensive and diversified services. As a result, the government has to tackle the problem of all-encompassing 'big government' with the aim of undertaking major reforms, and it must also recognise that it has to stop regarding the public sector as the only unit capable of providing the people with services. If it can rise to the challenge, public governance will, as a result, become greatly energised, whilst the scope of available services will be expanded considerably, the 'government business' pie will become significantly enlarged and the goals of 'privatising public services' and 'the socialisation of public management' will be achieved.

It is quite readily apparent that the model of government reengineering which is currently being practised by many of the advanced countries around the world has been characterised mainly by the total reorganisation of the roles and responsibilities of the government, and the adoption of subcontracting and outsourcing, along with the wholesale transfer of public services to the private sector. The adoption of such a model facilitates not only the maximum utilisation of civil society resources, but also demonstrates considerable enhancements to the efficiency and quality of public services, whilst suggesting a transformation of the role of governments from one of 'paddling' into one of 'navigating' (Osborne and Gaebler, 1992).

Nevertheless, in striving to achieve the optimum level of 'small government', the Taiwanese government still has to consider local contexts, provide support measures for the newly emerging business sectors, non-profit organisations and volunteers, and ensure the effective management and solution of society's problems which will undoubtedly arise from such national transformation.

Following the principle of 'localised and effectual management', the government has to draw on the resources of the various communities, religious groups, volunteers and schools, putting in place appropriate regulations and policies, tailor-made for local needs, whilst providing them with only minimum subsidies. The necessary policies should include areas such as providing authorisation for the supervision of projects by the private sector, simplifying relief systems, requesting businesses to take on additional responsibilities and encouraging the participation and supervision of projects by communities themselves, so that even with limited financial and human resources, the government should be able to fulfil each and every one of its function in the most effective way.

The government is also responsible for the management of a variety of problems that have arisen from cross-strait exchanges and necessary adjustments to the domestic economy; it therefore has a responsibility to welcome and embrace this new era of globalisation. Indeed, as Taiwan's President, Chen Shui-Bian, noted (ETToday.com, 2001):

> The liberalisation and internationalisation of Taiwan's financial and capital markets are the only direction the government will follow. The government must respect the market mechanism and refrain from intervening too much.

As has already been noted in the preceding pages, the government must now recognise the need for a number of its existing functions to be transferred to private sector businesses or groups as a means of strengthening its capacity to govern, rather than playing the role of 'full-dimensional' government, a role it has traditionally played in the past. Although it was always inevitable for some intervention in economic activities to be undertaken by capitalist states, the government must carefully consider the issues of 'what areas to intervene in', 'how much intervention' and 'the method for such intervention'. Governmental focus should no longer be on management or regulation of the state and the policies adopted by such governments should be flexible but consistent in order to assist their domestic enterprises and their people to establish for themselves a better management, investment and living environment.

Economic growth has been successfully created in Taiwan – on a miraculous scale – largely as a result of total reliance on the role played by the manufacturing sector; however, Taiwan must now prepare itself for the growing problems arising from its loss of global competitiveness and incorporate itself into international society by active pursuit of a more open role. Under the growing pressure of internationalisation and globalisation, and as a result of the commitments made in 2001 for accession into the WTO at the end of that year, Taiwan must now make some fundamental adjustments to its social structure. Discussions surrounding globalisation are not just about cross-border flows of capital, products and workers, but are also related to the challenges faced by national legal frameworks, policies and even national sovereignty. It is impossible for Taiwan to face the challenges of globalisation alone, and only by making preparations in advance will it be possible for Taiwan to avoid drowning in the flood of internationalisation.

For all economies, economic development in this new century must follow international trends, and for Taiwan in particular, its economic future will be determined by its ability to recognise the road to its destiny based upon the firm foundations built over recent decades. Living in this 'new economic era', characterised by borderless environments, the roles and functions of the government must be transformed without delay, with the aim of pursuing ongoing financial, fiscal, political, social (and perhaps most importantly, government) reforms.

Faced with the dilemma of global economic recession and government fiscal deficit, Taiwan must, on the one hand, recognise the need to rationalise its internal organisation and to economise, whilst on the other hand, actively explore the potential for the linking and sharing of new resources. Only by transcending the idea and the actual structure of 'small government' can Taiwan build a new winning formula that takes on the image of 'big government, big society and big business'. The issue no longer focuses on size, scale and numbers, but instead, on expansion and linkages, reduced intervention by 'political forces', efficiency enhancements amongst the island's 'administrative forces' and the spreading and deepening of participation by 'social forces'.

In the face of the wide-ranging socio-economic challenges and the challenges arising from political development and technological change, although we argue that the roles and responsibilities of the government should be greatly reduced, its remaining roles are nevertheless becoming increasingly important. Since small, market-oriented government has become the international trend, the government in Taiwan must actively seek to participate in global, collaborative economic development projects, so that the island's competitive edge can be transformed from its current basis of 'force' into competitiveness based upon 'capabilities', and from its current 'enterprise-based' competitiveness, to competitiveness based upon the 'nation'.

The government in Taiwan must now be aware that it has to prioritise improvements in the investment environment, with a particular focus on domestic investment, providing an environment beneficial to economic and industrial development, and thus leading to the creation of employment opportunities and the enhancement of national competitive capabilities. It must also devote itself to building an environment in which its people can live in peace and harmony with their neighbours, with the potential for achieving a secure livelihood. If it shows itself capable of all of this, not only will Taiwan be able to bring about another 'miracle' in the twenty-first century, but it will also make its people proud of 'living in Taiwan' and make Taiwan, for them, the best place to live in the world.

NOTES

[1] See: Accenture, 2001; see also: 'Singapore One Defined: A Review'.

[2] According to the World Economic Outlook published by the IMF on 18 December 2001, the economic growth rates (real GDP) of the Asian Four Little Dragons, at that time, were 2.6 per cent for South Korea, -0.9 per cent for Hong Kong, -2.2 per cent for Taiwan and -2.9 per cent for Singapore.

[3] The IMF forecast of the global economic growth rate for 2001 was adjusted downward from 3.9 per cent to 3.2 per cent at the beginning of the first quarter. Six months later, the estimate was put at 2.6 per cent, but as a result of the September 11 terrorist attack on the US, the IMF subsequently released a special report, on 18 December 2001, renewing the forecast and putting it at just 2.4 per cent.

REFERENCES

Accenture (2001), Governments: Closing the Gap between Political Rhetoric and eGovernment Reality, at http://www.accenture.com/xdoc/en/industries/government (30 March).

Brundtland Commission (1987), at http://sd.erl.itri.org.tw/form/brochure/brhol.htm, United Nations.

Chang, C.-C. (2001), 'The Impacts on Taiwan's Agricultural Sector after WTO', *National Policy Forum*, **1**(9): 34-50.

Crozier, M.S., P. Huntington and J. Watanuki (1975), *The Crisis of Democracy*, New York: New York University Press.

Department of Statistics and Information Science (2001), Survey report on the Public Perspective towards Contemporary Finance Issues in Taiwan, Taipei: Fu-Jen University.

ETToday.com (2001), 'The Government Should Respect the Market Mechanism', at http://www.ettoday.com/article/319-487234.htm (12 June).

Forum on National Sustainable Development at http://sd.erl.itri.org.tw/forum/brochure/brh01e.htm

Hammer, M. and J. Champy (1994), *Reengineering the Corporation: A Manifesto for Business Revolution*, New York: Harper and Collins.

Held, D. and A. McGrew (1999), 'Globalisation', *Global Governance*, **5**(4): 483-96.

Hogwood, B.W. and B.G. Peters (1983), *Policy Dynamics*, Brighton, UK: Harvester.

Hood, C. (1991), 'Public Management for All Seasons', *Public Administration*, **69**(1): 3-9.

Hsu, C.-M. (2001), 'Financial Disorder, Rising Unemployment and Government Helplessness', *National Policy Forum*, **1**(4): 134-6.

Hult, K.M. and C. Walcott (1990), *Governing Public Organisations*, California: Brooks and Cole.

IBRD (1994), *Governance: The World Bank Experience*, Washington, DC: International Bank for Reconstruction and Development.

IMD (1996-2001), *World Competitiveness Yearbook*, at http://www.imd.ch/wcy/ranking, Lausanne: Institute for Management Development.

IMF (2001), 'World Economic Outlook: The Global Economy after September 11', *World Economic and Financial Surveys*, at http://www.imf.org/external/pubs/ft/weo/2001/03/index.htm

Kettl, D.F. and J.J. Dilulio Jr. (1995), *Inside the Reinvention Machine: Appraising Government Reform*, Washington, DC: Brookings Institution.

Kickert, W. (1997), 'Public Governance in the Netherlands: An Alternative to Anglo-American Managerialism', *Public Administration* (Winter), **75**: 731-52.

Kim, S.S. (1999), 'East Asia and Globalisation: Challenge and Responses', *Asian Perspective*, **23**(4): 5-44.

Kirkpatrick, I. and M.M. Lucio (1999), 'Introduction: The Contract State and the Future of Public Management', *Public Administration*, **74**(1): 1-8

Lin, C.-Y. and M.-C. Chiang (1997), *Public Organisation Theory*, Taipei: National Open University.

Lovell, R. (1992), 'The Citizens' Charter: The Cultural Challenge', *Public Administration*, **70**(3): 395-404.

METI (2000), *The Economic Foundations of Japanese Trade Policy - Promotion of a Multi-Trade Policy* (August), Medical Education Technologies Inc., at http://www.meti.go.jp/English/report/data/g00W02le.pdf

North, D.C. (1990), *Institutions, Institutional Change and Economic Performance*, Cambridge: Cambridge University Press.

OECD/DAC (1996), 'Evaluation of Programmes Promoting Participatory Development and Good Governance', Paris: Organisation for Economic Cooperation and Development (unpublished draft synthesis report).

Osborne, D. and T. Gaebler (1992), *Reinventing Government: How the Entrepreneurial Spirit is Transforming the Public Sector*, New York: Penguin Books.

Peters, B.G. (1996), *The Future of Governing: Four Emerging Models*, Kansas: University of Kansas.

Ranson, S. and J. Stewart (1994), *Management for the Public Domain: Enabling the Learning Society*, Hong Kong: St. Martin's Press.

'Singapore One Defined: A Review' at http://www.s-one.gov.sg/overview/s1def01.html.

Smouts, M.C. (1998), 'The Proper Use of Governance in International Relations', *International Social Science Journal* (March), **155**: 83-89.

Song S.W. (2001), 'Globalisation and Global Governance on Taiwan's Public Policy', paper presented at the Knowledge Economy and Government Administration Conference, held in Taipei by the National Policy Forum (14 April).

Tsai, H.-M. (2001), 'Special Arrangements for Cross-strait WTO Economic Issues', *China Review*, **40**(4): 56-9.

UNDP (1996), 'Governance for Sustainable Human Development, Management Development and Governance Division' (unpublished draft document).

UNESCO (2002), 'Education for Democratic Governance: Review of Learning Programmes', prepared by Carlos Santiso and published by the Management of Social Transformation (MOST) Programme, SHS-2002/WS/11.

United Daily News (2001), 'IMF Modifies the Growth of Global Economics' (21 October 2001), Taipei.

4 The Transformation of Taiwanese Agriculture

Hsi-Huang Chen

INTRODUCTION

The remarkable success, in terms of the agricultural development which was enjoyed by Taiwan throughout the 1950s and 1960s, has since become widely recognised as an era responsible for laying the foundations for the island's wider economic development, and consequently, for the successful transformation of a society once heavily dependent upon agriculture, to one that is now based largely on commerce and industry. During the early stages of agricultural development in Taiwan, the focus had been placed on the pursuit of greater levels of land productivity, a strategy which had relied heavily upon the application of high labour intensity and capital intensity, whereas, in contrast, in the large-scale farming countries, the focus was generally placed on the pursuit of higher capital returns.

Following Taiwan's recent accession into the World Trade Organisation (WTO), which came as a result of many years of sustained effort, the island is now going through a period of acceleration in the overall pace of globalisation and trade liberalisation. The government in Taiwan is required to revise the island's existing agricultural policies in line with its WTO accession concessions, which will ultimately require the lowering of existing tariffs on imports, greatly increased market access, and the total elimination of subsidy measures, since many of these policies amount to trade distortions which directly contravene WTO regulations. Now that the island's agricultural trade regime is pushing towards an open market environment, it will clearly be extremely difficult for domestic production methods, with their emphasis on land productivity, to compete with the production methods adopted in the large-scale farming systems of other countries, where the emphasis is on higher levels of capital productivity; thus, the stage is now set for the wholesale restructuring of agriculture in Taiwan.

There seems to have been some general acceptance that the advent of the knowledge-based economy is limited to information technology (IT) or to the high-tech sector as a whole; however, traditional industries, such as agriculture, can also be developed into 'knowledge-based industries' through innovation and the inducement and application of knowledge. Indeed, it is clear that the island's agricultural sector must be transformed from its former traditional 'quantity economy' into a 'knowledge-based economy'. The new policies adopted within the agricultural sector should be competition-oriented, so as to include ways of promoting strategic alliances in agriculture, enhancing the development of bio-technology, developing an agricultural processing industry and also putting some effort into leisure agriculture. In such a way, it will be possible within the overall process of achieving sustainable agricultural development for the agricultural sector in Taiwan to become upgraded from primary and secondary, to tertiary status.

This chapter sets out to provide a review of agricultural development in Taiwan along with an examination of the main factors behind its success, before moving on to examine the challenges that must now be faced within the agricultural sector in the years ahead. Appropriate policies are proposed which could lead to further success in the twenty-first century, along with a description of the vision for the future of agriculture in Taiwan.

HISTORICAL REVIEW OF AGRICULTURAL DEVELOPMENT IN TAIWAN

After the end of the Second World War, small-scale farming in Taiwan experienced a period of more than fifty years of successful development; a period of continuous development which has played a number of different and critical roles, each of which were appropriate for the various stages of development, and as a combined force, were responsible for laying the foundation for the island's 'economic miracle'. The various stages can generally be described as follows:

Rehabilitation Stage (Meeting the Demand for Food) – 1945 to 1953

As a result of the devastating ravages of the Second World War, Taiwan's agricultural facilities had been severely damaged and generally lay in a state of ruin. Millions of soldiers and their families had subsequently retreated to the island from mainland China and, as a result, the government was struggling to restore the existing agricultural irrigation facilities, to increase the supply of fertilizers, to provide better varieties of seeds and root crops and to improve farming techniques so as to increase the overall level of food production. These issues were, at the time, regarded as being of the utmost urgency, and thus, the 'Rice-fertilizer Bartering System', the 'Fertilizer Distribution Regulations', the 'Food Management Act', the '37.5 per cent Rent Reduction Act', the 'Sale-of-Public-Lands Act' and the 'Land to the Tiller Act' were all put into effect. As a result of these measures, agricultural production was restored to the highest levels of the pre-war period.

Developing the Industrial Sector through Agriculture – 1954 to 1967

Once the government in Taiwan had ensured that the foundations for basic agricultural development had effectively been put into place, it then went on to promulgate the first four-year national economic development plan, with a policy being announced for 'Fostering Industry through Agriculture – the Development of Agriculture by Industry'.

The government was, on the one hand, providing reinforced incentives aimed at raising the island's overall level of farm production through measures such as the 'Integrated Pig-rearing Farm Programme', the 'Integrated Programme for Crops and Livestock', the 'Farm Financing Project' and the 'Regulations for Agricultural Extension', whilst on the other hand, in order to accelerate the transfer of capital funds from the agricultural sector to the non-farming sectors, it also introduced the 'Farm Land Tax in Kind' and the 'Compulsory Purchase of Paddy Rice' in 1954, as a means of pursuing a policy of food price capping.

Developing Industry in Tandem with Agriculture – 1968 to 1983

Following the take-off stage of the Taiwanese industrial economy, further advancements in economic development followed rapidly; however, despite industrial and commercial services leading the drive towards successful domestic economic development, the role of agriculture was still recognised, in specific terms of its provision of staple foods, and through its general contribution to the economy as a whole. In the early stage, agricultural production methods focused on the development of labour-intensive cash crops for export, such as mushrooms, asparagus and processed tomatoes, whilst in the later stage, capital-intensive production methods were encouraged, such as coastal and inshore fishing, along with commercial chicken and pig farming.

Throughout this period, the government continued to launch appropriate agricultural programmes and statutes, such as the 'Mechanical Acceleration Programme (1970)', the 'Agricultural Development Act (1973)', the 'Guaranteed Price for Paddy Rice Procurement Act (1974)', the 'Farmers'

Income Enhancement and Rural Reconstruction Act (1979)' and the programme for 'Enhancing Basic Construction and Boosting Farmers' Income (1982)'.

Adjustment and Renovation – 1984 to 1990

After thirty years of successful development, the agricultural sector, which was at that time a very traditional and very domestic-oriented sector, had reached the limits of its development under the island's scarce supply of natural resources. At the same time, as a result of requests from its various trading partners, imports of foreign agricultural products had begun to flow into the domestic market, with the inevitable result of a widening gap between the production and marketing structure due to the influx of foreign products. This resulted in the implementation of the 'Programme for Strengthening Agricultural Structure and Boosting Farm Income' and the 'Paddy Rice Diversion Programme'.

Although agricultural production in Taiwan did increase at an annual rate of 2.0 per cent, the contribution from agriculture to the island's gross national product (GNP) nevertheless declined from 6.3 per cent in 1984, to 4.2 per cent in 1990. Over the same period, employment in the agricultural sector was down from 17.6 per cent to 12.9 per cent of the island's total employment.

Multifunctionality – 1991 and Beyond

In order to meet the challenges of trade liberalisation, nature conservation, and environmental protection, Taiwan launched an 'Integrated Adjustment Programme' in 1991, which emphasised the growing importance of multi-functionality in a whole range of areas, including human resources, land, markets, techniques, organisations, fisheries, welfare and conservation. The release of the 'White Paper on Agricultural Policy' in 1995 declared a long-term policy of commitment towards integrating all of the elements of production, conservation and the living standards of the island's people, and thereafter, in 1997, the 'Cross-Century Agricultural Development Programme' was put into effect.

Nevertheless, despite the continuing growth in the scale of agriculture, the overall contribution to GNP accounted for by the agricultural sector continued to decline; indeed by 2000, it was down to just 2.1 per cent. The role of agriculture had thus completed its transformation from being an important element in the overall level of production achieved in Taiwan, to making non-economic contributions, such as open space and greening, and an emphasis on scenic value and nature conservation.

FACTORS INVOLVED IN SUCCESSFUL AGRICULTURAL DEVELOPMENT

Without the important contribution from the agricultural sector, the Taiwanese 'economic miracle' would never have taken place, and indeed, Taiwan's agricultural development has generally come to be recognised as an appropriate role model for adoption by other developing countries, particularly those whose economies are based on relatively small-scale farming. A number of institutional factors and areas of appropriate investment are regarded as having contributed significantly to this Taiwanese success story; these are outlined in the following sub-sections.

The Sino-American Joint Commission on Rural Reconstruction

The Sino-American Joint Commission on Rural Reconstruction (JCRR) was established to provide much needed sponsorship for a number of individual projects that were aimed at accelerating farm mechanisation, developing slope-land farming, encouraging the livestock industry, developing the food-processing industry and promoting food exports. The JCRR provided both technical and financial assistance to various agencies and organisations in support of both agricultural and rural projects for some considerable time (from 1950 to 1978), and these projects were responsible for providing a significant number of job opportunities within the island's agricultural sector.

Land Reform

The land reform programme significantly altered the overall structure of land ownership in Taiwan, with the proportion of owner-farmers rapidly increasing to 65 per cent, whilst the proportion of tenant-farmers fell to just 14 per cent. This transformation provided farmers with greater economic incentives to put additional effort and physical inputs into farm production. During the pre-reform period, gains from innovations aimed at increasing production had been accrued by the landowners rather than the cultivators, whereas after the land reform programme had been put in place, all such gains were enjoyed by the cultivators themselves.

Farming Organisations

There are currently four major rural organisations in Taiwan, the farmers' associations, the irrigation associations, the fishermen's association and the fruit-marketing cooperative. The farmers' associations are multi-purpose cooperative organisations, formed by the farmers themselves, aimed at promoting their interests, improving farming knowledge and skills, increasing farm production and income, and improving farmers' living conditions. Scattered around the island, the irrigation associations' main functions are the regulation of water usage for irrigation, the collection of water fees and the construction and maintenance of irrigation facilities. The major functions of the fishermen's associations are similar to those of the farmers' associations, the only difference being that their services are targeted solely at fishermen. The fruit-marketing cooperative is, as the name suggests, a single-purpose organisation specialising in the marketing of domestically-grown fruit, and only those farmers who are actively engaged in fruit growing are eligible for membership of this organisation.

Technical Research Institutions

New and innovative research ideas and technologies are essential elements in the improvement and boosting of agricultural production levels, with technical adaptation research, in particular, being of significant importance in the overall course of rural development. The Botanical Institute, which is part of Taiwan's Academia Sinica, deals primarily with basic scientific research, whilst the Agricultural Research Institute and six district stations are responsible for carrying out adaptation experiments on a regional basis. In addition, a number of other research institutes have been established over the years to cover areas of specific research into topics such as pesticides, tobacco, sugar, tea, forestry, fisheries, livestock, sericulture, bananas and food processing.

Supporting Services

Agricultural extension services, sponsored by the farmers' associations in conjunction with district agricultural improvement stations, serve as a bridge between agricultural research and the field testing and application of new farming techniques. Within the available credit services, the farmers' associations play a very active role in providing loans for production and marketing purposes, and although the funds come mainly from the deposits of the association members themselves, they are also supplemented by the government and a number of the island's domestic banks. Marketing services are also provided by the farmers' associations within each township, with the cooperative marketing of pigs, poultry, eggs, fruit and vegetables, along with the work of the fruit-marketing cooperative, all being aimed at increasing the bargaining power of farmers and maintaining the overall level of marketing efficiency.

Rural Infrastructure

The irrigation associations are responsible for water supply and for the construction and management of the overall irrigation system. As a result of the efforts of these associations, more than 60 per cent of all farmland is now covered by the irrigation system. With the exception of the most remote mountainous areas, a complete rural road system has been developed to provide total accessibility to rural villages for the purpose of transportation and marketing of farm products.

THE CURRENT SITUATION AND THE IMMEDIATE CHALLENGES

The aforementioned institutional and investment factors are not the only factors that have assisted in Taiwan's agricultural development; however, they have been responsible for the greatest contribution, and whilst these factors have been outlined separately here, they are nevertheless an integral part of the island's overall agricultural development.

Given that Taiwan's agricultural sector grew so rapidly in the early stages, but has since slowed down – or indeed, staggered to a halt in recent years – the competitiveness of the island's agricultural products has naturally dwindled. With the trend towards trade liberalisation and the globalisation of markets, the further development of agriculture in Taiwan is now facing a number of new challenges, whilst other factors such as changes in consumer habits, as well as ecological deterioration, are also providing daunting challenges for the island's decision makers. The challenges to current agricultural development are categorised and outlined below.

International Challenges

Accelerated liberalisation of agricultural trade
With the development of both regionalism and multilateralism, the pace of global trade liberalisation has accelerated much more rapidly than anyone might have expected. Furthermore, overt regionalism – such as the North American Free Trade Agreement (NAFTA), the Association of Southeast Asian Nations Free Trade Area (AFTA) and the South Common Market (MERCOSUR) – has become a significant part of the global trading system. Between 1947 and 1994, no fewer than 109 regional trade agreements were established under the former General Agreement on Tariffs and Trade (GATT), the forerunner to the WTO, and since 1995, at least sixteen new

regional trade agreements have been reported to the WTO as new additions to the global trading arena. Regionalism can serve as a building block for multilateral trade liberalisation, but it can also divert trade from non-member countries.

The multilateral process of global trade liberalisation under the WTO has continued to develop vigorously despite the collapse of the Third Ministerial Meeting held in Seattle in 1999, with the mandated negotiations in both services and agriculture having been included in the overall process, as scheduled, since 2000. The Fourth WTO Ministerial Conference, which was held in Doha, Qatar, in November 2001, succeeded in bringing to a conclusion a comprehensive round of negotiations. Within that round of negotiations, following discussions aimed at amending the 1996 Farm Act (which subsequently expired in June 2002), the US had submitted a comprehensive set of proposals aimed at building up a fair and more market-oriented trading system by accelerating the reduction of trade distortions whilst preserving the appropriate roles for governments in addressing the various agricultural concerns.

The European Union (EU) has also provided its full commitment to continuing the reform process with a wide array of proposals, such as those for achieving further reductions in support and protection, the need to provide different treatment for developing countries on the basis of their special needs, and a number of non-trade concerns. Furthermore, in its Ministerial Meeting in September 2001, considerable solidarity and determination was demonstrated by the Cairns Group in their efforts to establish a market-oriented trading system.

Nevertheless, when it comes to allowing unrestrained trading, the developing or less developed trading partners in Latin America and Africa have tended to be more conservative and cautious; however, within the WTO, there is a general recognition of the need for ongoing negotiations and debate covering the main sensitive issues in agriculture, such as specific issues of market access, domestic subsidies, tariff quotas and special tariff treatment, as well as genetically modified organisms and other non-trade concerns.

As the world's fourteenth largest trading economy, Taiwan has been actively participating in international trade organisations and seeking international cooperation in agriculture with many other countries. Taiwan demonstrated its commitment towards accelerating the pace of trade liberalisation with its initial submission for WTO accession in 1990. In September 2001, in its conclusion to 12 years of negotiations, the WTO Working Party on Taiwan's Entry agreed to forward the legal text for formal acceptance by the 142 member governments of the WTO, and Taiwan finally became a full member of the WTO in January 2002.

International concerns for food security

With the rapid economic development and population growth characteristic of many developing countries, there has been a worldwide increase in the demand for food, with the issue of food security now being afforded considerable concern. According to the forecasts of the Food and Agriculture Organisation (FAO), the global population is set to increase from the six billion people estimated in 1999, to around eight billion in 2025, representing a rise of one third in the overall demand for food. In addition, the production environment is likely to be further aggravated under the increasing uncertainty of production influenced by water resource misallocation, farmland diversion, the greenhouse effect, disorders in normal weather patterns and environmental degradation.

On a worldwide scale, around half of the total food production is undertaken by the developed countries, despite these countries accounting for only around a quarter of the world's population. Clearly, therefore, the inadequacies of the food supply are felt most in the developing countries. The FAO has indicated that around 800 million people in 67 lower income countries are suffering from malnutrition, and in the poorest of these countries, the situation could soon grow worse. Since 1997, despite the abundant world food supply and sluggish market prices, fears of food production insecurity have become widespread. Food availability does not guarantee food security, since this also depends on the ability to buy food and to use it effectively. Individual health and education levels, as well as local conditions, such as the safety and security of the water supply, will also affect the appropriate use of food. Thus, ways of alleviating the inherent insecurity in the global food chain, and ways of solving the problem of uneven food distribution, have now become urgent issues that need to be resolved in the twenty-first century, and yet, they are now much more complicated than ever before.

Given the unique and sensitive political situation in Taiwan, the issue of food security cannot be judged by trade or production factors alone. Any unexpected incident may turn the issue of food security into a sensitive political matter which could lead to sudden turmoil throughout the island. It is therefore imperative for the government to set up an appropriate mechanism for the overall management of food security, taking into account economic feasibility and social security, and to determine to what extent food security needs to be established with regard to the current cross-strait tension and the impending global food crisis.

The urgent need for environmental conservation

In 1972, the United Nations (UN) staged a conference in Stockholm on the subject of the Human Environment, during which there was a general recognition that defending and improving the human environment for both present and future generations was an imperative goal for mankind. The UN thereafter announced a declaration which included twenty-six environmental principles to which all nations were urged to adhere. Twenty years later, however, the global environment was deteriorating more rapidly than ever. Depletion of the ozone layer, changing climate patterns, expanding deserts and the extinction of various species are all the result of inappropriate and excessive exploratory behaviour stemming from the rapid growth in the global population and overall economic development.

Recognising the inherent urgency of environmental protection, in 1992, the UN staged a further conference on the subject of development and the environment in Rio de Janeiro, followed by the announcement of the 'Climate Change Convention', 'Biological Diversity', 'Forest Principles', and 'Agenda 21' which recognised the integral and interdependent nature of the earth, and the goal of achieving sustainable environmental protection. The 'Montreal Protocol', the 'Basle Convention' and the 'Kyoto Protocol' were subsequently announced to demonstrate the commitment towards achieving sustainable development. These environmental issues will need to be raised again if all the developed and developing countries continue to pursue economic development whilst blatantly ignoring environmental concerns.

Given its fifty years of rapid economic development, the over-exploitation of hillsides and forestlands in Taiwan, as well as water and soil resources, was inevitable. The excessive drawing of water from the underground tables in the coastal regions has caused significant land subsidence, quickly followed by the invasion of sea water. The overuse of fertilizers and pesticides, and the improper release of agricultural wastewater and waste materials into the environment have also resulted in pollution of the island's natural resources. Illegal hunting and gathering of wild fauna and flora have also damaged the overall biological diversity of the ecosystem, an area of conservation which has given rise to increasing worldwide attention in recent years.

Nevertheless, the citizens of Taiwan are also gradually beginning to sense the overall deterioration of their general living conditions, the decline in environmental quality and the loss of the island's limited natural resources. Indeed, Taiwanese people are now much more aware than ever before of the importance of issues such as nature conservation and environmental protection; therefore, the efforts of the agricultural sector are now focusing more on the conservation of natural resources, along with ways of finding the correct balance, in terms of the demand for economic development alongside the appropriate recognition and concern for environmental conservation.

Domestic Challenges

The domestic challenges that are now being faced by agriculture cannot, however, be regarded as the responsibility of the agricultural sector alone, and indeed, all of the following issues will need to be resolved with the active cooperation of other non-agricultural sectors.

Accelerated pace of structural readjustment

Historically, the main objective of agricultural policy was to keep pace with the food demand generated by a growing population. What is now craved by consumers is not only ways of ensuring that their basic energy requirements are met, but also that they have the opportunity to eat better, by way of access to wider varieties of nutritional food, characterised by high regard for food safety and sanitation. With such consumer-driven market forces, domestic agricultural production structures must be adjusted, and a high quality image has to be established so that consumer demands for convenience, freshness, health and variety may be satisfied. Only after gaining consumer confidence in domestic products can Taiwan's agriculture face the growing challenge from foreign products.

Upon WTO accession, Taiwan was required to fulfil its commitments to lowering tariff rates, reforming the non-tariff regime and reducing domestic subsidies. Given that the pace of trade liberalisation will continue to accelerate alongside the ongoing WTO negotiations on agriculture, it is inevitable that Taiwan's agricultural sector will face greater competitive pressure, particularly for those products that are required to comply with ordinary customs duties. Thus, some proportion of the island's agricultural resources and labour is expected to shift outwards. One of the most pressing needs, therefore, is to expedite improvements in domestic production and the overall structure of agricultural product marketing in order to meet the growing demands of consumer-driven markets.

Emerging technology in agricultural and farming operations

There have been many breakthroughs in agriculture-related technology in recent years. Genetically modified organisms have been developed using genetic engineering technology in breeding research. Precision agriculture has also been introduced using satellite positioning systems and geographical information on farming management; farmers can now easily determine the most productive field for farming with machinery efficiency and ample data information. E-commerce also allows farmers and ranchers to keep up with changing market information through the worldwide web, which will eventually change the fundamentals of agricultural marketing and the transaction structure.

The more that technology accelerates, the faster new products are being innovated and developed. As a result, product life cycles will be altered, and this will have enormous impacts on the agricultural sector. In order to meet such a challenge, a major issue to be tackled involves determining ways of assisting farmers to produce 'branded', 'graded' and 'standardised' products. A further issue of significant importance is the fact that this new biological technology-based industry cannot easily attract investment by entrepreneurs or the younger generation due to the huge initial investment required, the protracted return period and the uncertain area of profitability.

Rural reconstruction and the welfare of farmers
Agriculture in Taiwan is facing growing pressure for transformation under the impacts of trade liberalisation and social evolution. Ever since industrial and commercial services replaced agriculture as the new backbone of the economy, the discrepancy between urban and rural areas has increased considerably. Moreover, because of its biological characteristics, agriculture is affected more by natural environmental factors. Risks in production are extremely high as compared to industrial production, and thus, farm income is also very unpredictable. The status of agriculture needs to be redefined both in terms of the production function and non-economic factors, such as social welfare and conservation, with the main objectives being to improve the rural living environment and enhance both the level and the quality of the rural infrastructure so as to boost the welfare of farmers. The new outlook for farming villages will be heavily reliant on aggregate planning in the areas of culture, ethnicity and basic infrastructure.

Furthermore, the deteriorating quality of the agricultural workforce and the declining share of farm income as a proportion of overall household income is also worthy of attention. The agricultural workforce is of relatively low labour quality with an average age of 49 years. Of all farm households, 84 per cent fall into the category of 'part-time' farming, with 82 per cent of their total income coming from non-agricultural services. Apart from this problem of majority part-time farming households, agriculture transformation also faces issues of structural adjustment, including the reallocation of farmland, the mobility of the workforce under integrated planning, the setting up of mechanisms for appropriate land use, and refunds for agricultural development. There will be a considerable shift in the proportion of the senior population in Taiwan in the near future, and rural villages are no exception; hence a dramatic increase is expected in the number of farm operators aged 65 years, or older. Therefore, the government also needs to address ways of enhancing healthcare programmes for senior farmers in rural villages, including maintaining their ability to live independently and to enjoy a high quality of life.

The multi-dimensional impacts on farming organisations

Farmers' organisations used to play a comprehensive role in the process of agricultural development ranging from agricultural extension, credit and loan services, to policy implementation; however, political awareness is dramatically affecting the operation of farmers' organisations following the growing campaigns for a more democratic and multi-dimensional society. The former conservative, passive and pessimistic attitude has evolved into an active and optimistic attitude in which farmers are now fighting for their own rights. Nevertheless, the membership of farmers' organisations in suburban areas has declined significantly, whilst membership in the rural areas is now represented largely by the aged, following the outflow of young and middle-aged farmers from the rural villages. The reorganisation and restructuring of farmers' organisations into efficiency-oriented enterprises with the ability to develop new business, taking advantage of inherited culture and landscape resources, has therefore become necessary; however, the membership structure of farmers' organisations will continue to change following the liberalisation of farmland ownership, and therefore a critical issue is whether they will be capable of carrying out such structural reorganisation themselves.

New concepts created by the knowledge-based economy

Taiwan's economy was traditionally based upon a closed system of agriculture, within which greater attention was paid to agricultural production in pursuit of a high degree of self-sufficiency through labour-intensive land use. However, with the rise of industrialisation and globalisation, agricultural development in Taiwan has been moving away from its closed system of traditional, small-scale farming and the sale of fresh products at local markets, to progressively greater changes in farming structure, farmers' organisations, more processed farm products, and expansion of its international trading territory. Thus farmers are now considering the demands of the international market as a driving force in their farm production, and thus, as a major factor in their decision making. Research, development and innovation are key elements of the value chain in international logistics. Therefore, in order to ensure success in the international market, which will inevitably hinge on the confidence of consumers, there needs to be some systematical analysis of the supply and demand of international agricultural products.

A report by the Organisation for Economic Cooperation and Development (OECD, 1996) noted that the knowledge-based economy will dramatically transform the development pattern of the global economy, with knowledge and information replacing the traditional production factors of land, labour and capital, to become the driving force in productivity and economic development. Faced with such a new concept, agriculture will clearly have to be restructured from its current pursuit of 'quantity' to a much greater focus on this new 'knowledge-based' economy so as to promote 'added value' instead of 'added production'. Therefore, another important issue for agricultural development is finding ways of commercialising and marketing agricultural products by fully utilising the available technologies, industry culture and distinct local characteristics, in order to reflect the value of knowledge in the market and to increase its added value. In pursuit of such goals, the development of a knowledge-based agricultural economy is in full swing in Taiwan at this moment.

Increase in cross-strait exchanges

The activities involved in cross-strait exchanges include indirect trading and investment, and the exchange of agricultural technology, including gene plasma technology. There has been a dramatic increase in visits across the strait in recent times, all of which has produced a number of positive bilateral effects; however, issues such as product substitution and competition, smuggling, disease transmission and fishery disputes cannot be ignored since these clearly have adverse effects on Taiwan's domestic agricultural development. Generally speaking, Taiwan has an advantage in investment and technology, whilst the mainland has an advantage in agricultural gene plasma and basic technologies. Therefore, it is now necessary to find ways of avoiding confrontation, establishing a framework for orderly trading relationships through the formulation of a cooperative model for cross-strait interaction, and maintaining a win-win situation for the agricultural sectors on both sides of the strait.

Recent trends have shown that whenever there is an increase in the market price for certain sensitive domestic agricultural products, this is accompanied by a rise in smuggling activities of that product from the mainland. Such activities severely damage both local market order and farm income, whilst also violating regulations on pets and disease prevention. And since the public is not always alert to such unlawful imports, it is extremely difficult to carry out effective monitoring and inspection of such smuggled goods.

STRATEGIES FOR AGRICULTURAL TRANSFORMATION IN THE TWENTY-FIRST CENTURY

The New Programme for the New Century

As a new member of the WTO, in addition to the pressure of market competition caused by trade liberalisation, Taiwan must now put significant effort into resolving issues in areas such as the allocation of farmland, irrigation water and the agricultural workforce, as well as the adjustment of farmers' organisations, rural development and nature conservation. The current pace of self-adjustment in the agricultural sector has to be accelerated, with much greater emphasis upon renovation and improvement. By allocating priorities based upon macro-oriented strategies in areas such as the maintenance of competitiveness within the sector, food security and nature conservation, the agricultural sector in Taiwan will certainly be able to meet the needs of contemporary living and ultimately secure sustainable development for the years ahead.

In its 'New Programme for the Twenty-first Century', which formed the blueprint for Taiwan's agricultural development from 2001 to 2004, the government in Taiwan set out a number of missions and goals which included: (i) developing the knowledge-based economy and applying technical and cultural knowledge to the upgrading and competitiveness of the agricultural sector; (ii) ensuring food security, producing high quality, safe and sanitary products, and protecting consumer rights; (iii) increasing the living standards and quality of life within rural villages as well as setting up a farmers' social security safety net to further increase the income and welfare of farmers; and (iv) improving the quality and efficient use of agricultural resources, whilst also emphasising soil conservation and protection in order to promote harmony within the ecological environment. In order to achieve these aims, there are a number of areas to which significant attention will need to be paid, as outlined in the following sub-sections.

Promoting strategic agricultural alliances in Taiwan

In order to develop economies of scale and technical efficiency within the agricultural sector, and thus enable the sector to stand up to the competitive challenge from international trade in agriculture, Taiwan has to strengthen the integration of marketing and production. This has led to the Council of Agriculture (COA) forming a task force aimed at establishing 'strategic agricultural alliances' to organise the farmers' associations, and other related associations, into various unions, such as production, processing, distribution and recreation unions. Such methods should effectively enhance competitiveness and cooperation within the sector through specialisation, the diversification of risk and the maintenance of bargaining power, in order to establish the safeguards allowed under WTO accession, along with other new economic cushions against the influx of foreign products.

Developing the food-processing industry

Development of the food-processing industry and increased industrialisation in agricultural operations will lead to the upgrading of the structure of agricultural production from primary, to secondary, and ultimately, tertiary status, which will increase the effective utilisation of agricultural products.

Through the incorporation of technological know-how and an emphasis on the value of Chinese gourmet foods, medicinal meals and health foods, all perfected with processing, marketing, promotion and commercialisation, and finally, bundled with agricultural knowledge of high-tech, cultural and regional characteristics, the price of such agricultural products will no doubt increase to reflect their true value. Thus, the redefined food-processing industry is expected to gain the support of consumers whilst also bringing prosperity to the farmers.

Developing high-quality agricultural and recreational business
In order to enlarge the scope of farm operations, a number of agricultural products have been designated as main items for government focus based on the criteria of their competitiveness with foreign products, such as their market potential, technological advantage and special local characteristics. Specific items such as field crops, seeds and seedlings, flowers, new varieties of mushrooms, tropical fruits and organic paddy rice are listed as being targeted for further development. In the area of fishery farming, those items targeted for development are new fish varieties, aquaculture varieties, ornamental fish and cage farming, whilst in the livestock sector the aim is to raise high quality free-range chickens and pigs by incorporating high-tech and industry resources.

The attention of consumers has also recently been diverted to recreation and tourism. Imported products clearly cannot replace domestic recreational agriculture, within which emphasis must be placed upon local scenic areas and local characteristics; thus, the COA is now vigorously promoting agricultural recreational activities, and the hope is that these recreational activities can help to raise household income levels for farmers whilst allowing the opportunity for 'urbanites' to experience life in rural farm villages.

Strengthening management and increasing the efficiency of farm usage
The 'Agricultural Development Act', which came into effect in January 2001, deregulated farmland transactions and partition limits, with new farming leases no longer being subject to the '37.5 per cent Land Rent Reduction Act'. Given that existing agricultural enterprises and business entities may be interested in acquiring such farming rights, it is expected that there will be an increase in the level of transactions involving these rights.

The COA has also been working on enhancing the related regulations which provide support for farmers in terms of improving the production environment and the current level of marketing technology. Furthermore, by implementing its programme of integrated farmland utilisation, and thereby introducing entrepreneurial techniques and management, it is expected that the independent operation of farmers' associations will be realised in the near future.

Developing key agricultural technologies
By placing effort into setting up information systems and modernising the marketing environment, the key agricultural technologies of the future will not only focus on strategic items such as automation, biology and genetic engineering, but also on the development of economic, cultural and medical knowledge. In addition, through the dissemination of information and the use of the Internet, Taiwan will soon be able to establish multi-dimensional marketing channels and an environment of electronic farm operations, followed in turn by the establishment of technologically-oriented, as well as information and knowledge-based, agriculture. The COA has already established agricultural information systems based on a model that provides the reporting, checking and dissemination of up-to-date marketing information to farmers. This system will be further integrated with related information channels to eventually form a comprehensive information and knowledge-based system.

Reconstruction through the creation of rural commune zones
The pace of rural village reconstruction must be accelerated in order to narrow the gap between urban and rural development, and so as to revitalise the rural economy in the current atmosphere of trade liberalisation. This must include acceleration of the reconstruction of rural and fishing villages. A model of rural reconstruction will be established on the basis of commune zones incorporating factors such as industrial development, ecological scenery and regional culture, with the aim being to demonstrate the aesthetic beauty of local, natural features, and to create a new image of rural villages characterised by multi-functionality, including humanitarian, industrial, recreational and ecological issues.

Enhancing conservation and maintaining bio-diversity
The pursuit of green sustainable development will be the main theme in the twenty-first century, with the overall aim of preventing natural disasters, particularly in the mountainous regions, and upgrading ecological environment quality. The COA aims to enhance both green production and consumption by maintaining the ecological function of agriculture and by promoting bio-diversity conservation programmes. Complete restructuring and readjustment of water and land resources is planned, and under the guidance of food security and nature conservation, farmland will be released to introduce some measure of rationality into resource reallocation. A 'green belt' is to be formed by connecting less productive (or marginal) county land areas and devoting them to forestation (or reforestation) and other related conservation purposes. In addition, watershed protection, disaster prevention, water and soil conservation and various greening measures are to be implemented so as to ensure the safety of life and to protect the property of individuals.

THE VISION OF FUTURE AGRICULTURAL DEVELOPMENT IN TAIWAN

The Bases for Future Agricultural Development

The trend in agricultural development in Taiwan is expected to run along the same lines as in other developed, small-scale farming economies, such as that of Japan, with some diminution of the production function based on benefits to other functions such as rural living, the preservation of culture and scenery, and overall nature conservation. Future agricultural policy in Taiwan has to be constructed on the basis of greening technology, under an operational knowledge-based model, so that it can survive alongside the competitive global trading paradigm. It must also combine culture with recreation and nature resources to invoke interest in rural living, and to gain the support of consumers for domestic agriculture.

The future vision for modern agriculture in Taiwan is based on a number of premises, including technology, economy, culture, recreation and ecology, with a major aim being to ensure that agriculture is much more energetic in the future. Farmers should benefit more and rural villages should become much more aesthetically appealing. The ultimate vision is that all of the people in Taiwan will immerse themselves in an extremely high-quality environment with a high quality of life provided through agriculture.

Technology-based development

In order to create this new era, which we may refer to as the 'green revolution', a more efficient production and marketing system will need to be established for use in conjunction with advanced technology. In addition to developing biotechnology, there should also be a focus on new products equipped with distinguishing characteristics (such as anti-disease, better tasting, health-conscious, ready-to-eat, local features, and so on). The new technologies to be applied should be based on nutritional diagnosis, organic agriculture, biological and environmental controls.

Along with a drastic reduction in the amount of chemical fertilizers, insecticides, pesticides, feed additives and animal drugs currently being used in agriculture, the aim should be to produce a wide range of high-quality, safe and hygienic products that will satisfy the multi-dimensional demands of consumers. Furthermore, in order to mitigate any negative impact on the environment, the efficient utilisation of resources should be emphasised so that the aim of maintaining the environment through advanced agriculture can be achieved, thus laying the foundation for its future sustainability.

Economy-based development
The rapid changes in economic development on an international scale have already pushed us into the era of the knowledge-based economy, and the development of systems within which greater output value is produced with ever lower levels of input, thus creating greater added value through innovation, communication and application. Improvements are expected in Taiwan's overall agricultural structure, the enlargement of the scale of farming and breakthroughs in farming techniques, once the 'Agricultural Strategic Alliance' is fully implemented.

Agriculture in Taiwan is already at a crucial turning point and has to undergo total transformation without delay. Significant amounts of resources need to be injected into the future development of the strategic agricultural sector, and into the promotion of cooperation between agriculture and industry, if the island is to achieve real competitiveness in the agricultural sector. Although using modern technology to process traditional Taiwanese 'fancy foods' will upgrade the quality of these products, the application of good marketing strategies is also necessary, along with the establishment of well-known brands and competitive marketing channels, and the expansion of the overseas market. It is hoped that agriculture will become a competitive and energetic business, and consequently, that farmers will see increased benefits for their efforts.

Culture-based development
The COA is to construct an agricultural culture system on the basis of a programme entitled 'One County, One Special Crop and One Festival' which takes advantage of regional agricultural and cultural resources. A series of cultural activities are planned to be held during the major production seasons aimed at encouraging interest in rural villages and cherishing local traditional culture, as well as creating an atmosphere of high-quality consumption. Multi-purpose product usage will be enhanced in order to upgrade the level of food consumption and cultural observation, with the overall aim being to enhance the taste and appeal of agricultural products so that Taiwanese agriculture can satisfy both sensory and spiritual needs.

Recreational-based development
The COA aims to accelerate its planning in the areas of recreational fruit farming, the provision of assistance in recreational farm operations, the construction of coastal corridors and blue ocean highways, and the creation of ecological parks featuring the functions of recreation, tourism, nature conservation and education. In addition, it is intended that the recreational farms and fisheries, the forest parks and the resources of the farmers' and fishermen's associations are to be consolidated into one entity, referred to as

'One County, One Recreational Zone'. Schools are to be encouraged to consider using the recreational farms for their outdoor teaching activities, and the recreational farms will also connect with financial services, tourism, restaurants and large retailers to form strategic alliances with the ability of providing comprehensive service packages. The aim is that the people of Taiwan will eventually be able to enjoy educational farm tourism of the highest quality.

Ecology-based development

Finally, the COA is also set to promote the value of greening production and consumption, developing organic agriculture and creating ocean-based farming. Fisheries that are currently of 'fishing-type' will be transformed into 'farming-type' fisheries. The pace of the current campaign for 'foresting, greening and beautifying of the whole island' will be accelerated so that the goals of forest resource protection, bio-diversity and the efficient use of forest resources can be achieved. There are also plans to implement ecological policies based on converting retired farmland to forestry, encouraging the use of marginal land for forestation, applying ecological techniques to forestry, cultivating high quality forests and establishing a green belt for scenic landscape development. Local governments in Taiwan are also planning to build regional forest parks that can serve a secondary air-cleaning function. Planning for the use of national land in coastal and oceanic areas, including major coastal wetlands and the twenty-four mile coastal protection zone, is a top priority in the government 'to do' list, with regard to the better management and protection of ocean resources and achieving a balanced ecological system.

CONCLUSIONS

Taiwan's very successful experience in agricultural development during the 1950s and 1960s was essentially responsible for laying the foundations for the well-known Taiwanese 'economic miracle' which continues to stand out and achieve widespread recognition around the world. However, with the rapid development of the industrial and commercial sectors, the role of agriculture has changed, and it can no longer ignore multi-functionality issues in agriculture, including food safety, rural development, greening, the beautifying of rural villages and nature conservation.

The accelerated pace of trade liberalisation in Taiwan will be accompanied by an influx of foreign products which will have severe impacts on domestic agriculture, rural villages and farmers. Therefore, in order to take up the challenge, Taiwan has established a well-planned programme for the twenty-first century covering the period from 2001 to 2004. It is believed that agriculture can be transformed from a traditional 'quantity-oriented' sector into a 'knowledge-based' economy propelled by knowledge inspiration and innovation. The goals of this policy have shifted from a focus on production towards a theme of upgrading competitiveness. By integrating farmers' associations, achieving high technology and quality agriculture, enhancing biological development and promoting food processing and recreational agriculture, Taiwan's agriculture is set to evolve from a primary, to a secondary and ultimately, tertiary industry, based on its future sustainability.

REFERENCES

Chen, H.-H. (1990), *Strategies for Agricultural Development in Taiwan*, Taipei: Industry of Free China.

Chen, H.-H. (2001), *Agricultural Policy in Taiwan*, St. Louis: 2001 Congress of the World Agricultural Forum.

Council of Agriculture (1986), *Long-Term Agricultural Development in the Republic of China (1986-2000)*, Taipei: Council of Agriculture, Executive Yuan.

Council of Agriculture (1995), *White Paper on Agricultural Policy*, Taipei: Council of Agriculture, Executive Yuan.

Council of Agriculture (2001a), *The New Agricultural Programme Towards the 21st Century (2001-2004)*, Taipei: Council of Agriculture, Executive Yuan.

Council of Agriculture (2001b), *Meeting the Conclusions of WTO Accession and Agricultural Knowledge-based Economic Development*, Taipei: Council of Agriculture, Executive Yuan.

Mao, Y.-K. and C. Schive (1991), *Agricultural and Industrial Development in the Economic Transformation of the Republic of China on Taiwan*, Taipei: Council of Agriculture, Executive Yuan.

OECD (1996), 'Identifying Best Practices for the Knowledge-based Economy', *Science, Technology and Industry Outlook*, Taipei: Organisation for Economic Cooperation and Development.

Ong, S.-E. (1984), *Development of the Small Farm Economy in Taiwan*, Taipei: Council of Agriculture, Executive Yuan.

Yager, J.A. (1988), *Transforming Agriculture in Taiwan*, Ithaca: Cornell University Press.

5 The Transformation of Traditional Manufacturing Industries

Yun-Peng Chu

INTRODUCTION

Undertaking an in-depth study of the transformation of the so-called 'traditional' industries has never been an easy task, for at least three reasons. First of all, it is extremely difficult to define which categories of industries should in fact be classified as traditional. Secondly, even for those industries that are categorised as 'traditional', it becomes readily apparent that the technological level within some of the firms in these industries is already extremely high. Thirdly, it appears that the focus of such investigation is in fact a moving target, because both firms and industries evolve dynamically in a process which is rapid and ever-changing, particularly within a newly industrialising economy (NIE) such as that of Taiwan. Nevertheless, despite these inherent difficulties, we believe that it is of some interest, and indeed, some importance, to attempt to trace the evolution of the traditional industries, in order that we can try to predict the ways in which they can continue to develop in the future.

The term 'traditional industry', in the case of Taiwan in particular, normally encompasses virtually all of the industries in the manufacturing sector. We use the term 'virtually' because of the notable exceptions of the electrical and electronic apparatus/equipment industry, the aerospace industry and the biotechnology industry, each of which is now generally referred to as a 'high-tech' manufacturing industry, and each of which has largely ceased to be referred to in the 'traditional' sense.

In this chapter, we set out to show that the majority of these industries have, in one way or another, undergone significant transformation over recent decades, with the pattern of such transformation having roughly fallen into a typical cycle of a rise, followed by a levelling off, and finally the decline of certain industries alongside the resurgence of others, in a process widely recognised, and generally referred to, as the 'flying-geese' pattern.

103

Manufacturing production in Taiwan rose steadily during the 1960s, the 1970s and the first half of the 1980s. However, throughout the late 1980s, the traditional industries started to face considerable challenges, with the manufacturing sector as a whole showing clear signs of levelling off, largely as a result of the substantial currency appreciation at that time, and the continual rise in labour costs.[1] Nevertheless, there was an abrupt change to the situation in the early 1990s, with the overall resurgence of the manufacturing sector (see Figure 5.1).[2] Although the high-tech industry was no doubt the key player in the process, the non-high-tech or traditional industries were also responsible for very important contributions. Not only did these traditional industries show no signs of losing their competitiveness on an international scale, but some of them have even managed to enhance their competitive edge. It is, therefore, clearly worth exploring how these industries managed to survive and thrive in the face of the ever-changing economic environment, along with an examination of their performance against the backdrop of the experiences of other economies.[3]

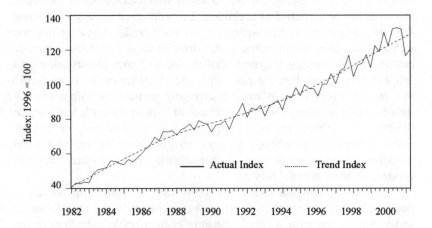

Figure 5.1   Manufacturing production index in Taiwan, and the current trend

CHANGING INTERNATIONAL COMPETITIVENESS AND SKILLED-LABOUR INTENSITY IN TAIWANESE INDUSTRY

We use the Taiwanese share of the imports of the United States, the European Union, Japan and mainland China to gauge the international competitiveness of its manufacturing industries; however, since data are only available from 1993 for mainland China, the period selected for investigation is therefore 1993 to 2000. Furthermore, we use the concept of skilled-labour intensity (SLI) in order to gain an understanding of the high-tech content across industries, with the ratio of those workers with college or higher education to the total number of workers for each sector (direct and indirect), being obtained from the business surveys.

Those industries in the manufacturing sector as a whole are divided equally into three groups, the high skilled-labour intensity (HSLI), medium skilled-labour intensity (MSLI) and low skilled-labour intensity (LSLI) groups, according to the size ratio defined above. Figures 5.2 to 5.4 provide details of the categorisation of exports by SLI in Taiwan, South Korea and mainland China, respectively.[4]

As Figure 5.2 shows, in the case of Taiwan, industrial upgrading has largely been successful. Within the overall structure of Taiwanese exports, the share of HSLI has risen from less than 30 per cent in 1993, to around 50 per cent in 2000, whilst the share of LSLI fell from in excess of 30 per cent, to around 20 per cent over the same period. As compared to South Korea and mainland China, Taiwan enjoys greater international competitiveness, as evidenced by the SLI; nevertheless, since China is clearly a latecomer in the international arena, any changes in the ratios for this country will have much greater significance than its absolute levels. Obviously, with the efforts being put in to catching up with other NIEs, mainland China has demonstrated stronger performance in recent years.

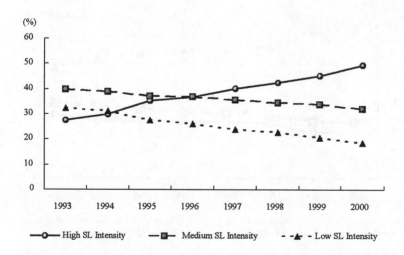

Figure 5.2   Categorisation of exports by skilled-labour (SL) intensities, Taiwan

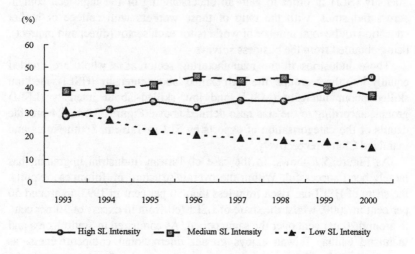

*Figure 5.3   Categorisation of exports by skilled-labour (SL) intensities,
                South Korea*

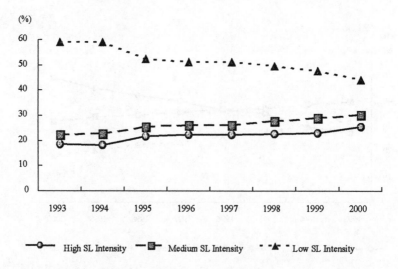

*Figure 5.4   Categorisation of exports by skilled-labour (SL) intensities,
                mainland China*

Taiwan's star performers in exporting throughout the period from 1993 to 2000 included steel surface treatment, steel processing, aluminium processing, scientific instruments, airplane parts, fibre glass products, shipbuilding and repairs, and data processing equipment. Those industries that were lagging behind were meat preparation, food and beverages, frozen food, preserved food, shoe manufacturing, plastic shoes and products, wooden products, wooden furniture, jewellery and gold products, clocks and watches, and lighting equipment. Although most of the industries lagging behind were traditional industries with low skilled-labour intensity, many of the star performers and medium range performers also belonged to the traditional industries.

The key determinant of whether a traditional industry will decline or prosper lies in the speed of its reform. Only by changing and improving their products or services, introducing innovations to production methods or the provision of services, and exploring new markets whilst also expanding old ones, can industries find the necessary impetus for further development.

THE TRANSFORMATION OF TRADITIONAL INDUSTRIES IN A KNOWLEDGE-BASED ECONOMY

Case Studies

We examine a number of case studies of successful industrial upgrading in order to illustrate the ways in which firms in the traditional industries have managed to sustain their rate of growth whilst maintaining competitiveness in an economy, such as that of Taiwan, characterised by a growing emphasis on knowledge and information. Along with changes in the level of international competitiveness and skilled-labour intensities, the advent of the knowledge-based economy has indeed both fostered and forced the transformation of these traditional industries.

The term 'knowledge-based economy', as defined by the Organisation for Economic Cooperation and Development (OECD), refers to an economy which regards the possession, allocation, production and utilisation of its knowledge resources as the most important factor of production. Within a knowledge-based economy, the accumulation and use of knowledge and information have replaced physical capital stock, human resources and hardware technology to become the major driving force behind sustainable growth and development. In an era with such great emphasis on knowledge and information, the crucial success of an individual, a business enterprise, a society, and even a nation, rests on the speed at which knowledge can be utilised to bring about rapid changes, and which can thereby facilitate constant innovation and perpetual improvement. After all, not all innovations have to be earth-shattering; even though they may seem small and insignificant, constant changes, combined with new ideas accumulated over time, can provide a dynamic driving force for the growth of an economy.

Rather than imposing hard and fast rules for delineating which of the industries are knowledge-based, and which are not, a knowledge-based economy represents both a concept and a process. Every industry can be knowledge-based, and every industry can succeed in innovating through the utilisation of knowledge. Even traditional industries can upgrade themselves by using knowledge to bring about rapid changes and creativity, strengthening their immunity to the almost inevitable fate of eventual decline, as predicted by the flying-geese model. Thus, the key lies not in whether or not the industry is traditional, but whether it adopts a policy of change and innovation through exploring novel products and services, changing the process of production and the means of sales promotion, and opening up new markets.

Various indices have been proposed to measure the success of industrial upgrading (for example, Wu, 2000; Chen, 2000; Lim, 2000; Wang, 2000), within which two common indicators are generally identified. The first indicator is the relative research and development (R&D) input, whilst the second is the success in terms of both innovativeness and the application of new knowledge and technology into the various aspects of production, including product design, the production process, the organisational structure of the enterprise, the organisation of management, and finally, marketing of the merchandise. These indices will be used to examine the case studies of industrial upgrading that follow.

The traditional industries in Taiwan have become more capital-intensive and skills-intensive, with their developmental trend being tied closely to the fluctuations in production costs. With the diminishing supply of cheap labour and the rising costs of land, these industries have suffered a general decline and have lost their former competitiveness, such that their survival in the international arena has come under considerable threat. Whilst some have been able to escape the finality of being phased out, others have nevertheless gone on to experience resurgence through upgrading.

We list eighteen enterprises within the traditional industries that have successfully gone on to transform themselves into new knowledge-intensive businesses with the following brief case studies highlighting some of these success stories, and serving to illustrate that innovation and change will determine whether an industry, knowledge-based or not, can survive and thrive in the ever-changing economic environment.[5]

ECLAT

Founded in 1977, ECLAT began mass production of budget-priced garments for the general public, with its success in the research of stretch fabrics leading to the production, in 1981, of Spandex knitting fabrics. ECLAT entered into technological collaboration with Dupont in 1989, and in 1993, established an R&D division and set up the ECLAT testing centre, which subsequently received 'Q-mark' certification from Dupont.

ECLAT's annual R&D expenditure amounted to NT$50 to NT$60 million, accounting for 1.0 to 1.2 per cent of its total business sales. In 1997, the company started its own brand-name product 'Eclon', which was registered as a trademark in over thirty countries. With its investment and expansion in dyeing mills, ECLAT achieved vertical integration of its automated and diversified production processes, research systems and marketing services on an international scale, and was subsequently listed on the Taiwan Stock Exchange in 2001.

Yulon Motor Company Limited
Yulon Motor Company Limited has placed significant emphasis on R&D, particularly with regard to new product designs. In 1999, the company embarked on a process of establishing an effective supply chain system (SCS), an enterprise resource planning (ERP) system and electronic business-to-business (B2B) operations, all of which were designed to link the core factory with its subsidiary factories. The various functions, including the management of production, delivery, capital stock, purchasing and quality control, are all accessible via the Internet; indeed the more traditional communication means, such as telephone, fax and computers, have been replaced by more efficient Internet exchanges. Simultaneous production operations can be achieved with these more advanced means of communication, thus enhancing overall production efficiency and industrial upgrading. The company found that it was able to recover all of the initial investment costs and expenditure on general maintenance within the first year of implementation.

Fu Sheng Industrial Company
Fu Sheng Industrial Company is the leading manufacturer of compressors in Taiwan. Its success in the research of screw air compressors pushed its business sales to record highs in 1995; thereafter, riding on the growing popularity of golf, it switched its production to the manufacture of golf club heads, and despite the global recession and the continuing decline of traditional industries, the company went on to become the number one producer in this field. From the factories which Fu Sheng has successfully established in both Taiwan and mainland China, the company's production and services have been completely redesigned to provide tailor-made services to meet the demands and needs of its wide range of customers.

Ho Chen Corporation
Ho Chen Corporation is Taiwan's leading manufacturer of bathroom and toilet equipment; however, with the real estate market having been hit hard in recent

years by the global economic downturn, this has indirectly affected sales of such equipment. In response to such difficult times, Ho Chen launched a range of newly designed products, the Legato series, which rapidly began to enjoy steady sales growth. The company's emphasis on the development of new value-added design products ensured that its business continued to flourish, whilst further technological advances also led to a new vitreous chinaware series. The new production techniques not only lowered production costs, but also added further value to the products, in terms of their attractive design and enhanced durability, making the new series even more appealing to customers.

Everbeauty

From its factories in Kaohisung and Taipei, Everbeauty emerged in 1988 as a manufacturer of disposable diapers having formerly been a supplier of construction materials. The inefficient communication that existed between the factories caused considerable delays in the exchange of materials, thus affecting production efficacy. Therefore, between 1992 and 1994, the company invested over NT$6 million in the computerisation of its operations. However, this initial effort failed to meet the needs of the company and the outlay proved futile. Learning from this lesson, over the next three years, the company invested a further NT$6 million in order to acquire new equipment and software, integrating its various operating systems, including finance and accounting, the purchase of raw materials, production processes, marketing and sales, and company auditing, and in 2000, it launched its first new electronic sales invoice. Although not all the new measures and modes of operations were welcomed by the company staff, as time went by, the efficiency proved overwhelming. Not only did the decision-making process become much more effective, but the computerised operations also saved on labour inputs. The staff was reduced from 400 to 300, thus cutting personnel expenses and labour costs considerably.

Transformation Benchmarks

Table 5.1 lists the different benchmarks of transformation undertaken by the various industries. As the table shows, within these examples of successful industrial upgrading, an increase in R&D expenditure was the most common change to be introduced. Another common aspect of transformation observed in over 90 per cent of the sample cases involved innovation in product design and in the companies' production processes. Although over 60 per cent of the companies listed had carried out a reform of their markets or relationship management, other aspects, such as the computerisation of operations, company reorganisation and corporate restructuring, had been undertaken by less than half of the companies.

Table 5.1 Transformation benchmarks achieved by companies in the traditional industries

Company	Increase in R&D Expenditure	Computerised Business Operations	New Products	New Production Processes	New Management Organisation	New Corporate Structure	New Markets
1 ECLAT	✓		✓	✓	✓		✓
2 Yulon Motor Co. Ltd.	✓	✓	✓	✓	✓		✓
3 ATOP	✓	✓	✓	✓	✓		✓
4 Chunghwa Picture Tubes Limited	✓		✓	✓			✓
5 Fu Sheng Industrial Co.	✓	✓	✓	✓			
6 Sinon Corporation	✓		✓	✓			
7 Chang-chun Synthetic Resin Corp.	✓		✓	✓		✓	
8 Rui-sheng Plastic Co., Ltd.	✓		✓	✓	✓		✓
9 Ho Cheng Corp.	✓		✓	✓			
10 Everbeauty Co. Ltd.	✓	✓	✓	✓			
11 Chatronic Industrial Technique Co. Ltd.	✓		✓	✓	✓		
12 Daily Polymer Corp.	✓		✓	✓			
13 Li Shin International Enterprise Corp.	✓	✓	✓	✓			✓
14 Minton Optical Industry Co. Ltd.	✓	✓	✓	✓			✓
15 Di-gu Diamond Co.	✓		✓	✓			✓
16 Prosperity Tieh Enterprise Co. Ltd.	✓		✓	✓			✓
17 Techco Chemical Co. Ltd.	✓			✓			✓
18 Compucase Enterprise Co. Ltd.	✓	✓	✓	✓		✓	✓

A common feature observed amongst many of these companies was their recognition of the need to adopt policies focusing on change and reform. ECLAT, Fu Sheng and Ho Chen had each been traditional labour-intensive industries focusing on the mass production of low-priced merchandise. Even before their current production levels had begun to show signs of decline, ECLAT and Fu Sheng had taken the initiative to explore new product designs and more advanced technological support. Taking advantage of their accumulated experience in production and undertaking huge investment in R&D, these traditional industries adopted the latest advances in technology and new knowledge to reform their current production processes and to develop new designs. It was this readiness to accept change and the recognition of the need for transformation, as well as an emphasis on R&D, that helped these firms to sustain their current level of competitiveness and to secure ongoing growth.

The methods adopted by Yulon and Everbeauty in pursuit of the transformation of their companies did not involve changes to their product designs or innovations to their production processes, but rather the reorganisation of the company or the corporate structure. Greater efficiency was achieved by these companies through computerisation of their operations and through overall integration of the production functions. These innovations brought new life and dynamism to the companies, helping them not only to revive their past levels of achievement, but also to go on to thrive in the new business environment.

Entrepreneurship

The transformation benchmarks outlined above are not the sole factors governing the upgrading and resurgence of industries, since the crucial determinant is shown to be entrepreneurship; however, this raises the question of how we define entrepreneurship. The following two examples serve to illustrate how entrepreneurial spirit can pave the way for the success of an enterprise.

Daily Polymer Corporation

Ever since its establishment in 1970, Daily Polymer Corporation's main area of business had been the production of synthetic resins for use in the manufacture of paints and adhesives. However, the company experienced a serious decline in business as a result of the global economic downturn and thus embarked on a policy of switching to the production of alignment film for liquid crystal display (LCD) screens. Such a switch was possible because polymer is an important component of alignment film; however, this was in fact an idea that was brought up by an employee during a brainstorming session which was aimed at determining new directions for the company's production lines.

Despite having identified a new venture which might have appeared as a natural choice (given the company's considerable expertise in working with polymer), it would clearly have taken considerable courage at management level, and no small degree of risk, to launch such a business from a new platform. Nevertheless, the company's daring spirit, entrepreneurship, and readiness to reform and transform itself contributed significantly to the smooth transition of the company and laid the foundations for its successful industrial upgrading.

Compucase Enterprise Company Limited
Our final example is Compucase Enterprise Company Limited which had evolved from being a manufacturer of automobile accessories to become a leading producer of computer cases. Such a drastic change was inspired by one of the company's clients. What began as a casual suggestion offered to the company by the client was finally realised as a result of innovative collaboration fuelled by an adventurous spirit.

Surprisingly, both Daily Polymer Corporation and Compucase Enterprise Company Limited did not undertake any major investment in R&D, nor did they hire any experts for advice. Rather, it was the innovative spirit of a member of staff or a client that sparked off the total upheaval of the company, and its eventual transformation. In short, therefore, it would seem that entrepreneurship embodies the spirit of innovation within which all eyes must remain wide open for new ideas and new directions, the willingness to accept what might initially be seen as an enormous amount of risk-taking once the goals are identified, and a spirit of dedication to realise the company's new ambitions once the decisions have been taken.

CONCLUSIONS

A retrospective examination of many of the various 'traditional' industries reveals that in a knowledge-based economy, transformation is often a prerequisite for survival and continuing development. Recognition of the need to undergo change takes great courage on the part of management, since they will then have to face many unknown risks; it also takes patience on the part of employees since they will be required to adapt to the changes, and to make the necessary adjustments. What is also of great importance is recognition of the fact that transformation does not miraculously occur overnight. Rather, the changes involved will be ongoing and often relentless. In the long run, the cumulative effects of these changes, although seen as small and perhaps even insignificant at times, will not only save an enterprise from further decline, but will also drive it towards its evolution into a new phase of development, and perhaps deliver prosperity to an otherwise ill-fated destiny.

That said, it would be useful in closing to comment on, and develop if possible, the general environment in which the traditional industries noted above had been struggling to survive, with an examination from three different aspects, starting first of all with an examination of the environment from an industrial policy aspect.

The Taiwanese government's industrial policy used to play a key role in assisting the development of industries through the granting of tax exemptions, development of industrial parks, development and assimilation of new technologies, and by making it possible for firms to secure cheap loans (Chu, 2001). However, the environment has changed considerably since the revision, in 1990, of the *Statute for Encouragement of Investment*, a revision which was undertaken as a means of placing greater emphasis on 'functional subsidies' (such as R&D and environmental protection) rather than the subsidisation of 'strategic industries'. Although the government has continued to play a major role in the development of the 'high-tech' industries, its role in the upgrading of traditional industries has become much more limited in comparison to preceding decades. Some of the technology enhancement schemes remain, and there would sometimes emerge a plan to save the traditional industries on a periodical basis; however, many of these plans have done more to serve political purposes than to signify any return to the former role of the government. Therefore the traditional industries in Taiwan have found themselves forced to pursue their necessary transformation with only limited help from the government.

Secondly, from an educational aspect, it is clear that such education has been responsible for laying the important foundations for Taiwan's initial industrial development. Within the island's population, the proportion of those aged 15 years or older, and in receipt of secondary and higher education, rose from 41.28 per cent in 1976, to 76.72 per cent in 2001, with a large proportion of these students becoming technicians or engineers. Clearly, Taiwan's traditional industries would not have been able to develop and survive the 1987 currency appreciation, if it were not for the continuous flow of high-quality graduates from within the island's education system. However, in recent years, a trend has emerged which essentially penalises the traditional industries, since Taiwan has also been reforming its higher education system in a way which allows vocational schools and professional colleges to convert themselves into regular high schools and universities. Students attending vocational schools once constituted 70 per cent of the total, but this is already down to around 50 per cent and the slide is continuing; thus the supply of high-school level technicians will gradually diminish and this could have a significant impact on firms in the traditional industries, particularly small and medium enterprises (SMEs). There is also a growing trend for the high-tech sector to absorb all of the talented engineering students, largely because this sector has a greater attraction to these graduates than the traditional industries. This clearly prevents the traditional industries from getting their hands on the sort of quality engineers that are crucial to the upgrading of these industries.

The third aspect is one of scale. Many of the manufacturing firms in the traditional industries are SMEs, but with technology advancing at a much more rapid pace than ever before, R&D becomes even more important, and this is an area in which SMEs clearly struggle. In many cases, firms needs to achieve a critical mass of researchers and equipment if they are to be successful in their R&D efforts, and it is clear that SMEs cannot afford such expenditure on an individual basis. It is also becoming apparent that Taiwan's old system of (flexible) networks of small suppliers sharing large orders from overseas is gradually disappearing. In its place we see the emergence of much larger scale plants, within which R&D activities are centralised. This phenomenon is already revealing itself, since the share of total exports accounted for by SMEs in Taiwan fell sharply from 54.8 per cent in 1993, to 29.0 per cent in 2000.

Our analysis of the general business environment in Taiwan reveals that, for the past decade or so, it has not really favoured the traditional industries; indeed, many firms within the traditional industries have either failed, or have moved to foreign countries to continue their operations. Many of those that have stayed in the hope that they can overcome the current problems will also eventually fail. Such a situation is only to be expected, because there has been a wholesale shift in the weight of the manufacturing sector from the traditional industries to high-tech industries. What is amazing is that in spite of the adverse conditions in the current environment, there have been so many cases of successful transformation.

NOTES

[1] See: Chu (1994).

[2] See: Ettlie (1988); for discussions on the reform of the manufacturing sector, see: Naya and Takayama (1990); NRC and NAS (1993); Molero (1995); Masuyama et al. (1997); JCIP (1997); Appelbaum et al. (2000); and Agrawal et al. (2000).

[3] See also Chu et al. (2001).

[4] The groupings of skilled-labour intensity for both South Korea and mainland China are categorised in accordance with the definition adopted in Taiwan.

[5] Many of the materials discussed here originated from Chu and Zeng (2000).

REFERENCES

Agrawal, P., S.V. Gokarn, V.M.K. Parikh and K. Sen (2000), *Policy Regimes and Industrial Competitiveness,* Singapore: Institute of Southeast Asian Studies.

Appelbaum, E., T. Bailey, P. Berg and A.L. Kalleberg (2000), *Manufacturing Advantage: Why High-Performance Work Systems Pay Off,* New York: Cornell University.

Chen, T.-J. (2000), 'Development Directions of the Knowledge-intensive Industries in Taiwan', paper presented at the Sixth National Conference on Scientific Technology, Taipei (November).

Chu, Y.-P. (1994), 'Taiwan's External Imbalance and Structural Adjustment: A General Equilibrium Analysis', *Asian Economic Journal,* **8**: 85-114.

Chu, Y.-P (2001), 'Market Grew and Matured as a Result of State Actions', *Journal of Development Planning Literature,* **16**(3-4).

Chu, Y.-P, T.-J. Chen and B.-L. Chen (2001), 'Rethinking the Development Paradigm: Lessons from Taiwan – The Optimal Degree of State Intervention', in P.-K. Wong and C.-Y. Ng (eds.), *Industrial Policy, Innovation and Economic Growth: The Experience of Japan and the Asian NIEs,* Singapore University Press, pp.197-244.

Chu, Y.-P. and Z.-S. Zeng (2000), The Knowledge-based Economy and Case Studies of Upgrading of Traditional Industries, in C. Lee (ed.), *The Myth and Retrospection of the Knowledge-Based Economy,* Taipei: Commonwealth Publishing, pp.145-63 (in Chinese).

Ettlie, J.E. (1988), *Taking Charge of Manufacturing,* San Francisco: Jossey- Bass.

JCIP (1997), *Made in Japan: Revitalizing Japanese Manufacturing for Economic Growth,* Boston: The Massachusetts Institute of Technology, and the Japan Commission on Industrial Performance.

Lim Y.-T. (2000). 'A New Measurement of the Level of S&T, International Comparisons and Some Econometric Applications in Knowledge-based Economies', paper presented at the Conference on the Measurement of Industrial Technological Competitiveness in the Knowledge-Based Economy, Taipei (23-24 August).

Masuyama, S., D. Vandenbrink and C.S. Yue (1997), *Industrial Policies in East Asia,* Tokyo: Nomura Research Institute, and Singapore: Institute of Southeast Asian Studies.

Molero, J. (1995), *Technological Innovation, Multinational Corporations and New International Competitiveness,* New York: Harwood Academic Publishers.

Naya, S. and A. Takayama (1990), *Economic Development in East and Southeast Asia: Essays in Honor of Professor Shinichi Ichimura,* Singapore: Institute of Southeast Asian Studies, and Hawaii: East-West Centre.

NRC and NAS (1993), *Learning to Change: Opportunities to Improve the Performance of Smaller Manufacturers,* Washington, DC: National Research Council and National Academy of Sciences.

Wang, C.-C. (2000), 'Development of Traditional Industries in a Knowledge-based Economy', paper presented at the Sixth National Conference on Scientific Technology, Taipei (November).

Wu, R.-I. (2000), 'Analysis of Technological Competitiveness of Industries in Taiwan', paper presented at the Conference on The Measurement of Industrial Technological Competitiveness in the Knowledge-Based Economy, Taipei (23-24 August).

6 The Road to Financial Globalisation

Ho-Mou Wu

INTRODUCTION

For well over a decade, Taiwan has been continually striving to integrate the modern practices of the global financial markets into its own economy, and for the most part, it has been successful in terms of opening up its market to foreign investment and in pushing domestic investors to become more globally-oriented. Nevertheless, whilst there have undoubtedly been some significant improvements in the island's overall level of competitiveness over the past decade, particularly with regard to the effective restructuring and deregulation of its financial markets, there is still considerable room for further improvement in many areas.

In reviewing and reengineering its earlier efforts, which had subsequently become obsolete, over the years, the Taiwanese government introduced a range of new initiatives, including promotion of the free movement of financial capital, enhancement of efficiency within the financial sector and the strengthening of financial supervision. The overall aim of the government was to ensure the creation of a stable financial environment with transparent policies, so as to promote a lively capital market and a healthy banking sector.

Following in the wake of the Taiwanese presidential election of 2000, the new government formed by the Democratic Progressive Party (DPP) and led by Chen Shui-Bian, also embarked upon a massive scale programme of restructuring within the island's financial sector, under the belief that the promotion of globalisation and liberalisation of the financial sector would constitute the most important ingredients for Taiwan's further economic development in the twenty-first century. Taiwan's experience, as a result of all of these measures, essentially demonstrates that globalisation and liberalisation go hand in hand. In this chapter we will examine the impact of recent events and policies on Taiwan's financial sector, and discuss how the policies on financial liberalisation and globalisation can fundamentally affect the prospects for a growing economy.

THE CHALLENGES OF FINANCIAL GLOBALISATION

The Flow of International Funds

Taiwan's financial sector has now entered a new era in which the most important issue is clearly globalisation. With the barriers to entry into Taiwan's markets now falling, competition is inevitably increasing and global investment flows are rapidly gaining pace, forcing new conditions upon Taiwan, not only with regard to its financial institutions, but also with regard to the impacts that they will inevitably have on the island's markets. Clearly, international capital flows will always have very profound, long-term effects on the reorganisation and restructuring of the financial sector within any economy; hence, the effects of international capital flows on Taiwan's financial sector are also resulting in the reshaping of the island's economic future. Alongside these effects, the rapid pace of development in mainland China has also led to major capital outflows from Taiwan; thus, the incessant trend towards globalisation clearly poses a major challenge to Taiwan's economic future.

From about 1970 to 1990, an upward trend became readily apparent in the total amount of capital flows within Asia and many other developing countries (Table 6.1). By the 1990s, the capital outflow from Taiwan towards the emerging markets was largely taking the form of foreign direct investment (FDI), whilst in terms of stock investment, the movement of international funds towards Taiwan's market was on the rise during the early 1990s, but then saw a significant decline in the aftermath of the 1997 Asian financial crisis. An examination of Table 6.1 also highlights another important category of international capital flows, 'other investment flows', which include short-term loans and deposits; this is a category of capital flow which has played an increasingly important role ever since the onslaught of the financial crisis.

The international capital flows, both into and out of Taiwan, between 1985 and 2002, are characterised by the following stylised facts:

1. With regard to its relative size, since the 1990s, Taiwan's capital outflows have settled at a stable level of about 3 per cent of the island's GDP.

2. In the eighteen-year period from 1985 to 2002, there were fourteen years when the balance of capital flows was outward.

3. The 1990s had generally seen the category of 'other investment flows' becoming a major, and unstable, determinant of total capital flows. In 2002, it became the most important component, thereby inducing a net capital inflow into Taiwan.

Table 6.1 International capital flows into Taiwan

Year	Net Capital Flows			Direct Investment			Stock Investment			Other Investment		
	US$ million	% of exports	% of GNP	US$ million	% of exports	% of GNP	US$ million	% of exports	% of GNP	US$ million	% of exports	% of GNP
1985	-3,171	-10.34	-5.03	263	0.86	0.42	-46	-0.15	-0.07	-3,388	-11.05	-5.37
1986	6,942	17.45	8.98	261	0.66	0.34	71	0.18	0.09	6,610	16.62	8.55
1987	10,395	19.43	10.03	10	0.02	-	-372	-0.70	-0.36	10,757	20.11	10.38
1988	-11,451	-18.93	-9.07	-3,160	-5.22	-2.50	-1,712	-2.83	-1.36	-6,579	-10.87	-5.21
1989	-12,131	-18.34	-7.95	-5,347	-8.08	-3.50	-902	-1.36	-0.59	-5,882	-8.89	-3.86
1990	-15,150	-22.56	-9.23	-3,913	-5.83	-2.38	-1,006	-1.50	-0.61	-10,231	-15.23	-6.24
1991	-2,228	-2.93	-1.21	-784	-1.03	-0.43	45	0.06	0.02	-1,489	-1.96	-0.81
1992	-6,910	8.51	-3.18	-1,088	-1.34	-0.50	444	0.55	0.20	-6,266	-7.72	-2.89
1993	-4,629	-5.46	-2.03	-1,694	-2.00	-0.74	1,067	1.26	0.47	-4,002	-4.72	-1.75
1994	-1,397	-1.51	-0.56	-1,265	-1.36	-0.51	905	0.98	0.37	-1,037	-1.12	-0.42
1995	-8,190	-7.36	-3.05	-1,424	-1.28	-0.53	493	0.44	0.18	-7,259	-6.53	-2.70
1996	-8,633	-7.48	-3.05	-1,979	-1.71	-0.70	-1,045	-0.91	-0.37	-5,609	-4.86	-1.98
1997	-7,291	-5.99	-2.49	-2,995	-2.46	-1.02	-7,953	-6.53	-2.72	3,657	3.00	1.25
1998	2,495	2.26	0.93	-3,614	-3.28	-1.35	-2,412	-2.19	-0.90	8,521	7.73	3.17
1999	9,220	7.61	3.17	-1,494	-1.23	-0.51	9,079	7.50	3.12	1,635	1.35	0.56
2000	-8,019	-5.43	-2.55	-1,773	-1.21	-0.57	-528	-0.36	-0.17	-5,718	-3.88	-1.82
2001	329	0.27	0.11	-1,371	-1.12	-0.46	-1,291	-1.06	-0.45	2,991	2.45	1.04
2002	8,386	6.46	2.90	-3,441	-2.65	-1.19	-9,185	-7.07	-3.18	21,012	16.18	7.27

Note: Net capital flows = Direct Investment + Stock Investment + Other Investment; a negative sign indicates capital outflows.

Source: *Taiwan Statistical Data Book*, Annual Report, Central Bank of Taiwan, Ministry of Economic Affairs.

4. After 1997, stock investments became another major determinant of capital inflows and outflows. As a result of the increasing deregulation of the financial sector, a large capital inflow occurred in 1999; however, this soon declined, highlighting another unstable force for fluctuations in capital inflows into Taiwan.

5. Although direct investments have been relatively small, they have nevertheless been the cause of steady capital outflows over the past fifteen years.

During the past two decades, the capital inflow into Taiwan has responded to the globalising trend in the international capital market, particularly in the late-1980s to early-1990s when direct investment and other investment flows increased sharply. Taiwan has also experienced a steady flow of direct investment outflows over the past ten years, focusing largely on mainland China and other Asian countries, and thus making Taiwan more globally oriented than ever before.

Taiwan's Competitiveness Compared to Neighbouring Financial Centres

Since taking the initiative to become an Asia-Pacific Regional Operations Centre (APROC) in 1995, Taiwan's financial sector has seen much deregulation and reform, largely implemented with speed and efficiency, and generally in line with the practices of neighbouring financial centres, including Hong Kong and Singapore. Comparing these three economics, Singapore has the largest trade volume in terms of currency exchange, with volume topping US$94 billion in 2000, whilst Taiwan has the smallest, with volume of just US$5 billion. The stock exchange volume, on the other hand, is an altogether different matter. In 2000, Taiwan's stock exchange value topped US$990 billion, putting it in first place; Hong Kong came second, with US$370 billion, whilst Singapore was third, registering just US$95 billion.

Taiwan has a relatively active stock market because it has a large number of publicly listed companies, and having recently deregulated the market, it has become very attractive to foreign investors. Nevertheless, Taiwan still has the smallest share of foreign investors and foreign publicly listed companies, the categories in which Singapore and Hong Kong both lead, and where Taiwan can obviously make improvements; and Taiwan clearly lags behind in terms of openness to foreign banks. In a comparison of the number of foreign banks in Taiwan, Singapore and Hong Kong, although Hong Kong leads in this category, there has been some recent weakness in its ability to retain these institutions, whereas Singapore has proved itself quite adept at attracting foreign banking institutions over recent years (Table 6.2).

Table 6.2   Foreign banks in Taiwan, Singapore and Hong Kong

	1995	1996	1997	1998	1999	2000	2001	2002
Taiwan	38	41	46	46	41	39	38	36
Singapore	128	131	140	142	133	132	133	120
Hong Kong	183	178	178	168	150	143	138	135

Source: MAS Annual Report, www.info.gov.hk/hkma, http://www.boma.gov.tw

In the third category, offshore assets, although Taiwan managed to achieve a level of US$50 billion in 2000, this figure still represented only one tenth of the total offshore assets of both Hong Kong and Singapore. It is clear, therefore, that Taiwan continues to lag behind in its attempts to create a truly global financial sector, not only in terms of its total offshore assets, but also with regard to the number of institutions participating in the offshore financial sector; in 2000, there were 68 such institutions in Taiwan, as compared to 268 in Hong Kong, and 195 in Singapore.

Although, in 1992, Taiwan decided to allow foreign companies to begin participating in the issuing of securities in the domestic stock market, the regulations governing such issues were still rather strict and constraining, particularly with regard to punitive taxes; local policies demonstrated their continuing failure to meet the degree of liberalisation being achieved within the markets of the neighbouring countries. The end result was that only two foreign companies began issuing deposit receipts in Taiwan, whilst the total number of locally listed foreign enterprises also remained very limited. When comparing this to the situation in both Hong Kong and Singapore, where about thirty foreign enterprises have successfully achieved local listing, this also demonstrates that Taiwan clearly has much room for improvement within this category.

According to the Swiss Institute for International Competitiveness (IMD), by 2000, there had been some distinct advantages achieved within Taiwan's financial industry, particularly in the areas of overall stock market volume, the relatively high deposit ratio as compared to the amount of lending, the active venture capital market, the island's impressive level of bank assets as compared to its GDP and a good overall credit rating for the economy. The IMD's analysis suggested that Taiwan's competitiveness could be improved by removing the restrictions on investment in local assets by foreign companies and initiating improvements to the infrastructure of the stock exchange, inviting more foreign firms to participate within the financial market, liberalising the insurance industry and encouraging local companies to seek out foreign listing opportunities.

From a long-term perspective, there are still opportunities for Taiwan to become an Asia-Pacific financial centre; this is particularly so when we consider its strong manufacturing base, high savings ratio and globalisation efforts. Nevertheless, improvements can still be made, in addition to those discussed above, in speeding up the deregulation of the financial sector, modernisation of the regulating agencies, recruitment of international professionals and the promotion of greater proficiency by its people with regard to the use of the English language. Its advantages, including its major strength of a lively capital market, as already discussed, and a general consensus to pursue the further deregulation of the financial sector, may allow Taiwan to compete with Hong Kong and Singapore in the future, as a regional financial centre.

THE BANKING SYSTEM IN TAIWAN

The Changing Function of Indirect Finance

The flow of funds within an economy, from surplus units to spending units, can be conducted through either the financial markets (direct finance) or financial institutions (indirect finance). As in Germany and Japan, funding in Taiwan's financial sector is largely based upon financial institution channels, in particular, the banking industry, and here, the importance of the banking industry in Taiwan's financial sector is self-evident, with around 73 per cent of all funding being channelled though this medium in 2002. Taiwan's banking industry is currently characterised by the following features:

Increased number of banks
In 1992, the government provided approval for the entry of an additional fifteen commercial banks, thereby entirely reshaping the banking community based upon a greater number of participants. In 1997, many credit cooperatives were given approval to become commercial banks, which resulted in the rapid growth of the number of financial institutions (Table 6.3). By 2002, the total number of branch offices in Taiwan had climbed to over 5,000.

Increased competition from direct finance
The total accumulated amount of direct financing – the sourcing of funds through the financial markets as opposed to the banking industry – increased from around 10 per cent in 1991, to 27 per cent in 2002 (Table 6.4), indicating that direct financing has become an important source of funding over the past ten years.

Table 6.3 Composition of the banking sector in Taiwan

	1991	1992	1993	1994	1995	1996	1997	1998	1999	2000	2001	2002
Domestic Banks												
HQ	25	40	41	42	42	42	47	48	52	53	53	52
Branches [a]	1,046	1,212	1,382	1,577	1,807	1,936	2,176	2,404	2,576	2,693	3,005	3,068
Foreign Banks												
HQ	36	36	37	37	38	41	46	46	41	39	38	36
Branches [b]	47	50	53	57	58	65	69	72	71	70	69	68
Credit Cooperatives												
HQ	74	74	74	74	73	73	64	54	50	48	39	37
Branches	425	439	482	530	556	595	505	446	416	394	373	358
Farmers and Fisheries Cooperatives												
HQ	311	312	312	312	312	312	314	314	314	314	285	278
Branches	785	803	822	865	930	972	991	1,007	1,020	1,022	927	887
Investment Trusts												
HQ	8	7	7	6	5	5	5	4	3	3	3	3
Branches	62	55	61	53	49	55	61	43	36	36	33	29
Others [c]												
HQ	17	24	29	31	32	33	33	34	34	33	29	30
Branches	1,275	1,294	1,310	1,328	1,345	1,358	1,379	1,396	1,412	1,421	1,434	1,463
Totals												
HQ	471	493	500	502	502	506	508	500	494	490	447	436
Branches	3,640	3,852	4,111	4,410	4,745	4,981	5,181	5,368	5,531	5,636	5,841	5,873

Notes:
a The number of branch offices operated by domestic banks does not include overseas offices.
b Figures for foreign banks include only the number of branches operating in Taiwan.
c Others include life insurance companies and postal deposit branches.

Source: Monthly Statistical Report, Central Bank of China, ROC.

Table 6.4   Financing channels in Taiwan [a]

Unit: NT$100 million

Year	Indirect Finance (1)		Subtotal	Direct Finance [b] (2)	Total (3) = (1) + (2)	(1)/(3) (%)	(2)/(3) (%)
	Bank Loans	Bank Securities Investment					
1991	61,257	6,759	68,016	8,247	76,264	89.19	10.81
1992	77,041	8,822	85,863	9,973	95,836	89.59	10.41
1993	89,783	12,783	102,566	11,297	113,863	90.08	9.92
1994	104,656	13,409	118,065	14,608	132,673	88.99	11.01
1995	114,237	16,120	130,357	19,023	149,380	87.27	12.73
1996	118,673	22,632	141,305	24,024	165,329	85.47	14.53
1997	132,615	21,541	154,156	35,029	189,185	81.48	18.52
1998	139,763	26,630	166,393	44,768	211,161	78.80	21.20
1999	145,854	27,074	172,928	50,660	223,587	77.34	22.66
2000	153,091	27,855	180,946	58,716	239,661	75.50	24.50
2001	149,457	31,830	180,287	62,720	244,007	74.30	25.70
2002	145,902	34,691	180,593	69,002	249,595	74.35	27.65

Notes:
[a]   All figures are accumulated amounts.
[b]   Direct Finance = Securities issues – bank securities investments.

Source: Financial Report, Central Bank of China, ROC.

Declining asset quality

As Table 6.5 shows, although the non-performing loan ratio within local banks was below 2 per cent in 1994, by 2001, the figure had risen sharply to around 8 per cent, reflecting a considerable decline in asset value. However, following protracted efforts by the government and banks, this was reduced to 6.8 per cent in 2002.

Table 6.5   Non-performing loans in Taiwanese banks

Unit: %

Year	Domestic Banks and Local Trusts	Foreign Banks	Farmers' and Fisheries' Cooperatives	Total
1994	1.82	0.34	2.46	1.90
1995	2.88	0.82	4.02	3.00
1996	3.74	1.00	7.10	4.15
1997	3.74	1.07	8.53	4.18
1998	4.41	1.64	10.57	4.93
1999	4.96	3.20	13.70	5.67
2000	5.47	3.22	15.68	6.20
2001	7.70	3.53	16.39	8.16
2002	6.39	2.36	15.37	6.84

Source: Financial Report, Ministry of Finance, ROC.

Declining bank profits

As the return on assets (ROA) fell below the levels established in the 1980s, there was a corresponding decline in the profitability of banks; namely a fall from the high level of 0.65-0.73 per cent to around 0.26 per cent in 2001, and even into negative territory in 2002 (Table 6.6). The return on equity (ROE) also fell with the decline in the profitability of banks (Table 6.7).

Table 6.6   Post-tax earnings/assets (ROA) in Taiwanese banks

Unit: %

Year	Large Commercial Banks	Small/Medium Sized Banks	Foreign Banks	Investment Trusts	Bills Companies
1991	0.62	0.68	0.53	0.78	2.25
1992	0.55	0.58	0.62	1.91	1.38
1993	0.60	0.69	0.54	3.15	1.16
1994	0.65	0.81	0.56	2.52	1.60
1995	0.59	0.69	0.78	1.85	-0.18
1996	0.66	0.65	0.72	2.10	0.94
1997	0.73	0.59	0.98	2.14	0.74
1998	0.59	0.08	0.87	2.20	0.20
1999	0.54		0.45	-0.68	0.75
2000	0.47		0.62	-3.92	0.70
2001	0.26		1.19	-2.03	0.46
2002	-0.47		1.18	-1.77	0.34

Source: Annual Financial Report, Ministry of Finance, ROC.

Table 6.7   Post-tax earnings/equity (ROE) in Taiwanese banks

Unit: %

Year	Large Commercial Banks	Small/Medium Sized Banks	Foreign Banks	Investment Trusts and Cooperatives	Securities Companies
1991	14.22	17.74	12.18	9.47	20.56
1992	8.69	14.70	14.38	18.07	16.05
1993	9.86	16.66	12.90	30.73	13.67
1994	10.52	15.17	13.19	15.48	15.22
1995	9.64	12.71	16.72	12.18	-1.88
1996	10.30	10.50	15.05	13.19	9.05
1997	10.43	8.83	22.51	8.76	6.43
1998	7.61	1.16	17.56	8.31	1.83
1999	0.91		11.44	-5.78	7.42
2000	6.05		30.19	-30.55	9.62
2001	3.61		30.98	-26.85	6.41
2002	-7.35		30.74	-30.0	4.38

Source: Annual Financial Report, Ministry of Finance, ROC.

The stock market, which had been particularly exuberant between 1994 and 1997, had contributed significantly to the return on equity within the banking sector; however, the earlier returns of 10 per cent and higher saw their peak in 1997 and thereafter, began to fall. By 2001, returns stood at just 3.61 per cent, and even fell into negative territory in 2002.

Formation of Financial Blocs

Starting in late 2001, the government approved the establishment of fourteen financial holding companies (Table 6.8), most of which included one of Taiwan's major banks within their group. This has resulted in a profound change in the competitive environment for all financial industries in Taiwan.

Table 6.8   Financial holding companies (FHCs) in Taiwan

Unit: NT$100 million

Financial Holding Company	Business Startup Date	Total Asset Value *	Bank Subsidiary
Hua Nan FHC	19 Dec 2001	642	Hua Nan Bank
Fubon FHC	19 Dec 2001	1,719	Fubon Bank
China Development FHC	28 Dec 2001	1,677	China Development Ind'l. Bank
Cathay FHC	31 Dec 2001	1,381	Cathay Bank
E. Sun FHC	28 Dec 2001	239	E. Sun Bank
Mega FHC	4 Feb 2002	1,684	Chiao Tung Bank
Fuh-Hwa FHC	4 Feb 2002	400	Fuh-Hwa Bank
Jih Sun FHC	5 Feb 2002	294	Jih Sun International Bank
Taishin FHC	18 Feb 2002	538	Taishin Bank
Shin Kong FHC	19 Feb 2002	247	None
Waterland FHC	26 Mar 2002	209	None
SinoPac FHC	9 May 2002	532	SinoPac Bank
Chinatrust FHC	17 May 2002	934	Chinatrust Commercial Bank
First FHC	2 Jan 2003	492	First Bank

Note: * All company assets are valued as at 31 December 2002.

The Future for Taiwan's Banking Industry

Over the years, Taiwan's banking industry has become burdened with mounting non-performing loans, and despite the government's efforts to persuade banks to write off these bad loans, this has met with only limited success. Although the Central Deposit Insurance Corporation has taken over more than thirty non-performing cooperative banks, much greater effort is urgently required. The Ministry of Finance has estimated that NT$600 billion is needed to support the writing off of bad loans, but private estimates suggest that the figure is closer to NT$1 trillion. There are a number of directions in which joint efforts could be undertaken by the government and the banking system in the future as a means of establishing sound practices within the banking industry; these are described below.

Establishing a strong safety net
Many banks have been trying to enhance the level of reserves needed to support their deposits, particularly as the island's citizens have become increasingly concerned about the current level of banks' reserves. Both the government and the banks should therefore aim to work closely to establish a sound system of deposit insurance.

Reestablishing the credit creation function of banks
As a result of the significant increase in non-performing loans within the banking system, the credit creation function of banks has been seriously eroded. The widely used practice of selling bad assets to Asset Management Corporations (AMC), as seen in Korea, Malaysia and other Asian countries, could be adopted in Taiwan as a means of helping the domestic banks to get back on their feet. Clearly, the government could provide a number of incentives to speed up this process of adjustment.

Respecting the market mechanism
For some considerable period of time, a number of policies pursued by the Taiwanese government have resulted in the island's state-owned banks being forced to provide virtually unlimited credit lines to certain industries, or companies, based purely upon policy considerations, and even after the privatisation of these banks the government has still retained considerable influence as a major shareholder; these banks have therefore had to deal with non-market intervention as a way of life. In the future, policy tasks should be identified, with their costs being approved under budgetary procedures, and the banks should ultimately be allowed to function within the credit market with total independence.

Encouraging financial innovation and initiatives by banks
Although, during the past decade, approval was given for the opening of many new banks and branches – which has ultimately resulted in serious competition and 'over-banking' – the variety of financial products has continued to be severely restricted by government regulations. In the future, banks should be given more room to design new products and services, and to develop their own niche in the market.

Enhancing prudential supervision and regulation
In the aftermath of the Asian financial crisis, effective regulation has become the focus of banking reform. Taiwan should therefore adopt the Core Principle of Effective Banking Supervision, established by the international banking community, and should also implement the Basle II agreement on capital adequacy regulations in the very near future.

TAIWAN'S STOCK AND BOND MARKETS

Taiwan's Stock Market

Taiwan's stock market includes trading in the Taiwan Stock Exchange (TSE), where 638 listed stocks are traded, and the Gretai Securities Market (GSM, otherwise known as the over-the-counter (OTC) market), where 384 small-capitalisation stocks are traded (Table 6.9). Bonds are also traded in the GSM, as will be discussed later.

Table 6.9 Primary market trading in the TSE and GSM

Unit: NT$ billion

Year	TSE Listed Companies			GSM Companies		
	Total No.	Capital Issued	Market Value	Total No.	Capital Issued	Market Value
1991	221	643	3,184	9	4	11
1992	256	761	2,546	11	4	10
1993	285	908	5,146	11	4	10
1994	313	1,100	6,504	14	10	27
1995	347	1,347	5,108	41	173	246
1996	382	1,661	7,529	79	264	833
1997	404	2,106	9,696	114	315	1,027
1998	437	2,734	8,393	176	381	888
1999	462	3,083	11,804	264	514	1,468
2000	531	3,661	8,191	300	677	1,051
2001	584	4,096	10,248	333	681	1,412
2002	638	4,443	9,091	384	627	862

Notes:
a There are 24 companies listed as full delivery stocks, and traded under a separate bracket, with a total par value of NT$89.85 billion. Nine listed companies are suspended from stock trading by the TSE with a total par value of NT$58.71 billion.
b The total number of GSM listed companies has included TIGER Board stocks since April 2000. There were 11 listed companies on the TIGER Board at the end of 2002, with capital issued amounting to NT$7.94 billion.
c Figures for emerging stocks within the GSM are not included in these totals.

The development of the Taiwanese stock market from 1993 to 2002 is shown in Table 6.10, which clearly demonstrates the relative importance of individual investors, who account for more than 80 per cent of all trading activities in the TSE. Institutional investors, both domestic and foreign, are not as important in the Taiwanese stock market as in the markets of other countries. It is also clear from the table that, although having increased over the past decade, foreign participation in the Taiwanese stock market is still quite limited. At the end of 2002, the total of 638 companies listed on the Taiwan Stock Exchange was less than the 812 companies traded in Hong Kong, but greater than the 385 companies traded on the Singapore exchange.

As for its size relative to GDP, Taiwan's stock market capitalisation is comparable with the standards set by the developed countries. As Table 6.11 shows, Taiwan's capitalisation ratio in the TSE is lower than the ratios of both the Hong Kong and the Singapore markets, but higher than those of either Korea or Tokyo. This may have something to do with Taiwanese investors' enthusiasm for the local exchange, which may also explain the high level of stock market trading activities. As compared with other stock exchanges in Asia, Taiwan's trading value is considerably higher, and particularly so when compared to either the Hong Kong or Singapore exchanges. Although the relative capitalisation levels within the Hong Kong and Singapore markets are higher, Taiwan's stock market is much more active, as can be seen from Table 6.12. As the table shows, Taiwan is also a clear leader, in terms of trading value, when compared to other stock markets within Asia.

Taiwan's stock exchange turnover rate is also high, as shown in Table 6.13, which clearly indicates that Taiwan has quite a liquid market. Consistent with the importance of individual investors, as indicated in Table 6.10, most of this turnover activity in the Taiwan stock exchange is accounted for by individual investors.

The relatively high attractiveness of margin transactions is also quite noticeable in the Taiwan stock market. Of the total market trading value of US$635.2 billion in 2002 (Table 6.12), the trading value of margin transactions stood at US$278 billion at the end of 2002, whilst short sales stood at US$101 billion, indicating the significant importance of margin transactions in the Taiwan exchange.

Another feature of the Taiwan stock market, which is clearly worthy of mention, is that in the aftermath of the Asian Financial Crisis, financial supervision became much stricter in Taiwan. Government officials began monitoring the market and using the newly established National Stabilisation Fund (NSF) to protect the stock market against any abnormally wide fluctuations.

Table 6.10 Breakdown of stock exchange trading values

Year	Domestic Institutional Investors (NT$ million)	(%)	Foreign Institutional Investors (NT$ million)	(%)	Domestic Individual Investors (NT$ million)	(%)	Foreign Individual Investors (NT$ million)	(%)
1993	993,235	5.37	89,689	0.48	17,415,108	94.13	1,683	0.02
1994	2,260,990	5.81	264,463	0.68	38,944,012	93.51	3,321	0.00
1995	1,378,309	6.69	283,994	1.38	18,940,022	91.92	2,611	0.01
1996	2,265,425	8.62	556,733	2.12	23,445,164	89.25	2,670	0.01
1997	5,694,864	7.55	1,289,018	1.71	68,428,214	90.73	10,849	0.01
1998	5,144,250	8.63	964,754	1.62	53,480,509	89.73	9,083	0.02
1999	5,520,478	9.36	1,420,107	2.41	52,043,211	88.22	8,121	0.01
2000	6,306,518	10.27	2,222,145	3.62	52,855,308	86.10	5,707	0.01
2001	3,569,410	9.70	2,168,800	5.90	31,081,540	84.40	2,950	–
2002	4,868,110	11.10	2,897,570	6.60	36,105,220	82.30	3,370	–

Source: Taiwan Stock Exchange.

Table 6.11 Regional stock market capitalisation, relative to GDP

Unit: %

Year	Taiwan	Hong Kong	Singapore	Tokyo	Korea	London	New York	Thailand*
1993	86.70	331.90	523.16	67.88	42.07	126.30	69.36	68.24
1994	102.90	205.66	446.48	76.67	50.42	116.95	64.13	93.58
1995	71.87	216.27	173.30	68.97	40.10	125.63	82.76	88.68
1996	100.62	290.32	159.40	64.92	29.29	149.47	95.60	54.40
1997	119.20	241.52	148.38	53.44	9.49	159.83	109.90	22.94
1998	96.24	206.61	107.44	64.74	35.67	165.61	120.69	30.90
1999	127.06	383.46	227.12	105.18	75.27	201.08	123.60	46.00
2000	84.77	377.58	166.7	67.03	32.0	181.4	117.4	23.77
2001	107.79	308.54	136.1	55.09	46.0	152.1	109.4	31.30
2002	93.43	284.05	114.94	51.83	–	–	86.3	–

Note: * Figures refer to estimated GNP value.

Source: Taiwan Stock Exchange.

132

Table 6.12 Trading values of regional stock exchanges

Unit: US$ billion

Year	Taiwan	Hong Kong	Singapore	Tokyo	Korea	London	New York	Thailand
1993	352.8	156.8	80.0	793.0	210.9	843.0	2,259.5	86.4
1994	736.9	147.2	81.0	859.0	286.6	930.0	2,453.6	84.2
1995	390.2	106.9	59.1	878.0	185.7	1,024.9	3,082.5	61.7
1996	476.5	182.5	54.8	932.0	178.0	1,178.0	4,063.3	51.4
1997	1,310.2	453.6	74.1	894.5	170.7	1,989.5	5,777.7	28.8
1998	896.0	206.2	58.5	750.8	145.1	2,888.0	7,317.9	21.0
1999	917.3	230.0	107.4	1,675.6	733.4	3,399.4	8,945.2	37.3
2000	993.3	376.7	95.2	2,315.5	556.1	4,558.6	11,060.1	21.1
2001	546.1	241.0	71.8	1,660.5	380.6	4,550.5	10,489.3	31.1
2002	635.2	194.0	62.8	1,565.8	532.8	3,998.4	10,311.2	41.3

Source: Taiwan Stock Exchange.

Table 6.13   Stock exchange turnover rates

Unit: %

Year	Taiwan*	New York*	Tokyo*	Korea*	London	Hong Kong	Thailand	Singapore
1993	252.42	53.00	25.86	186.55	80.50	61.00	66.19	26.20
1994	366.11	53.00	24.93	174.08	77.10	55.00	64.04	26.70
1995	227.84	59.00	26.77	105.11	77.60	38.00	43.06	17.80
1996	243.43	62.00	28.94	102.98	78.60	41.00	50.91	13.60
1997	407.32	65.71	32.93	145.56	44.03	90.92	49.56	56.28
1998	314.06	69.88	34.13	207.00	47.10	61.94	68.86	63.95
1999	288.62	74.62	49.37	344.98	56.71	50.60	78.14	75.16
2000	259.16	82.40	58.86	301.56	63.81	62.99	64.91	64.97
2001	206.95	87.62	56.52	218.24	76.1	46.55	73.8	56.07
2002	217.41	88.98	65.21	254.53	89.17	42.78	97.14	59.81

Notes: * Pre-1996 values refer to trading volume.

Source: Taiwan Stock Exchange.

Following the initial activation of the NSF in 2000, the regular application of this 'stabilising instrument' produced artificial price support for the stock market, and subsequently proved itself to be ineffective. This has been a lesson learned in Taiwan, and the Ministry of Finance has announced that the NSF will not be so easily activated in the future unless the market is hit by a major event affecting national security.

Taiwan's Bond Market

The bond market in Taiwan has overall responsibility for the issuing and trading of government, financial and corporate bonds; Table 6.14 provides details of the changes in the composition of such bond issues in Taiwan over the past ten years. By the end of 2002, the total amount of government debt had expanded to NT$2,214 billion, whilst there had also been a rapid increase in financial debentures, issued by banks, to NT$377 billion over the last two years. In the meantime, corporate bonds have also begun to show a dramatic increase in recent years, reaching a level of NT$1,007 billion in 2002.

Foreign bonds, which are issued by regional banks in other countries, constitute the final component of Taiwan's bond market. By the end of 2000, twenty-four different foreign bonds had become available to investors in Taiwan, with a total net value of just NT$107 billion, thus representing a much smaller draw than local government bonds or locally issued corporate bonds.

Table 6.14 Bond issues in Taiwan

Unit: NT$ billion

	1993	1994	1995	1996	1997	1998	1999	2000	2001	2002
Government Bonds										
Issues	237	148	125	235	174	146	283	363	457	463
Redemptions	66	73	56	116	125	137	82	127	79	80
Circulated	722	798	867	986	1,035	1,044	1,245	1,480	1,858	2,214
Financial debentures										
Issues	58	33	45	37	27	47	36	46	119	214
Redemptions	61	26	42	41	51	24	31	52	8	39
Circulated	87	94	97	93	69	92	98	92	203	377
Corporate Bonds										
Issues	13	30	44	184	111	235	138	181	198	286
Redemptions	19	19	22	26	38	39	66	64	97	87
Circulated	60	71	92	250	323	519	590	707	809	1,007
Totals										
Issues	308	211	214	456	313	428	456	590	774	936
Redemptions	146	118	120	183	214	200	178	244	184	206
Circulated	869	963	1,056	1,329	1,427	1,655	1,933	2,279	2,870	3,598

Source: Financial Monthly Report, Central Bank of China, ROC.

Taiwan's bond market had limited appeal in the early years, given the competition with other financial instruments. Most bonds have substantial face value; therefore, insufficient funds have been available to purchase these bonds, simply because most trading activities in the TSE are undertaken by individual investors. Nevertheless, there has been a rapid increase in the relative importance of bond transactions in the GSM (OTC market) in recent years as more institutional investors have begun to trade in bonds (Table 6.15).

Taiwan's money market, which includes the issuing and trading of treasury bills, commercial papers, bankers' acceptances and transferable certificates of deposits, has also become quite active, largely in line with the trend towards overall market liberalisation. Trading in commercial papers has been the most popular of these financial instruments, accounting for over 70 per cent of the total, followed by quite a liquid market for certificates of deposits. In contrast, the treasury bill market has not been so active and there has been a decline in the relative importance of bankers' acceptances (Tables 6.16 and 6.17). However, the total transaction volume, and new issues of all money market instruments, have both shown a positive trend over the past decade, with total issue value increasing by around 40 per cent and total trading value up by around 60 per cent.

The Prospects for Taiwan's Capital and Money Markets

The future for Taiwan's stock market
There are at least three directions for the possible future development of the Taiwan stock market, each of which is described in the following sub-sections.

Improving the corporate governance of listed companies. In the wake of the financial distress associated with a number of listed companies in recent years, it has become apparent that there is an urgent need to strengthen corporate governance, including the establishment of effective boards of directors for listed companies, the greater scrutiny of the dealings of corporate leaders and closer examination of financial documents. Newly listed companies are already required to include outside directors on the board; however, there is also an urgent need to place limits on the extent to which corporate executives can borrow using their company shares as collateral. Clear standards should also be applied to limit the amount of influence that affiliated businesses can have on company affairs. Affiliated overseas business groups should also be examined, with special emphasis being placed upon separating business operations and financial investment dealings. Boards of directors of all listed companies should be required to take these issues seriously and to ensure that they abide by the regulations in the future.

Table 6.15 Stock and bond transactions in the Gretai securities market

Unit: NT$ billion

Year	GSM Stock Transactions	Bond Transactions				Total Transaction Volume	Bonds/Stocks * (%)
		Corporate	Government	Financial	Foreign		
1991	464	–	3,742,982	510	–	3,743	39
1992	671	1,896	10,732,662	76	–	10,735	181
1993	649	–	748,789	–	–	13,156	145
1994	568	–	1,033,192	–	–	15,973	85
1995	2,796	2,747	1,767,639	–	2	20,821	205
1996	453,509	21,275	2,595,894	–	5	28,287	212
1997	2,310,659	27,084	2,517,709	–	26	40,372	102
1998	1,198,158	71,636	6,867,974	–	1,689	54,957	178
1999	1,899,925	98,118	6,941,900	–	172	52,178	167
2000	4,479,662	203,081	16,203,155	–	245	68,887	197
2001	2,326,900	263,860	52,365,960	10,000	360	55,327	268
2002	2,794,700	852,170	59,613,180	53,700	286	63,600	258

Note: * Bonds/stocks represents trading value ratio at the GSM.

Source: Securities and Futures Commission, Ministry of Finance, ROC.

137

Table 6.16 Financing in the Taiwanese money market

Unit: NT$ billion

	1993	1994	1995	1996	1997	1998	1999	2000	2001	2002
Treasury Bills										
Issues	60	50	15	98	57	55	315	95	85	180
Redemptions	110	65	25	89	52	20	220	200	80	50
Circulated	30	15	5	15	20	55	150	45	50	180
Commercial Papers										
Issues	3,843	5,201	6,141	6,773	8,872	11,498	9,391	9,033	8,927	7,525
Redemptions	3,675	5,174	6,029	6,326	8,671	11,030	9,664	9,268	9,081	7,758
Circulated	509	536	648	1,095	1,297	1,765	1,491	1,256	1,102	870
Bankers' Acceptances										
Issues	829	1,145	1,707	1,817	1,019	487	66	46	36	40
Redemptions	743	1,094	1,625	1,822	1,155	581	90	49	38	40
Circulated	142	192	274	268	132	37	13	10	8	8
Certificates of Deposit										
Issues	1,237	1,054	1,231	955	1,401	1,652	905	1,151	854	633
Redemptions	1,339	977	1,192	1,064	1,179	1,716	1,055	1,036	1,020	708
Circulated	363	441	480	372	594	529	379	494	327	251
Totals										
Issues	5,969	7,451	9,093	9,644	11,349	13,691	10,677	10,325	9,902	8,378
Redemptions	5,866	7,310	8,871	9,300	11,057	13,348	11,029	10,553	10,219	8,556
Circulated	1,044	1,184	1,407	1,750	2,042	2,386	2,033	1,805	1,488	1,309

Source: Monthly Report, Central Bank of China, ROC.

Table 6.17 Trading value in the Taiwanese money market

Unit: NT$ billion

	1993	1994	1995	1996	1997	1998	1999	2000	2001	2002
Treasury Bills										
Bought	308	785	–	68	92	46	381	347	107	1,865
Sold	289	76	1	47	74	34	294	339	84	1,696
Commercial Papers										
Bought	9,984	13,961	15,267	16,449	25,072	34,558	30,361	31,091	28,169	23,890
Sold	7,843	11,029	11,658	13,623	21,180	28,093	24,682	25,851	22,048	19,232
Bankers' Acceptances										
Bought	1,783	2,561	3,907	3,804	2,548	1,387	136	85	56	53
Sold	1,272	1,831	2,860	3,151	2,079	1,165	145	90	53	43
Certificates of Deposit										
Bought	5,271	3,750	4,465	4,047	2,989	1,432	2,203	3,868	4,508	4,177
Sold	4,502	3,568	3,903	3,831	2,696	1,205	1,452	2,244	3,035	2,001
Totals										
Bought	17,347	20,353	23,641	24,375	30,708	37,424	33,081	35,391	32,840	30,033
Sold	13,906	16,508	18,423	20,656	26,033	30,500	26,575	28,524	25,220	23,015

Source: Monthly Report, Central Bank of China, ROC.

Increasing transparency in the capital markets. There has been recent renewed emphasis on financial disclosure laws and greater attention is now being paid to the core operations of businesses. Corporate auditing and accuracy in financial reporting can be improved by ensuring the explicit adherence to the law by accountants. Accountants should also be allowed to act independently of their clients, to ensure clear and accurate financial data. At the same time, insider trading and other means of manipulating the market should be tackled; periodic checks should ensure the proper disclosure of all necessary information on listed TSE and OTC stocks. Indeed, all financial instruments should come under this broadened scope of monitoring since, together with listed stocks, the possibility also exists of undue manipulation of futures and bonds.

Respecting the market mechanism and attracting institutional investors. There is a danger that Taiwan's market could become artificially influenced by government intervention. Therefore, the government should firmly commit to its recently announced pledge that the NSF will be deployed only when it is absolutely necessary, that is, when faced with a major threat to national security. It is clear that Taiwan does need to develop an infrastructure of competitive trading comparable to international standards in order to instil greater confidence, which might then encourage more domestic and foreign institutional investors to join the market. This is important, as the future of the island's stock market will ultimately depend on the confidence of investors, with particular regard to the market mechanism.

The future for Taiwan's bond and money markets
There is still a considerable amount of room for improvement in Taiwan's bond and money markets. In the foreseeable future, Taiwan's growing number of companies should be able to obtain their much needed finances not only from the stock market but also from the bond market, which will greatly enhance the development of Taiwan's new economy. The directions for future reform should include the following:

Government bond issues. Government bonds should be issued on a regular basis so as to encourage investor trading, and thus effectively establish more liquid markets for bonds at various maturity levels. The established term structure of interest rates for government bonds could also form the basis for evaluating other corporate bonds.

Bond trading infrastructure. Taiwan's bond market is not very active, particularly when compared to stock trading, and there is therefore a clear need for the wholesale modernisation of the bond trading infrastructure.

Taiwan needs to establish a primary dealer system and an appropriate mechanism for margin trading and short selling, along with a 'when-issued' market prior to the actual issue of government bonds, a credit rating system for corporate bonds and a unified system of trading regulations, so that it can effectively meet the international standards for bond trading.

Broadening of bond trading. Bond trading should be broadened so as to attract foreign and individual investors. As already noted, trading in the bond market is mostly undertaken by domestic institutional investors; therefore, in order to attract individual investors, the government should reduce the minimum amount of funding required for bond investment and promote the intermediation of bond trading through financial institutions. A reduction of the current level of transaction tax would clearly be helpful in this respect. Furthermore, the restrictions on foreign investors should be lifted in order to encourage the active participation of international capital.

Liberalisation of the money market. Liberalising the money market is a necessary element in the pursuit of effective development of the capital market. Most companies have generally relied on commercial papers for short-term financing in the money market, and since most trading is mediated through bills finance companies, the now obsolete restrictions on trading by these bills companies should be lifted in order to promote a more liberalised money market. Not only should bills finance companies be allowed to trade foreign short-term instruments, but they should also be able to offer money market mutual funds to domestic investors. The bills companies can become financially sound if they are allowed to have more diversified business investments and operations. In the meantime, internal auditing could also be strengthened to ensure that these companies have proper control of the credit risk associated with the underwriting and trading of money market instruments.

THE DERIVATIVES MARKET IN TAIWAN

The Futures and Options Market

Following its establishment in 1997, Taiwan's Futures Exchange (TAIFEX) began trading in TSE Capitalisation Weighted Index Futures Contracts on 21 July 1998. One year later, on 21 July 1999, the TAIFEX introduced the Taiwan Electronics Share Index Futures and the Taiwan Financial Index Futures. On 9 April 2001 the Small Capitalisation TSE Index Futures came into being, followed, on 24 December 2001, by the introduction of the TSE Index Options.

The options on individual stocks were also introduced in late 2002. The average daily transaction volume in the Taiwan Futures and Options market has doubled each year since its establishment. Total volume in these futures and options reached a daily average of 32,033 contracts by 2002 and increased to 61,716 contracts during the first quarter of 2003, with the most rapid growth coming from the options market (Table 6.18). This impressive rate of growth has been consistent over the past four years, indicating that Taiwan's derivatives market still has considerable opportunities for further growth.

Table 6.18   Average daily transaction volume in the futures and options markets in Taiwan

Unit: Lots

	1999	2000	2001	2002	2003[*]
TSE Index Futures	3,653	4,944	11,659	16,661	16,387
Electronics Futures	714	1,512	2,807	3,367	3,929
Financial Futures	155	654	1,596	1,479	4,031
Small Cap TSE Index Futures	–	–	2,334	4,210	3,814
Stock Options	–	–	–	–	2,057
TSE Index Options	–	–	856	6,316	31,498
TAIFEX Total Volume	4,522	7,110	18,396	32,033	61,716
TAIFEX Vol/SGX-DT Vol (%)	54.0	63.0	119.0	–	–
SGX-DT Volume	8,448	11,286	15,522	–	–

Note: [*] The daily transaction volume for 2003 covers January to March.

Source: Taiwan Futures Exchange.

On 5 May 2000, a reduction in transaction tax from 0.05 per cent to 0.025 per cent was applied to Taiwan futures transactions in an effort to broaden the market; the policy change clearly had the desired effect with a general increase in daily volume. Other changes were also implemented, including an increase in the position limit for institutional investors from 600 contracts to 1,000 contracts, which also helped to attract more investors. The fluctuations in the stock market over the last few years also contributed to public interest in trading futures and options. Although Singapore's SGX-DT started trading index futures based on Taiwan's stock market in 1997, even before the existence of the TAIFEX, over the past two years, Taiwan's market for derivatives has become increasingly active (Table 6.19), and in the first quarter of 2003, trading value in the TAIFEX actually exceeded the SGX-DT level by around 50 per cent.

However, trading volume in Taiwan's derivatives market is mostly attributed to individual investors; in the first quarter of 2003, such investors were contributing around 85 per cent of the total trading volume in the futures market (Table 6.20), and around 60 per cent of the total trading volume in the options market (Table 6.21).

Table 6.19   Comparison of trading values in the TAIFEX, TSE and
SGX-DT

Unit: NT$100 million

2003 Monthly Total	TAIFEX (A)	TSE (B)	A/B (%)	Trading Days (C)	Daily Trading Value (A/C)	SGX-DT (D)	A/D (%)
Jan	4,663	21,006	22.20	19	245	159	154
Feb	3,734	9,636	38.75	16	233	168	139
Mar	4,080	9,538	42.85	21	194	124	157
Total	12,477	40,180	31.05	56	223	451	147

Table 6.20   Futures transaction volume by individuals, institutional
investors and futures proprietary traders, March 2003

Unit: Lots

	Electronics	Financials	TSE Index	Small Cap Index	Total	Share (%)
Open Interest	4,008	2,994	14,451	4,748	26,201[a]	
Individual Investors						
Bought	48,082	45,411	283,618	77,339	454,450	84.37
Sold	47,589	46,936	285,009	78,450	457,984	
Institutional Investors						
Stock Proprietary Traders						
Bought	481	197	1,676	–	2,354	0.41
Sold	357	100	1,614	–	2,071	
Investment Trusts						
Bought	699	274	1,675	–	2,648	0.49
Sold	708	160	1,781	–	2,649	
Foreign Investors						
Bought	5,172	5,373	6,158	–	16,703	2.85
Sold	5,488	4,081	4,578	–	14,147	
Others						
Bought	893	760	6,252	733	8,638	1.67
Sold	928	765	7,232	529	9,454	
Futures Proprietary Traders						
Market Makers						
Bought	–	–	–	–	–	–
Sold	–	–	–	–	–	
Others						
Bought	7,259	3,002	41,655	4,046	55,962	10.21
Sold	7,516	2,975	40,820	3,139	54,450	
Total Futures Trading Volume	62586	55017	341,034	82,118	540,755[b]	100.0

Notes:
[a]   Figure represents 14.0 per cent of all open interest trading in futures and options.
[b]   Figure represents 40.0 per cent of combined futures and options trading.

Source: TAIFEX.

Table 6.21   *Options transaction volume by individuals, institutional investors and futures proprietary traders, March 2003*

	TSE Index	Stock Options	Total	Share (%)
Open Interest	149,895	13,583	163,478 [a]	
Individual Investors				
Bought	445,863	10,522	456,385	59.30
Sold	418,702	11,040	429,742	
Institutional Investors				
Stock Proprietary Traders				
Bought	–	–	–	0.00
Sold	–	–	–	
Investment Trusts				
Bought	190	–	190	0.00
Sold	125	–	125	
Foreign Investors				
Bought	34,877	4	34,881	0.02
Sold	19,496	–	19,496	
Others				
Bought	10,144	1	10,145	0.00
Sold	5,820	–	5,820	
Futures Proprietary Traders				
Market Makers				
Bought	271,708	15,159	286,867	37.79
Sold	308,105	14,646	322,751	
Others				
Bought	18,068	10	18,078	2.89
Sold	28,602	10	28,612	
Total Options Trading Volume	780,850	25,696	806,546 [b]	100.0

Notes:
[a]   Figure represents 86.0 per cent of all open interest trading in futures and options.
[b]   Figure represents 60.0 per cent of combined futures and options trading.

Source: TAIFEX.

Since the TAIFEX adopted a system incorporating market makers for options trading, these market makers, i.e. futures proprietary traders, have accounted for around 38 per cent of all options trading (Table 6.21). A summary of the total transaction volume, and the relative shares accounted for by futures and options, is provided in Table 6.22.

The Way Ahead for Taiwan's Futures Markets

There are several possible directions for the further development of Taiwan's futures and options market, as described in the following sub-sections.

Table 6.22   Summary of total futures and options trading, March 2003

Investors	Futures & Options Transactions		
	Bought	Sold	% Share
Individual Investors	910,835	887,726	66.76
Institutional Investors			
Stock Proprietary Traders	2,354	2,071	0.16
Investment Trusts	2,838	2,774	0.21
Foreign Investors	51,584	33,643	3.16
Others	18,783	15,274	1.26
Futures Proprietary Traders			
Market Makers	286,867	322,751	22.62
Others	74,040	83,062	5.83
Total Trading Volume	1,347,301		100.0

Source: TAIFEX.

The introduction of more derivative products

Although the TSE index futures and options have been quite successful within the TAIFEX, these products do have some major shortcomings. The most prominent of these is the fact that the TSE index includes all stocks listed in the TSE, some of which are illiquid and rarely traded; hence, the arbitrage mechanism, which is a crucial element in ensuring that derivative prices are kept in line with the spot price, became increasingly difficult to implement.

It has been suggested that the TAIFEX should adopt a selected sample of TSE stocks as the trading target for derivatives; the introduction of a new index futures in the TAIFEX based on fifty selected stocks compiled by the FTSE, has also been considered. Together with the Exchange Traded Fund (ETF), based on these fifty stocks launched in the TSE, this new Taiwan-50 index futures may function better in terms of its pricing, and may thus attract more investors.

Taiwan's fixed-income securities have not been sufficiently active to enable them to serve their proper function of raising much needed capital for growing companies. Besides promoting the market for corporate bonds and commercial paper, as discussed in the previous sections, the development of the interest-rate futures market would also enhance the functioning of the spot market for fixed-income securities.

With the simultaneous building up of a sound trading infrastructure for commercial paper and bonds, the TAIFEX could develop an efficient trading system for 30-day commercial paper futures and 5-year Treasury bond futures. Creating such a foundation for trading fixed-income instruments would help enormously in terms of globalising the appeal of Taiwan's financial market.

Taiwan should also try to develop an additional, centralised market for currency derivatives. So far, Taiwan has only the OTC market for currency forwards, options and swap contracts. Restrictions are also imposed on the participants in currency trading; only the financial institutions and corporations with foreign traders are allowed to trade Taiwan dollar currency derivatives. However, with the increasing degree of globalisation of Taiwanese corporations, the need for trading Taiwan dollar currency futures and options in a centralised market such as the TAIFEX is being strongly felt. The trading of Taiwan dollar currency derivatives will also provide a channel for foreign investors to hedge their risk. This is an important step, which has to be taken, if Taiwan's financial market is to become truly global in the future.

Modernisation of the trading infrastructure

With the rapid increase in trading volume (refer to Table 6.18), several instances of malfunctioning have occurred in the TAIFEX computer system during 2002 and the early part of 2003. In order to regain the confidence of investors, the TAIFEX will need to undertake modernisation of its computer system in order that it can effectively handle the increasing trading volume. The settlement procedure and trading rules should also be reviewed, in order to make them as convenient as the current practices in other countries.

Encouraging the participation of institutional investors

As already discussed, and as indicated in Tables 6.20 to 6.22, Taiwan's market is mainly dominated by individual investors; therefore, in order for the financial market to function, and in order to promote the economic development of Taiwan, there has to be some way of attracting institutional investors to use the financial market for their financing needs. The degree of participation of institutional investors in the financial market can provide an indicator of the usefulness of the financial system for the real side of economic development.

The effective liberalisation of the derivatives market could also clearly help in the continuing development of the underlying market for stocks and bonds. Once there are sufficient derivative instruments traded within an efficient exchange, including an infrastructure comparable with that of its international counterparts, then it will be possible to attract more foreign and domestic institutional investors. It is important for Taiwan to recognise the need to modernise its trading infrastructure and speed up its product innovation in the futures and options markets, in order to ensure that its financial system provides the appropriate support for the development of a growing economy in the future.

CONCLUSIONS

Looking back over the past decade, it is clear that Taiwan's financial system has improved considerably, with stable growth in many respects, thanks largely to the liberal and constructive policies set forth by the government. However, the promotion of Taiwan as an Asia-Pacific Financial Centre has been rather slow in reaching its goal. There is also still considerable room for improvement in Taiwan's banking system and its financial market.

In recent years, since the commencement of the Asia-Pacific Regional Operations Centre (APROC) plan, Taiwan has adopted a number of policies aimed at supporting both deregulation and liberalisation, with a great deal of additional support for globalisation as a means of increasing the island's competitiveness. In the future, these policies should be followed with vigour if Taiwan is to stand any chance of building up its overall economic strength. With its growing companies needing the support of the financial sector in order to effectively compete on a global scale, Taiwan must ensure that all businesses are allowed to obtain financing within a liberalised and competitive environment, so that they can continue to grow in the new economy. The effort to modernise and globalise Taiwan's financial sector has hence become a crucial issue for the island's future.

As Taiwan sets out to modernise and globalise its financial sector, incisive changes have to be implemented in order to help the financial industry to become truly competitive and productive. In addition to the adoption of liberalisation and internationalisation as the guiding principles, joint efforts by the government and the financial industry will be required to pursue the directions outlined in this chapter. In following such principles, it is recommended that the government should refrain from any excessive intervention, thus creating a genuine competitive environment.

Taiwan's financial industry has the ability to compete at an international level, particularly in those areas that are already deregulated and open to the global market. It is recommended that the trading infrastructure should be made comparable to other modern markets, and that improvement to the regulatory environment should be sought with a much greater emphasis on legal stipulations and enforcement. There is also a clear need for the strengthening of corporate governance, so that Boards of Directors and other corporate officials are not allowed to wield undue power. The regulatory framework should be based upon the principles of transparency, with greater reliance upon the proper disclosure of information to outside investors by banks and listed corporations.

This chapter has looked at many aspects of the financial sector and has envisioned a plan for the pursuit of Taiwan's goal of establishing itself as an Asia-Pacific Financial Centre. It should be pointed out, however, that the plan is totally reliant upon the full support of the government and upon its pledge to continue to pursue deregulation and adhere to the principles of globalisation and liberalisation. Any attempt to affect, or to support, the price of any individual market segment (be that in the foreign exchange, interest rate or stock markets) constitutes a major drawback. The government should instead be involved in regulatory reform, ensuring that appropriate laws are in place, and also ensuring strict adherence to these laws. Such policies will undoubtedly help Taiwan to attract more international business, whilst protecting the interests of local citizens and promoting greater competitiveness of its growing companies. Based upon the principles of globalisation, deregulation and the rule of law, Taiwan can no doubt develop a successful financial system and perhaps, one day, be able to achieve its goal of becoming an Asia-Pacific Financial Centre.

REFERENCES

Barton, D., R. Felton and R. Song (2000), 'Building Asian Boards', *McKinsey Quarterly*, (Special Edition), **4**: 64-73

BIS and IMF (1997), *Electronic Money: Consumer Protection, Law Enforcement, Supervisory and Cross-border Issues*, Bank for International Settlements and International Monetary Fund.

Casserley, D. and G. Gibb (1999), *Banking in Asia: The End of Entitlement*, London: John Wiley and Sons.

Chu, Y.-P. (2001), 'Liberalization Policies Since the 1980s', in Mai, C.-C. and C.-S. Shih (eds.), *Taiwan's Economic Success Since 1980*, Cheltenham, UK: Edward Elgar, pp.89-119.

Coombes, P. and M. Watson (2000), 'Three Surveys on Corporate Governance', *McKinsey Quarterly (online)*, **4**.

Johnston, R.B. and Ì. Ötker-Robe (1999), 'A Modernized Approach to Managing the Risks in Cross-Border Capital Movements', *IMF Policy Discussion Paper, No.99/6*.

Liu C.-Y. (1992), 'Money and Financial Markets: The International Perspective', in G. Ranis (ed.), *Taiwan: From Developing to Mature Economy*, Boulder, Colorado: Westview Press, pp.195-221.

López-Mejía, A. (1990), 'Large Capital Flows: A Survey of the Causes, Consequences and Policy Responses', IMF Working Paper.

Low, C.K. (2000), *Financial Markets in Hong Kong*, Singapore & New York: Springer-Verlag.

White W.R. (1996), 'International Agreements in the Area of Banking and Finance: Accomplishments and Outstanding Issues', *Bank for International Settlements Working Paper, No.38*.

Yang Y.-H. (2001), 'The Financial System and Financial Reform', in Mai, C.-C. and C.-S. Shih (eds.), *Taiwan's Economic Success Since 1980*, Cheltenham, UK: Edward Elgar, pp.347-77.

Yoshitomi M. and S. Shirai (2000), *Technical Background Paper on Policy Recommendations for Preventing Another Capital Account Crisis*, Asian Development Bank Institute.

7 The Globalisation of Business in Taiwan

Chi Schive and Tain-Jy Chen

INTRODUCTION

The outstanding performance of Taiwan, with regard to its achievements in economic development over the latter half of the twentieth century, has earned it the nickname of the 'Taiwan miracle'. The island has many records in economic development, such as high growth rates, equitable income distribution, low inflation rates, significant industrial restructuring and further advancements in many other areas. Clearly, there must be many explanations for these achievements and the policy initiatives behind them. Nevertheless, if we were asked to summarise the complexity of Taiwan's economic development in a single word, the gradual 'opening' of the island's economy may well be the word at the core of all arguments. If we can assume that this is the case, then this chapter sets out with three specific purposes.

We begin by presenting a brief summary and description of Taiwan's evolution towards achieving its goal of an 'open' economy. This is followed by an examination of the rich experiences and the general processes involved in Taiwanese companies, including many small and medium enterprises (SMEs), achieving multinational corporation (MNC) status; here, the move to mainland China is elaborated.

Finally, we regard it as essential to examine the implications of the large number of Taiwanese companies that have established a presence overseas, in a process known as production fragmentation, within which parts and components produced abroad are rapidly turned into final products for the market. These days, Taiwanese manufacturing companies are no longer concentrating on production, but instead have come to see the development of new products and the mastering of logistic services as the keys to survival. 'Global logistics', the new model of carrying out business, is now set to sharpen Taiwan's competitive edge in this new century.

THE EMERGING OPEN ECONOMY – PRE-2000

The classic work of Adam Smith, *An Inquiry into the Nature and Causes of the Wealth of Nations*, is most memorable for its recognition and discussion of the most vital of all issues in economics, economic growth: the embodiment of all consequences for human welfare. Smith noted that the engine for economic growth was to be found in the division of labour, in the accumulation of capital, and in technological progress. He also placed significant emphasis on the importance of a stable institutional framework, within which the invisible hand (the market) could function, and then went on to explain how an open trading system could allow poorer countries to catch up with richer ones.

As an open economy, Taiwan has reaped enormous benefits from the world trade boom of the 1960s, and beyond, with the consequent trade development being responsible for boosting the mobilisation of Taiwan's large, and fairly well-skilled, rural labour force into industry. This protracted period of mobilisation had begun in the 'import-substitution' phase of the 1950s, and then proceeded, to a much greater degree, in the 'export-promotion' phase. The trade promotion policies adopted by the government at that time were extremely effective in terms of helping Taiwan to make the best possible use of its comparative advantages; indeed, Taiwan subsequently went on to demonstrate comparative advantages in labour-intensive production in the 1960s, capital-intensive and skills-intensive production in the 1970s and 1980s, and technology-intensive production in the 1990s.

As regards the specific policies adopted by the government, Taiwan's economic development over the past five decades could be described as a process of gradual liberalisation, a long, drawn-out process of ensuring that the economy was to become much more free and open. By means of adding the ingredients for liberalisation into general policy reforms, as well as into overall industrial policy design, Taiwan was successful in bringing in many policy changes over a considerable period of time.

The two major reforms, which took place around 1960 and in the mid-1980s, were clearly linked to foreign factors, although other factors were also involved (Schive and Hsueh, 1999), whilst the more recent reform, in the mid-1990s, was triggered by the drive towards globalisation and was laid out in the plan to develop Taiwan as an Asia Pacific Regional Operations Centre (APROC) and in its bid for World Trade Organisation (WTO) accession.

The first of these reforms, around 1960, included the simplification and devaluation of the exchange rate for the local currency, the New Taiwan (NT) Dollar, and the promulgation of the Statute for the Encouragement of

Investment. Since then, there has been general consistency in policy reform towards free trade and free competition, despite some obvious periods of hesitancy; there were even times when some of the measures adopted could not be described as compatible with the move towards free trade, and indeed protectionism never really died. In general, however, Taiwan continued to move forward, in a stable manner, towards developing an open economy, and during the whole process the influence from abroad, at critical moments, did help to promote the reforms.

When export promotion was proposed in the late 1950s as an appropriate replacement for the previous import-substitution policies, it was largely seen as an assault on the popular move towards inward-looking policies. Industrialists and government decision-makers alike voiced some concerns as to whether Taiwan was ready for overseas competition, and there were also considerable fears that devaluation could worsen the economy's terms of trade, resulting in the importation of inflation from abroad. Against this backdrop, the measures that were designed to achieve industrialisation were effectively limited to the development of industries producing goods for highly protected markets. However, the domestic market was soon to become saturated with light industrial products, characterised by their low-capacity utilisation, and consequently, the market became characterised by increasing domestic competition and depressed pricing trends in these products.

In providing their assistance to help forge ahead with the new reforms, several well-known Chinese economists, including the late Professors S.C. Tsiang and T.C. Liu, attempted to explain to many key decision-makers the implications of the proposed changes to the existing outward-looking policy. Nevertheless, although these analyses did help to boost the confidence of the officials with regard to their proposed policy directives, the decisive factor behind the policy switch was clearly driven by the strong message coming out of the US Aid Mission in Taiwan (Li and Chen, 1987; Schive and Hsueh, 1999; Schive et al., 2001).

The reforms that had been undertaken in the 1960s represented a far-reaching movement towards total liberalisation. The value of the NT Dollar, for example, was adjusted towards a level that would be determined by the market, and this was accompanied by the simplification of the overall foreign exchange system, moving first of all from a multiple system to a dual system, and thereafter to a unitary system. Rail charges and electricity power charges were raised to cover full costs, and considerable progress was made towards reducing bureaucracy in general, and industrial land acquisition in particular, through the *Statute for the Encouragement of Investment* in 1960, and the setting up of the first export processing zone in Kaohsiung in 1966.

The subsequent reforms of the mid-1980s represented a painfully slow response to the mounting trade surplus, the undervalued domestic currency and the extremely high level of excess savings. The appreciation of the NT Dollar met with great opposition from the exporting industries; indeed, there was a general feeling that trade liberalisation might well hurt the 'fledgling' industries. There was also staunch opposition to financial liberalisation, which was largely based on the fear of losing control of the economy as a result of the elimination of tight financial regulations.

Meanwhile Taiwan found itself under the threat of strong US retaliation as a result of the island's huge trade surplus over its major trading partner. Thus, in order to demonstrate its determination to improve this imbalance in bilateral trade, the Taiwanese government set up a task force to tackle the various trade and economic problems between the two parties. Indeed, the government's introduction of the Guidelines for Trade and Economic Relations with the US can be seen as an overall summary of liberalisation proposals for the 1980s, with foreign exchange rate controls and trade barriers being removed accordingly. The average nominal tariff rate was drastically reduced each year, with a particularly significant shift from 22.83 per cent in 1986, to 9.65 per cent in 1990. In addition, liberalisation of the services market was undertaken along with vigorous promotion of privatisation.

By the end of the 1980s, the Taiwanese mindset had been totally reinvented, and liberalisation had proceeded along what was essentially a virtuous circle. The more the economy was opened up, the greater the economics benefits from liberalisation that were witnessed and experienced throughout all areas of the island's community. Furthermore, as Taiwan had now established itself as a newly industrialised economy, it was very keen to integrate itself into the wider international community; however, the island's application for entry into the General Agreement on Tariffs and Trade (GATT) – the forerunner to the WTO – was driven not only by a desire to participate within organisations at an international level, but also as a means of taking advantage of the global system of free trade.

Within the overall process of WTO accession negotiations, the services sector became the most challenged area, with the rationale for the move towards membership being reinforced by the efforts to develop the Taiwanese APROC plan. The extent of the revision of huge amounts of legal statutes and regulations, which represented the core of the APROC plan, far exceeded that of any of the reforms over the previous twenty years. Taiwan's accession to the WTO was finally approved in November 2001, and another round in the island's mission of achieving total liberalisation was generally completed. However, after many years of pushing for accession, it remains to be seen whether the long awaited entry will bring greater happiness for the people of Taiwan.

THE EMERGENCE OF TAIWANESE MULTINATIONALS

The Major Players of the 1970s

Taiwanese companies began to venture abroad only in the 1970s, some ten years after the proliferation of inward investment. Officially, the first case of outward investment from Taiwan was undertaken in 1959 when a local firm invested in US$100,000 worth of machinery at a Malaysian cement plant. After a lull of some two years or so, a jute bag manufacturer restarted Taiwan's capital outflow by setting up a plant in Thailand in 1962.

Throughout the 1960s, Taiwan's foreign direct investment (FDI) hovered at an annual rate of around US$800,000; however, outward investment as a whole has been on the increase ever since the early 1970s, at a whopping annual rate of 23.78 per cent, and by 1981, 163 investment projects had been reported and approved by the government (Schive and Hsueh, 1990). Nevertheless, not all of the ventures were successful; indeed, 48 of the total had failed completely, with 38 of these defunct ventures having actually gone into operation, but having then seen their investors withdrawing due to personal business failures or the Vietnam War.

Of the 54 companies with at least one surviving subsidiary by the end of 1981, Formosa Plastics, the largest manufacturing concern, had made applications for a total of twelve foreign ventures, but had only succeeded in bringing four of these into actual operation. Since then, the company has initiated numerous investments in the US petrochemical industry, with a total capital commitment of US$24 million, including the acquisition of a vinyl chloride monomer (VCM) plant in 1983. A proportion of the VCM produced at the plant was shipped back to Taiwan in order to take advantage of the low material costs.

Tatung, Taiwan's second largest manufacturing MNC, had eight projects approved and in operation by 1981, and since then, the company has added an Irish TV production plant to its worldwide network, whilst within the trade industry, a semi-governmental trading company established a worldwide network of twelve overseas subsidiaries. Pacific Wire and Cable Co., the third largest manufacturing MNC in Taiwan, had five projects approved by 1981, but one of these was later dropped; this company led the emergence of a new trend in Taiwan's outward investment by setting up a high-tech joint venture, Mosel, in the Silicon Valley (Schive and Hsueh, 1987).

By 1981, the lion's share (40.7 per cent) of Taiwanese FDI was being received by the US, whilst the economies of the Association of Southeast Asian Nations (ASEAN), accounted for a further 32.6 per cent. The remaining investment was widely distributed, mainly throughout Latin

America and Africa. As regards the industrial composition of this investment, 24.1 per cent of the remitted capital went to the electrical and electronics industry, with 53.7 per cent of this total being placed in the US. The chemical, trade, non-metallic products and plastic products industries attracted between 12 per cent and 16 per cent of the total outward FDI.

The primary reasons for investing abroad at that time were: (i) to secure supplies of raw materials; (ii) to pursue profits by supplying host-country markets; (iii) to facilitate exports; and (iv) to gain access to technology in the host country. Those who represented the first category of investors included plywood producers, a fishing company and a pineapple cannery, with Thailand, Malaysia, Indonesia and Costa Rica being the host countries for these ventures. Firms in the food and beverage, textile, plastic and plastic products, and non-metallic materials industries, were motivated to invest overseas by a desire to supply the domestic markets of the host countries. In order to undertake this type of investment, a parent firm must have sufficient experience and available technology to be able to compete with local firms and other MNC subsidiaries, and indeed, the Taiwanese investors in these four industries all share the common characteristic of an extended period of development and experience in their particular area of expertise. The monosodium glutamate and cement industries, for example, were established in the 1950s, whilst the PVC and PE plastics industries were both well developed by the late 1950s and late 1960s, respectively. Thus, investors in these four industries were well equipped with the necessary technology and marketing experience prior to their venture into the potentially risky foreign markets.

The third type of FDI is that which aims to facilitate Taiwanese exports, a category within which we find the electrical, electronics and trade industries. The US has continually attracted more than half of such investment, mainly because the impact on Taiwan products from the restrictive US trade policies is significantly dampened if the Taiwanese firms export semi-finished products, rather than final goods, to the US. An example of this is Lihtzer, Taiwan's largest sewing-machine manufacturer, which established a trading company in the US in the mid-1970s.

Another way of penetrating such fenced markets, particularly those which involve quota systems, is 'quota hopping', i.e., setting up overseas production in third-party countries as a means of effectively bypassing quota restrictions. Such methods have been evident in the case of the footwear industry in Latin America, and in some textile ventures established in Singapore and some of the French colonies, all of which are aimed at the markets of the European Union.

The final motivator to becoming an MNC is often seen in the high-tech industries. In 1979, United Microelectronics Co. (UMC) was organised to commercialise several innovations developed in a government-funded research institute, the Industrial Technology and Research Institution (ITRI). In order to ensure the continuous inflow of advanced technology, UMC set up a subsidiary, Unicorn, in the Silicon Valley, which maintained close relations with three other R&D companies – controlled by overseas Chinese businessmen – so as to monitor new technology and to boost the company's marketing skills. These three R&D companies were simultaneously operating in Taiwan's science-based industrial park in Hsinchu and in the Silicon Valley, and each one has been successful in developing a substantial number of patents in the design and manufacture of very-large-scale integrated (VLSI) circuits. This rather unusual type of FDI can only be explained by the desire to access US technology.

The investors of the late 1970s and early 1980s were the leading players in their specific industries in Taiwan, thus proving the hypothesis that MNCs from the developing economies will tend to be large in size, although not necessarily large by international standards. In fact, within most of the industries, the large companies have tended to become MNCs sooner or later, with all but five of Taiwan's MNCs being among the top 500 companies in Taiwan. Many of the large companies which are not engaged in foreign ventures are either subsidiaries of foreign companies or domestic market-oriented public enterprises. Despite the technology of Taiwanese MNCs not being as capital-intensive as that of MNCs from the developed countries, Taiwan's MNCs have developed their level of competitiveness by making the best use of their company-specific strength, along with the comparative advantages of the host countries. Thus, the main competitive advantages for Taiwanese MNCs have tended to be their smaller-scale production techniques and their superior marketing and technological skills, all of which allowed them to introduce and develop products, and thereby successfully enter the host markets.

The Globalisation of Taiwanese Business from the mid-1980s

In the mid-1980s, Taiwanese business firms embarked upon a course towards complete globalisation; these firms were focusing on protecting their export markets because, at the time, they were being undermined by rising labour costs and the value of the local currency. As a result, the target locations for such investment were naturally the low-wage economies of Southeast Asia and mainland China. Most of the Taiwanese firms served as subcontractors for MNCs which were marketing brand-name products and which had full control of the marketing channels. The globalisation strategy for these Taiwanese firms was therefore to strengthen their buyer relationships. It was clear that once these firms began investing so as to increase their production capacity, gain possession of multiple production sites, offer a full range of products and secure a stable supply of components and parts, there would be a corresponding increase in their overall value, as perceived by their buyers.

The investment strategy of the Taiwanese firms was also to serve more than one client, so that their manufacturing facilities could be effectively reallocated should one client choose to end the relationship. Most of the facilities in which Taiwanese firms were investing were for general purposes, rather than being firm-specific, and could therefore be switched from one client to another. More importantly, however, their investment in local linkages was the prime means of securing their market position.

Since partnerships with international buyers were the key to decisions on FDI, the overseas subsidiaries of the Taiwanese firms tended to be wholly-owned rather than joint ventures; in cases of joint ventures, these would be with international buyers rather than with local investors. Efforts made by the Taiwanese firms to strengthen their buyer relationships included enlarging the scale of production, developing more products under the horizontal division of labour, spreading production bases between different countries in order to build up their global logistics capacity and pursuing vertical integration so as to secure the supply of inputs.

Taiwanese firms sought to enlarge their production scale as a means of increasing their clientele, and thus improving their bargaining power. In the event of rising market demand, large and dominant contract manufacturers could juggle the priorities of their manufacturing schedules so as to favour particular clients. Moreover, the establishment of large production capacities could place these Taiwanese firms as primary, rather than secondary, sources of supply. Since buyers often prefer the flexibility of both the product-mix and the volume of each order, the horizontal division of labour would also help to provide such flexibility.

Multiple manufacturing bases further reduce the risks of production failure and disruption to supply. This is of particular importance when we consider the general market imperfections and the all-too-regular examples of government intervention in the developing countries. Many of the Taiwanese manufacturers investing in mainland China were attracted by the overall reduction in costs, whilst those investing in Southeast Asia generally aimed to capture the comparative advantage of a less regulated production environment. What was also clearly of significant importance to them was that by establishing multiple production sites, they would be able to serve their customers better. Nowadays, not only do brand-marketers demand direct shipment to customers, but they also require delivery within very tight time-frames; therefore, the establishment of a production base close to the major markets clearly provides the producers with an enhanced ability to cater for such demands. Proximity to the market is also a must if Taiwanese firms are required to provide after-sales services, an area of responsibility also previously held by the brand-holders.

Finally, vertical integration of key components and parts clearly increases the reliability of the supplier, along with an increase in the overall awareness and knowledge of these devices. For example, where a computer manufacturer has control of the supply of liquid crystal display (LCD) panels, a key component in lap-top computers, this not only ensures a stable production and shipment schedule, but also better product quality. Knowledge about the characteristics and functions of key components and parts also enhances the level of product innovation. Since key components or materials represent the essential segment of the value chain, control of this segment creates a much more powerful position for the supplier in the production network.

To summarise, the FDI undertaken by Taiwanese firms has resulted in the reshaping of the relationships that previously existed between contract manufacturers and their clients, and in many cases, Taiwanese firms have shown themselves capable of providing not only manufacturing services, but also product design. Within the subcontracting business, as opposed to the conventionally known 'original equipment manufacturers' (OEM), these firms are referred to as original design manufacturers (ODM), and despite their identity remaining anonymous to consumers, many of these Taiwanese firms have become leading global suppliers of their products. Indeed, their share of the world market has become so significant that they could even shake the competitive position of some of the leading brands. Such has been the success of these companies, in terms of advancing their know-how in product engineering and assembly, that they have surpassed all of their peers, and indeed, their clients; they have nevertheless shown their unwillingness to establish their own brands, even though it is clear that they could mount an effective challenge to their clients. This phenomenon, involving the emergence of a multinational firm without a brand name, or even a breakthrough in know-how, has not yet been sufficiently covered by the theories of international business.

One activity that is still missing from Taiwanese investment is diversification into unrelated technological fields. Although there are many examples of horizontal diversification commonly found amongst Taiwanese investors, these have been mainly in the same product category, or at least in the same industry category. As discussed earlier, the main purpose behind horizontal diversification is to improve the buyer relationship; therefore, diversification into unrelated technological fields, which requires improvements in managerial know-how and organisation strength, is rarely observed amongst Taiwanese investors.

GLOBAL LOGISTICS

From OEM to ODL

Prior to the mid-1980s, Taiwan's domestic industries – which lacked both the advanced technology and the capacity and capability for in-house design – had found themselves limited to OEM tasks, primarily assembling or processing intermediate goods – which would very likely be imported goods – for export to the markets of the developed economies. The necessary technology and management skills were essentially brought in through OEM orders and/or inward investment from Japan and the US. During the late 1980s and early 1990s, however, following the rapid expansion of Taiwan's foreign trade, the island quickly became very active as a source of FDI, first in the ASEAN economies, and then in mainland China, with the overall investment rising to billions of US dollars each year. In this new role as a major provider of FDI, Taiwan had begun exporting intermediate goods, equipment, technology and managerial know-how to other countries in the Asia-Pacific region where the final goods were then manufactured for shipment to markets throughout the world. Over the same period, domestic firms, which by then had gained some considerable technological expertise and the capacity for creative design, had graduated to the ODM stage, designing and developing products, made to order, for businesses on a global scale.

Since the mid-1990s, the introduction of networks, combined with the availability of powerful personal computers and drastically reduced telecommunication service charges, has enabled companies to communicate and exchange data far more rapidly than ever before, and at considerably lower costs. At the same time, consumers have become more sophisticated, and competition and the pursuit of growth have kept companies in constant search of better business practices to improve their level of efficiency. With business transactions increasingly being conducted over electronic networks, such as the Internet, there has been a fundamental shift in the organisation of basic corporate operations. Whilst some companies have found it to their advantage to outsource their non-core activities, others have discovered that they can now perform functions central to their businesses better, faster and more efficiently than ever before. Moreover, the combination of rising consumer demand for technical support, and an increasing need to foster customer loyalty so as to maintain market share, has driven the larger manufacturing MNCs towards a much greater focus on the customer end of the value chain. Some business consultants even believe that the real money in manufacturing today is to be made well downstream of the production function. In an extension of this scenario, MNCs might well decide to shed their logistics operations in order to concentrate on building up customer relationships, whilst Taiwanese manufacturers could extend their supply chain by moving into global logistics management (see Figure 7.1).

In the past, the major information technology (IT) manufacturers in Taiwan were required to build up their product inventory in advance, guided by their OEM order forecasts for the year ahead. These inventory products were then shipped to multinationals in the US and Japan, where the distribution, delivery and after-sales service functions were handled. However, this situation has changed dramatically in recent years, as the major MNCs in the IT field, such as Dell and Compaq, have chosen to adopt a build-to-order (BTO) strategy so as to effectively shorten their supply chains, either as a means of reducing inventory costs, or totally eliminating inventory cost, in order to safeguard their market share. Under the BTO model, customers are able to order products in varieties and configurations that are precisely tailored to fit their specific needs, with their orders being assembled, and their products shipped, in a pre-defined and precise manner. In order to successfully implement this just-in-time (JIT) type of distribution strategy, the major foreign MNCs have shifted the responsibility for inventory, delivery and after-sales functions to their OEM/ODM suppliers, i.e., they are engaged in marketing without inventory. Nevertheless, most of the foreign IT production orders received in Taiwan are nowadays directed mainly at the largest domestic players, such as ACER and Mitac, companies with proven capacity and capability in global logistics management; thus, any SMEs that hope to land larger international orders will increasingly find themselves relying on the logistics networks of these bigger domestic firms.

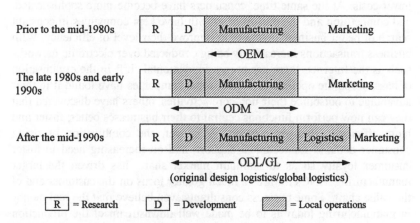

Figure 7.1 Changes in local business operations

As a logical extension of this strategy, OEM producers will ultimately have to start manufacturing and/or warehousing products not necessarily at their home base, but in locations that are specified by the clients placing the orders, so that these orders can be filled in the shortest possible time. The implication of this is that Taiwanese IT manufacturers will have to invest heavily in global logistics management in order to maintain their competitive edge in the international markets.

From Production Fragmentation to Operational Integration

As discussed earlier, it was the response to the strengthening of the NT Dollar in the mid-1980s, along with rising wages and land prices, that led many of Taiwan's industries to relocate their labour-intensive production operations to other countries. Attracted by the cultural similarities, and the high degree of complementarity existing between Taiwan and other Asian economies, Taiwanese entrepreneurs have been investing heavily in Southeast Asian countries and in mainland China since about 1986. Although such outward investment, as reported to the government, amounted to only US$7.5 million in the 1960s, and US$51.7 million in the 1970s, thereafter, the amount virtually doubled each year, surging from US$56.9 million to US$1,552 million between 1986 and 1990. Nevertheless, the data provided by the host countries actually suggests that this investment was much, much larger, with the disparity between Taiwanese government figures and host country figures, in some cases, being more than 100-fold. Host country data for this period also shows that Taiwan was one of the leading investors in both Southeast Asian economies and mainland China.

As overseas investment by Taiwanese companies expanded, the tendency to distribute production orders between onshore and offshore suppliers became more pronounced. In 1998, for example, domestic manufacturers allocated almost 11 per cent of their total orders to their overseas production facilities (Table 7.1). Information electronics firms, as a whole, have moved much faster in this direction than other industrial groups, outsourcing as much as 18 per cent of their total orders to foreign production sites in 1998, whilst producing only 77 per cent of their domestic orders at their own factories (Table 7.2). The data storage and telecom segments of this industry allocate even higher proportions of their total orders to overseas production. With production more geographically fragmented in the high technology industries than in traditional industries, and with the high technology sector accounting for a rapidly increasing share of total manufacturing output, the development of an advanced global logistics management capacity is therefore essential to Taiwan's future economic well-being.

Table 7.1   Procurement order sharing in Taiwanese manufacturing, 1998

Unit: %

	Composition	Share of Production	
		Domestic	Foreign
Manufacturing Totals	100.00	89.35	10.65
Information electronics	35.71	82.03	17.97
Electronics, electrical machinery	34.90	82.06	17.94
Precision instruments	0.81	80.92	19.08
Metal machinery	23.91	97.62	2.38
Chemicals	23.35	89.05	10.95
Consumer products	17.04	93.50	6.50

Source: MOEA (1999).

Taiwanese companies pass on orders to various overseas manufacturers for five main reasons: (i) to lower their production costs; (ii) on the request of their customers; (iii) based on the availability of their overseas subsidiaries; (iv) as a result of the inability of domestic production to absorb all orders received; and (v) because of the lack of availability of domestic facilities for certain types of production.

Around 22 per cent of all orders filled by overseas production go to Japan, the US and Europe, whilst around 41.5 per cent go to mainland China, and 32 per cent go to Southeast Asia. The information electronics industry has a higher than average ratio, with 23.8 per cent going to Japan, the US and Europe, 49 per cent going to mainland China, and 25.5 per cent going to Southeast Asia. The proportions for the electronics and electric machinery industry are similar.

Since Taiwan is severely lacking in domestic natural resources, Taiwanese industries have always depended heavily on the importation of raw materials, and this reliance on imported components has generally changed in line with the evolution of the industry. Upstream industries, for example, were developed as a result of the backward integration of the 1970s, and Taiwan was then able to rely on its own supply of components, with the one notable exception of key parts; this reliance was generally known as the result of secondary import substitution. However, given the increasing trend towards finer specialisation since the late 1980s, there has been an overall increase in the reliance on imported components. In 1998, Taiwan's manufacturing sector obtained 42.2 per cent of its raw materials, semi-finished products and components from overseas, compared with 52.3 per cent for the information electronics industry. The manufacturing sector as a whole purchased 50.7 per cent of all its imported inputs from Japan and the US, whilst in the information electronics industry, the figure was 61.0 per cent (see Table 7.3).

Table 7.2 Comparison of domestic and foreign procurement order sharing in Taiwanese manufacturing, 1998

Unit: %

	Domestic production		Foreign production			
	In-house Production	Subcontracted	Japan, US and Europe	Mainland China	Southeast Asia	Others
Manufacturing Totals	84.95	4.40	2.37	4.42	3.38	0.49
Information, electronics	76.97	5.06	4.28	8.83	4.59	0.28
Electronics, electrical machinery	76.94	5.12	4.37	8.64	4.66	0.28
Data storage processing	68.42	5.05	8.89	10.45	6.92	0.27
Telecommunications	73.86	3.81	0.09	7.14	15.10	0.00
Electronic components	82.06	4.93	1.95	8.15	2.68	0.23
Precision instruments	78.12	2.79	0.61	17.08	1.37	0.03
Metal machinery	92.61	5.01	0.71	1.29	0.26	0.12
Chemicals	86.95	2.10	1.44	2.46	6.00	1.05
Consumer products	88.20	5.30	1.95	2.25	1.63	0.67

Source: MOEA (1999).

163

Table 7.3 Sources of materials and intermediate goods for Taiwan-based firms, 1998

Unit: %

	Information Electronics	Electronics & Electrical Machinery	Data Storage Processing	Telecommunication Devices	Electronic Components	Precision Instruments
Total intermediates	100.00	100.00	100.00	100.00	100.00	100.00
Domestic	47.70	47.32	49.76	44.95	32.29	64.26
Foreign	52.30	52.68	50.33	55.05	60.71	35.74
Japan	17.91	17.93	12.85	9.00	23.15	16.97
US	14.06	14.29	17.58	22.40	12.87	3.78
Europe	7.28	7.39	2.95	6.59	15.09	2.46
Mainland China	1.85	1.86	1.73	3.59	2.06	1.50
Southeast Asia	6.71	6.82	8.44	13.18	5.57	2.16
Others	4.49	4.39	6.79	0.28	1.97	8.87

Source: MOEA (1999).

The movement towards greater specialisation can be seen as a two-way process. The expansion in demand for Taiwanese products abroad has not only deepened product specialisation in the island's domestic industries, but has also stimulated the demand from Taiwanese manufacturers for a host of specialised inputs from the overseas markets. In short, the producers of Taiwan's end products were involved in a shift towards manufacturing without machinery, with the niches of these producers coming from their development and logistics capabilities.

Supportive Industries

Success in global-logistics management demands a strong logistics information system, a framework for standardised operational procedures, the frictionless integration of production and supply operations and extensive managerial talent in international business. We should therefore examine how far Taiwan has come in recent years towards satisfying these requirements.

Since the early 1990s, Taiwan has shifted the emphasis from promoting industrial growth to the reengineering of the macroeconomy in ways that strengthen its international operational capability, and which have thereby laid the foundations for the establishment of a regional operations centre. The island's liberalisation efforts and physical development plans have focused on the expansion of regional telecommunications, as well as sea and air transport, with a view to upgrading the overall logistics infrastructure. In the meantime, the increasing importance of transshipments, and strategic alliances with major international players, has translated into steadily expanding markets for Taiwan's manufacturing sector, which, over the past thirty years, has succeeded in integrating its production operations and building a solid technological base.

Along with the efforts to liberalise the transportation sector, in 1995, an air express handling unit was also set up, followed by the establishment of two regional air transit hubs by UPS and Federal Express, in 1996 and 1997, respectively. The rapid expansion in transnational operations, particularly within the IT industry, raised the volume of air cargo shipments by 41 per cent during the four-year period ending in 1998. As a result, during 1998, at a time when most Asian economies were still overshadowed by the Asian financial crisis, Chiang Kai-shek International Airport was the only Asian air terminal able to maintain steady growth in air cargo shipments. Another positive factor explaining the rapid expansion in air transport operations is Taiwan's favourable geographic position as a gateway to the Western Pacific, with flight times from Taipei to other regional urban centres, including Hong Kong, Manila, Seoul, Shanghai, Sydney and Tokyo, being shorter, on average, than those from other less centralised locations.

Not long ago, Kaohsiung Harbour in southern Taiwan, the world's third-largest sea cargo/container terminal, handled less than half the volume of seaborne cargo passing through either Hong Kong or Singapore. However, following the implementation of reforms in the stevedore system and customs clearance procedures, and the extensive construction of new warehousing facilities, Kaohsiung has experienced remarkable growth in its cargo handling operations. Benefiting from a more liberal cross-strait regulatory environment, the port's new offshore centre has reported a 26 per cent average increase in total cargo handled on a quarterly basis since its inauguration in April 1997. The expansion, deregulation and modernisation of Taiwan's air and sea transportation networks have therefore succeeded in making the island a high performing regional transportation hub and global logistics centre.

CONCLUSIONS

Taiwan's successful economic development over the latter half of the twentieth century benefited from a series of open-door policies which first of all created a favourable environment for exports and FDI. The island was then able to accumulate an enormous amount of foreign exchange reserves from increasing trade surpluses during the first half of the 1980s, signifying the overall success of the previous policies. The direct impact which soon followed was a sharp appreciation of the NT Dollar and the unprecedented outward movement of significant amounts of investment from Taiwan, which posed a new operational challenge to Taiwanese businesses. Taiwan had to accommodate this new development by opening up its economy even further and by the overall upgrading of its industry. The globalisation of Taiwan's business operations, in particular, production, together with the subsequent availability of transportation, telecommunications and even financial networks, all prepared Taiwanese companies for a new way of carrying out business, i.e., their subsequent move into global logistics.

This new business model for Taiwan came as the trend towards globalisation was also emerging. Having effectively shifted into a global logistics mode, there were two other factors that would enhance Taiwan's position as it followed this new model into the future, namely, the accession of both Taiwan and mainland China into the WTO, and direct links, in terms of both air and sea transportation, across the Taiwan strait. The first of these has already materialised, with both parties having been welcomed into the WTO community late in 2001, and as a result, a further division of labour across the Straits is now expected. This implies that production fragmentation will intensity and transportation costs will be lowered, at least to a level which cannot be ignored, and that both of these trends will directly facilitate the further development of global logistics for Taiwanese companies.

Global logistics is a win-win strategy for all parties involved in a long supply chain. Consumers at the finished-product end will enjoy cheaper commodities with faster delivery times. The integrators, the Taiwanese manufacturers, will remain competitive in a widely opened and common global economy with logistics capability being the new trend, whilst at the other end of the chain, the many producers, most of whom are in the less developed countries, will continue to enjoy the benefits of their comparative advantage from the further division of labour. The world is shrinking in terms of the distance between countries, yet it is expanding as far as market boundaries are concerned. That is what global logistics is all about.

REFERENCES

Li, K.T. and M.-T. Chen (1987), *Overview of Taiwan's Economic Development Strategy*, Taipei: Lien-Ching (in Chinese).

MOEA (1999), *Survey on Manufacturing Activities*, Taipei: Ministry of Economic Affairs, Statistics Department, (July) (in Chinese).

Schive, C. and K.T. Hsueh (1987), 'The Experience and Prospects of High-Tech Industrial Development in Taiwan: The Case of the Information Industry', presented at the 1987 Joint Conference on Industrial Policies in the Republic of China and the Republic of Korea, Taipei: Chung-Hua Institution for Economic Research.

Schive, C. and K.T. Hsueh (1990), *The Foreign Factor: The Multinational Corporation's Contribution to the Economic Modernisation of the Republic of China*, Stanford: Hoover Press.

Schive, C. and K.T. Hsueh (1995), *Taiwan's Economic Role in East Asia*, Washington, DC: Centre for Strategic and International Studies.

Schive, C. and K.T. Hsueh (1999), 'How was Taiwan's Economy Opened up? The Foreign Factor in Appraisal', in G. Ranis, S.-C. Hu and Y.-P. Chu (eds.), *The Political Economy of Taiwan's Development into the 21st Century*, Cheltenham, UK: Edward Elgar.

Schive, C., K.T. Hsueh and R.Y.-S. Chyn (2001), 'Taiwan's High-Tech Industries', in L.K. Cheng and H. Kierzkowski (eds.), *Global Production and Trade in East Asia*, Boston: Kluwer Academic Publishers.

Vernon, R. (1977), *Storm over the Multinationals*, London: Macmillan.

8 Taiwan's Knowledge-based Service Industry

Jiann-Chyuan Wang

INTRODUCTION

Taiwan's traditional industries have found themselves mired in a continual downturn in recent years, with even the high-tech industries, those based on information technology (IT), having been confronted with extremely sluggish growth as further developments in computing technology have become less radical. Since computer manufacturing now appears to be approaching maturity, the question arises as to what the future will be for Taiwan's continuing industrial development.

Wang and Sun (2000) proposed that the potential development of Taiwan's domestic industries could involve: (i) conversion to high-tech domains based on multi-disciplinary expansion, including areas such as telecommunications, information appliances and software; (ii) improvements to internal capacity and competitiveness through mergers or acquisitions; (iii) moving upstream in the value chain to improve the added value of products by investing in innovation and design, the development of key techniques and devices, and improvements to processes; (iv) combining manufacturing, marketing and services to move into the downstream segment of the value chain, for example, withdrawing from the competition to focus on pure manufacturing through the implementation of global logistics management in developing industrial countries; or (v) developing the 'knowledge-based service industry' (KSI) to combine manufacturing or service industries with a technological background, such as IC design, logistics management, telecommunications services, biological detection, technical agency, and so on (Table 8.1). On the basis of these proposed transformation choices, it becomes apparent that there is a need for significant amounts of working capital, workforce and know-how, in terms of research and development (R&D), design, marketing and logistics management. Hence, this represents an enormous task for Taiwan's economic system, based, as it is, on small and medium enterprises (SMEs).

Table 8.1   Index of revealed service trade comparative advantages

	1992	1993	1994	1995	1996	1997	1998
Total Service Exports							
Taiwan	0.54	0.64	0.61	0.61	0.62	0.62	0.65
US	1.36	1.35	1.38	1.39	1.40	1.38	1.39
Japan	0.62	0.62	0.64	0.67	0.73	0.73	0.71
Netherlands	1.06	1.10	1.14	1.10	1.12	1.19	1.17
UK	1.19	1.17	1.19	1.23	1.21	1.26	1.33
Korea	0.59	0.65	0.74	0.79	0.77	1.80	0.78
Canada	0.64	0.61	0.62	0.61	0.63	0.62	0.62
France	1.38	1.43	1.21	1.18	1.15	1.12	1.09
Germany	0.66	0.69	0.65	0.69	0.71	0.70	0.66
Italy	1.19	1.12	1.08	1.06	1.04	1.10	1.08
Singapore	0.94	0.91	0.94	1.03	0.97	0.98	0.71
Transportation Exports							
Taiwan	0.60	0.65	0.73	0.78	0.72	0.62	0.64
US	1.25	1.21	1.20	1.23	1.22	1.16	1.09
Japan	0.98	0.94	0.94	0.99	1.03	1.03	1.09
Netherlands	1.87	1.89	1.87	1.87	2.01	2.17	2.05
UK	1.12	1.09	1.10	1.09	1.10	1.11	1.15
Korea	1.02	1.16	1.36	1.36	1.28	1.51	1.46
Canada	0.56	0.53	0.53	0.53	0.54	0.55	0.53
France	1.15	1.24	1.16	1.22	1.23	1.20	1.18
Germany	0.68	0.72	0.69	0.70	0.73	0.73	0.73
Italy	0.88	0.86	0.81	0.79	0.76	0.79	0.77
Singapore	0.67	0.66	0.69	0.75	0.74	0.75	0.77
Other Service Exports							
Taiwan	0.67	0.87	0.72	0.71	0.77	0.83	0.88
US	1.13	1.11	1.25	1.24	1.26	1.27	1.36
Japan	0.82	0.85	0.91	0.97	1.05	1.02	0.97
Netherlands	1.09	1.21	1.30	1.19	1.19	1.24	1.24
UK	1.47	1.40	1.49	1.49	1.49	1.59	1.68
Korea	0.48	0.51	0.60	0.66	0.71	0.68	0.56
Canada	0.72	0.71	0.72	0.70	0.73	0.70	0.69
France	1.78	1.82	1.30	1.21	1.13	1.05	1.01
Germany	0.63	0.68	0.67	0.78	0.83	0.80	0.77
Italy	1.23	1.05	0.93	0.92	0.91	0.98	0.97
Singapore	1.12	1.10	1.22	1.42	1.33	1.40	0.82

Source: Hsueh et al. (2003).

Clearly, by serving as a medium for business restructuring and improving competitiveness, the effective division of labour will help to improve Taiwan's economy with the growth of those firms that are based on R&D, management, logistics and design. It will also lead to the transformation of Taiwan's industries from their traditional manufacturing basis, into high value-added sectors, such as R&D, design, marketing and management. Thus, it seems clear that the flourishing growth of the KSI and its intermediate functions will play a crucial role in Taiwan's industrial transformation. Set against this backdrop, this chapter sets out to discuss the advantages, disadvantages and the vision of Taiwan's KSI, outlining several suggestions for government policy.

THE KNOWLEDGE-BASED SERVICE INDUSTRY

The Importance of a Knowledge-based Service Industry

On a global scale, there is a rapidly growing and widely recognised need for industrial transformation, and given the coming era of the knowledge-based economy, Taiwan's economy is now moving into a new phase of industrial development in line with such a need. The features of this new knowledge-based economy, according to Wu and Wen (1999), include not only the creation and diffusion of knowledge, but also the fundamental aim of adding value to knowledge, thus underlining the importance of improving the added value of industries through the creation and application of knowledge in the development of a knowledge-based economy. Since Taiwan's manufacturing industry as a whole is faced with declining profits, caused by increasing labour and land costs, as well as the rising awareness of environmental protection and labour rights, it would clearly be beneficial for Taiwan to pursue the development of a KSI, which would help to promote the developing industries and enhance the competitiveness of the existing manufacturing industries, thus increasing their added value.

The planned integration of Taiwan's manufacturing and service sectors will no doubt promote the island's advantages in the marketplace, separating it from the pure 'manufacturing' competition that currently exists between Taiwan and other developing economies. A specific example of this shift is the competitiveness of Taiwan's information industry, which comes mainly from the establishment of a global logistics system that combines manufacturing and services, including design, distribution, maintenance and other activities, and which has been extremely successful in leading Taiwan's manufacturing firms to forge ahead of many firms in other developing countries (Wang and Sun, 2000). As well as the huge market potential thrown up by a KSI, there is also very clear potential for the creation of numerous job opportunities in logistics, telecommunications, the Internet and e-commerce (Nomura Research Institute, 2000).

A further source of inspiration for the development of the knowledge-based service industry comes from the incessant push for further development in the advanced countries. In the US, for example, the service industry accounts for as much as 70 per cent of GDP and also generates around 70 per cent of the nation's employment opportunities. In contrast, the service industry in Taiwan accounts for around 65 per cent of GDP, and supplies only around 56 per cent of all employment opportunities. Not only does this demonstrate that there is significant room for improvement in the quality and competitiveness of Taiwan's service industry, but the numbers also reveal the enormous potential that the industry has with regard to creating further employment opportunities. As Table 8.1 shows, Taiwan's 'revealed service trade comparative advantage' (RCA) index has never exceeded 1; furthermore, as Table 8.2 reveals, Taiwan's balance of trade in services has consistently been in deficit (Hsueh et al., 2003).

Table 8.2   Balance of trade in services

Unit: US$ millions

	1992	1993	1994	1995	1996	1997	1998
Taiwan	-9,128	-7,896	-7,865	-9,037	-8,121	-7,744	-7,401
US	57,300	60,770	65,740	74,340	85,050	89,980	80,700
Japan	-43,960	-43,080	-48,060	-57,350	-62,240	-54,150	-49,420
Netherlands	265	676	1,411	2,262	3,835	5,756	5,201
UK	9,910	9,890	10,000	14,050	13,960	20,340	20,290
Korea	-2,884	-2,126	-1,801	-2,979	-6,179	-3,200	628
Canada	-10,812	-10,418	-8,146	-7,345	-6,433	-6,563	-4,755
France	19,378	16,861	19,512	17,973	16,254	17,493	18,705
Germany	-27,721	-31,538	-39,021	-45,362	-44,018	-41,294	-42,978
Italy	-4,438	50	1,448	6,569	8,055	7,764	4,170
Singapore	6,551	7,413	10,014	12,056	10,255	11,095	330

Source: Hsueh et al. (2003).

Based on protracted discussions within the investigation committee of the Japanese Ministry of International Trade and Industry – discussion which went on for over a year and a half – the Ministry subsequently published its vision of the development of Japan's industrial structure for the twenty-first century (Nomura Research Institute, 2000). The report pointed out that an 'integrated service industry' holds considerable potential for business and for the supply of many employment opportunities (see Table 8.3).

Table 8.3 *Innovation and integration within the service industry*

Industry/Area	Examples of New Commodities and Services	Employment Number Projection (x10,000 persons)			Market Size Projection (Japanese Yen Trillions)		
		Current status	Year 2010	Growth	Current status	Year 2010	Growth
Type of Innovation							
Information/Communications	Electronic commerce, content industry, electronic government, GIS.	125	245	120	38	126	88
New Product Technology	New generation materials, high level production control, automation.	73	245	120	38	126	27
Oceans	Fundamental fisheries.	59	80	21	4	7	3
Biotechnology	Medical supplies, food, chemical products, energy, environment.	3	15	12	1	10	9
Civil Aviation	New generation aviation, airport construction, extreme experiments.	8	14	6	4	8	4
Energy Conservation	Solar energy, wind power, ESCO.	4	13	9	2	7	5
Type of Integration							
Medical/Welfare	Home medical, Internet clinic, medical instruments.	348	480	132	38	91	53
Life/Culture	Regional commerce, career learning, leisure travel, fashion.	220	355	135	20	43	23

Table 8.3 (Contd.)

Industry/Area	Examples of New Commodities and Services	Employment Number Projection (×10,000 persons)			Market Size Projection (Japanese Yen Trillions)		
		Current status	Year 2010	Growth	Current status	Year 2010	Growth
Type of Integration							
Distribution/Logistics	Internet sales, third party logistics, logistics information services.	49	145	96	36	132	96
Business Assistance	Production outsourcing, consulting services, electronic commerce, accreditation services.	92	140	48	17	33	16
Urban Redevelopment	New transportation systems, intelligent-type living environment.	6	15	9	5	16	11
Human Resources	Movement of personnel, personnel intermediate agencies, job training.	6	11	5	2	4	2
Internationalization	Global logistics, global logistics consulting services, overseas life assurance.	6	10	4	1	2	1
Housing	Apartment remodelling, secondary products logistics, new construction materials.	3	9	6	1	4	3
Environment	Low pollution vehicles, resource recycling, environment-related equipment.	64	140	76	15	37	22
Total (approx)		1,060	1,800	740	200	550	350

Source: Nomura Research Institute (2000).

173

The opportunities include materials distribution/logistics (such as Internet shopping and the integration of materials consulting and distribution), life/culture (the integration of communications, leisure, travel and self- realization activities), and career support (the integration of outsourcing services, accreditation industry and career planning consulting). Since this direction is in general conformity with the development of the 'knowledge- based service industry', judging by the developmental experiences of the US and Japan, Taiwan's KSI seems to be heading for an optimistic future. The study by the Nomura Research Institute (2000) notes that in order to catch up and to remain competitive in the twenty-first century cyber community, manufacturing industry, in general, must also incorporate a certain degree of service activities such as finance, marketing, electronic commerce and management (Figure 8.1).

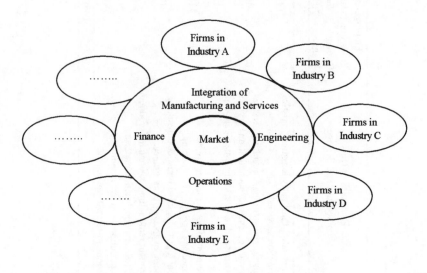

Source: Nomura Research Institute (2000).

Figure 8.1 The integration of industries

Definition of a Knowledge-based Service Industry

Having provided an illustration of the importance of a knowledge-based service industry, it seems fitting to go on to provide a definition of what a KSI actually is. The US Department of Commerce defines a KSI as an industry that incorporates the services of science, engineering and technology, or one that assists in the implementation of these industries (OECD, 2000). This covers areas such as business services (including computer software, computer and data processing, R&D, engineering and other relevant services), telecommunications, financing, education, medical care, and so on.

According to this definition, a KSI can be regarded as 'an industry providing services focusing on the provision of know-how or intellectual property (IP) to support those manufacturing or service industries with a technology background' (Wang and Tu, 2000). Such a definition suggests that a KSI should have the following features:

1. High R&D intensity (since knowledge comes mainly from R&D inputs);

2. Products (physical or invisible) that are produced for the needs of the manufacturing or services industry based on technology; and

3. A greater proportion of technical and R&D personnel than administrative staff, with a large proportion of these employees possessing college degree or above.

The Scope of Knowledge-based Service Industries

Having introduced the definition and features of a KSI, we now go on to examine the various definitions of KSIs provided by the US, the OECD and Singapore, followed by the scope of KSIs in Taiwan.

According to the OECD, a KSI should be involved in financing, insurance, telecommunications, property appraisal, business services, social services, warehousing and distribution; and in Singapore, a KSI is described as an industry which provides Internet services, software, R&D, multimedia and broadband services, e-commerce, information and media, logistics (logistics management) or education.

Since these various definitions of a KSI are extremely wide-ranging, we should take extra care not to ignore the fact that there may be some other important technology-based services hidden within the manufacturing sector, or that there may be others that are still emerging in the new era of the knowledge-based economy. For example, the recently extended activities of manufacturing, such as logistics, IP management and industrial design can all be classified as part of a KSI. The management information systems (MIS) departments or logistics departments in large firms could even be separated from the parent company as independent KSIs if they could be self-sustaining (Wang and Tu, 2000). Table 8.4 illustrates the current and emerging KSIs in the case of Taiwan.

Table 8.4   Taiwan's current and emerging KSIs and the relevant authorities

Industry Classification and Relevant Areas		Regulatory Authority [a]
Telecommunication Services	Telecommunications	MOTC
	Fixed line networks	MOTC
	Multimedia and broadband	MOTC
Banking and Financial Services	Insurance and banking	MOF
	Futures and funds	MOF
	Venture capital	MOF
Business Services	Accounting services	MOF
	Legal and business services	MOEA
	Management consulting (including R&D consulting)	MOEA
	Financing firms (certification)	MOF
	Advertising (including Internet advertising)	MOEA
	Design (including product and machinery design)	MOEA
	Leased facilities	MOEA
	Property and technology appraisal	MOEA
Education	Environmental detection	EPA
	Education and training services	MOE
	Academic research and services	MOE
	Publishing services	MOI
	Film making (Information and media)	GIO
	Radio and TV broadcasting (digital TV)	GIO
Medical Care	Medical examination	DOH
	Medical research	DOH
	Contract Research Organisation (CRO)	DOH
	Health and medical treatment services	EPA
Information Services, Engineering and Professional Design Services	Computer software services	MOEA
	Computer solution services	MOEA
	Data processing and information (including application service providers)	MOEA
	Network service provider (ISP and ICP)	MOEA
	IT IS	MOEA
	Technical agency	Dependent on service domain
	Factory design and planning	MOEA
	IP administration	MOEA
	IC design	MOEA
	Product design	MOEA
	Automatic engineering firms	MOEA
Personal Service	Career planning services [b]	–
	Human resource management services	CLA
	Skills training services	CLA
Environmental Hygiene and Anti-Pollution	Environmental detection services	EPA
	Environmental protection engineering services	EPA
	Anti-pollution services	MOEA

Table 8.4 (Contd.)

Transportation and	Warehousing and logistics distribution	MOF
Distribution	Customs brokerage	MOF
	R&D in natural sciences [b]	–
Research and	Multi-disciplinary R&D [b]	–
Development	Market surveys and opinion polls [b]	–
(R&D)	Translation services [b]	–
	Commodity inspection and quarantine	MOEA

Notes:

[a]   MOTC = Ministry of Transportation and Communications; MOEA = Ministry of Economic Affairs; MOF = Ministry of Finance; EPA = Environmental Protection Administration; MOI = Ministry of the Interior; CLA = Council of Labour Affairs; GIO = Government Information Office; DOH = Department of Health

[b]   These fields relate to areas where there are discrepancies between the authority specified by law and the target business authority, or where the authorities are not yet established.

Source: The table generalises the ideas of Ming-Chi Wu, Director of the Second Division of the Industrial Development Bureau, MOEA, and Chi-Tsung Yu, Director of the NICI Commission of the Executive Yuan.

AN OVERVIEW OF THE KNOWLEDGE-BASED SERVICE INDUSTRY IN TAIWAN

Current Status

As Figure 8.2 shows, on a global scale, 'business services' accounted for the lion's share of KSI production value in 1997, topping US$2.8 trillion, followed by financing (US$1.8 trillion), medical care (US$1.6 trillion), telecommunications (US$0.8 trillion), and education services (US$0.4 trillion). Dramatic growth is projected in the capacity of telecommunications and education services, along with the emergence of the Internet, telecommunications and the knowledge-based economy.

A more detailed examination of individual countries reveals that the US produced the greatest knowledge-based services, accounting for US$2 trillion of the total global capacity of US$7.41 trillion in 1997, whilst Japan came in second with US$1.35 trillion. In Asia, Taiwan was ranked third with a capacity of US$91.66 billion, just behind Japan and South Korea, but ahead of Hong Kong and Singapore. Within the various subcategories of Taiwan's KSIs, business services contributed the greatest proportion, at

US$34,478 million, followed by financing services (US$29,715 million), medical care (US$16,237 million), telecommunications (US$6,688 million) and education services (US$4,543 million).

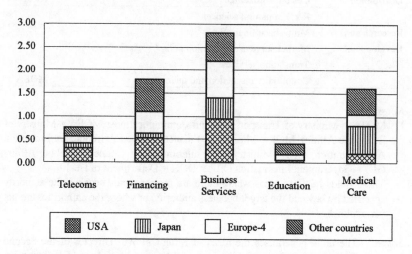

Note: Europe-4 refers to Germany, France, Italy and the United Kingdom.

Source: OECD (2000).

Figure 8.2   Five major KSIs and their global production values

Obviously, since the markets for telecommunications and education services are relatively small, there is still considerable room for further development. In addition, as pointed out by Wang and Chen (2000), Taiwan's KSI accounted for 33.7 per cent of GDP in 1996, with a growth rate in value added of 11.1 per cent in the same year (Table 8.5).

Table 8.5   The growth of Taiwan's knowledge-intensive industries

Unit: %

	Proportion of GDP			Value-added Growth		
	1991	1994	1996	1991-4	1994-6	1991-6
All Industries	-	-	-	9.8	10.2	9.9
Knowledge-intensive Industry	37.7	39.2	40.6	11.2	12.1	11.5
Knowledge-intensive Manufacturing Industry	6.1	5.7	6.8	7.6	20.5	12.6
Knowledge-based Service Industry	31.7	33.5	33.7	11.9	10.6	11.3

Source: Wang and Chen (2000).

Taiwan's Vision of the Knowledge-based Service Industry

Following the analysis of the current state of Taiwan's KSI, we can now attempt to explore its strengths and weaknesses, concluding with the sketching of a blueprint for the future development of Taiwan's KSI. A SWOT analysis is provided in Figure 8.3, showing the strengths and weaknesses of Taiwan's KSI and the opportunities that exist for future development.

Strengths	Weaknesses
Solid manufacturing bases, particularly in terms of the competence of the IT industry. Adequate supply of qualified engineers. Sound development of the venture capital sector. Capability of integrating resources in Chinese- speaking areas and market operations. Flexibility of small and medium enterprises to changes in the environment. Aggressive entrepreneurship. The widespread popularity and usage of the Internet.	Insufficient investment in R&D and own-brand marketing. High-tech manufacturing absorbs too much of the innovative talent, resulting in a shortage. Out-of-date financial system ('physical capital' remains the main collateral for financing). Unsatisfactory infrastructure (legal system, telecommunications facilities, no evaluation of non-physical property, insufficient IP rights protection, incompetence in foreign languages and lack of cultural development). Educational reform fails to react to the knowledge-based economy. The industrial system is based on SMEs, thus scale, competitiveness and the application of information are all limited.
Opportunities	Threats
The demand for transformation enhanced by the government's attention to industrial upgrading. Exploration of the mainland China market. The growing popularity of Chinese culture, leading to related product opportunities. The provision of a gateway to the mainland Chinese market for European, American and Japanese firms. The requirement for e-solutions and knowledge in current industries. The growing demand for training in the knowledge-based economy. The emerging market for regional information applications.	Financial crowding out from mainland Chinese firms. Unstable cross-strait relations. Reinforcement of policy unification. Barriers created by IP rights and financial strength of European and American firms. Problems with access to mainland China.

Source: Based on the conference on 'The Development and Strategies of KSIs' (convened and hosted by Acer Inc., in Aspire Park on 22 October 2000).

Figure 8.3 SWOT analysis of the KSI in Taiwan

So the question now remains as to what constitutes the vision of future KSI development in Taiwan. Since it is clearly very difficult to illustrate exactly what will constitute Taiwan's KSI in the early stages, all we can reasonably hope to do here is to provide some indication of the future direction of KSI development in Taiwan, as follows.

First of all, for industry as a whole, private sector effort, with the support of the government, can contribute to the prosperity of Taiwan's KSI in areas such as information services, financial consulting, design, R&D, materials flow and logistics management; the added value and core competitiveness of the manufacturing industry should also be successfully transformed and improved to facilitate new economic development. Secondly, the promotion of Taiwan's competitiveness in total information application and broadband networks can help to establish Taiwan as a centre for Asia-Pacific software supply and a design centre for the Chinese-speaking regions. Thirdly, Taiwan can be positioned as a centre for global logistics management within which Taiwan-based firms are helped to develop their capacity to integrate domestic and international investment resources and to strengthen their global competence. Fourthly, the successful implementation of the KSI can create more job opportunities, thus tackling the worrying problem of rising unemployment stemming from the migration of traditional industries.

Since Taiwan's KSI is still at an embryonic stage, it is supported by Article 8 of the *Statute for Industrial Upgrading* which offers a tax holiday to those firms classified as part of a KSI, a policy aimed at promoting their continuing development. In addition, the 'Action Plans for the Knowledge-based Economy' laid out by the Council for Economic Planning and Cooperation (CEPD) in 2000, established a number of policy measures to promote Taiwan's KSI as follows: (i) assisting firms to set up R&D consortia and providing tax reductions to promote large R&D cooperation projects; (ii) expanding government funds to participate in venture capital investment in order to assist start-up knowledge-intensive firms; (iii) speeding up industrial automation so as to provide additional scope for the development of knowledge-intensive firms; (iv) restructuring the education system and cultivating human resources to provide much needed highly skilled personnel for the KSI; and (v) establishing the relevant infrastructure to facilitate the development of the KSI.

Through the successful development of its KSI, Taiwan will transform itself into a mature knowledge-based economy, overcoming the rising costs of land and labour and staying ahead of the competition from developing countries in the ASEAN and mainland China. Furthermore, a flourishing KSI can help to balance Taiwan's industrial structure which, in the past, relied heavily on the electronics industry and exports. Combining manufacturing and service activities will also add value to the existing manufacturing industry, increasing firms' profit margins and restoring their competitiveness. As to the island's industrial structure, Taiwan will move one step further towards establishing its service industry, which will create more job opportunities, increasing its share of GDP from the current 56 per cent, to around 60 per cent to 65 per cent over the next five to ten years.

In terms of the balance in service trade, as Taiwan has now become a full member of the WTO, its commitment to market opening within various service sectors will be accompanied by an increase in the importation of services; however, with continued growth in the island's GDP, the corresponding requirement for upgrading of services from the manufacturing industry, and China's potential market for service exports, Taiwan's KSI sector will clearly have enormous potential for export growth. It should be noted, however, that since Taiwan's domestic market is limited, relevant firms within the KSI may have to rely on markets in the Chinese-speaking regions as their hinterland (including mainland China, Taiwan and Hong Kong) in order to achieve economies of scale. This developmental trend may well lead to Taiwan's economy becoming increasingly dependent on China.

PROMOTION OF THE KNOWLEDGE-BASED SERVICE INDUSTRY IN TAIWAN

Given the current development, strengths and weaknesses of Taiwan's KSI, in order to effectively implement the island's KSI, the government should provide the necessary support for its promotion. In this section, we follow the classification of Rothwell and Zegveld (1981) to introduce supportive strategies from environmental, supply and demand perspectives.

Environmental Measures

The government can encourage appropriate investment in Taiwan through the provision of a favourable environment for firms, in terms of IP rights protection, the appropriate infrastructure, and taxation policies, as follows:

Protection of IP rights and the establishment of an appraisal system
Apart from the clear protection of IP rights, successful transactions in the exchange of technology and knowledge lie in the proper pricing and fair handling of the two factors. Since traditional accounting systems can no longer satisfy the requirements of businesses in the KSI, it would benefit the emergence of the KSI immensely if the government were to strive to develop an appraisal system for IP in accordance with the approaches to knowledge commercialization taken by the OECD and other developed countries.

Improving infrastructure

The effective development of the KSI in Taiwan can only take place under a sound infrastructure, which would essentially include the appropriate supply of telecommunications facilities, the construction of Internet networks, the establishment of standards, relevant laws and regulations, network certification, security, and so on.

Promoting knowledge management

Knowledge management covers the creation, recording, organization, access to, and usage of, knowledge. The effective management of knowledge serves as a key to business competitiveness and, from a governmental perspective, the implementation of knowledge management creates an environment for innovation, exchange and distribution based on knowledge, leading to a prospering KSI. Here are some suggestions for the Taiwanese government's implementation of KSI management:

Developing performance indicators for comparison with other countries. The key to knowledge management lies in accurate records. Regrettably, Taiwan's KSI is not yet properly defined and some of the secondary data is scattered around in various industries, thus there are no records held due to development in progress. Clearly, the Directorate of Budget, Accounting and Statistics, or some other responsible authority, should now be attempting to clarify the definition and scope of Taiwan's KSI, systematically establishing and collecting some 'indicators of performance' so that the government can analyse the current status and offer guidance by undertaking comparisons with other countries, thereby gaining a better understanding of the overall developmental trend.

Developing the e-marketplace and interaction in technology exchange. The quality of agents plays a crucial role in the organisation, exchange of and access to knowledge, with a successful e-marketplace functioning as an appropriate technical agent. The e-marketplace provides information on domestic firms, products and relevant business news; this should be publicised, since those who intend to secure foreign investment in Taiwan need to be able to process international transactions comprising of product search, quotations and orders through these means. The private sector should take the initiative in the implementation of the e-marketplace, with the government offering information and appropriate channels for coordination with professional and business associations.

Innovative thinking to promote KSI development. Implementation of the KSI relies upon innovative thinking by the government, which should make appropriate adjustments to its current education policy, tax incentives, laws, the management of industrial parks, inappropriate controls of industry, and a general revision of its 'manufacturing-based' mentality. For example, the projects that are sponsored by the Industrial Development Bureau focus on 'factories'; therefore, some of the new KSI firms that do not have factories are excluded from such projects; thus, rapid changes need to be made to tax incentives, project planning, and so on, as it is extremely unlikely that the KSI can thrive without such support. The government should even consider establishing a long-run project team to investigate and organise the complete solutions and schemes for the exclusive purpose of meeting KSI targets.

Provision of personnel, capital, skills and an appropriate environment. Since Taiwan does not have sufficient domestic resources, there is a general need for all parts of society, including business, politics, academia and research institutions, to fully evaluate the current situation and concentrate on several domains of comparative advantages, such as multimedia, e-commerce, design and the distribution of logistics.[1] This should accelerate the allocation and gathering of capital and core personnel and help to break through critical mass in these domains. In addition, the government should seek out successful enterprises, cultivating them as firms of exemplary international competitiveness for the guidance of other firms. The 'Five-Year Project for the Development of the Software Industry' proved to be a remarkable achievement with the government providing software firms with full support in terms of products, technology, human resources and environment, and ultimately enhancing the overall competitiveness of the software sector.

Supply Side Measures

Policies concerning supply lead to the government having a direct impact on business investment through capital, manpower, technology and information, all essentially aimed at enhancing business competitiveness. One of the major bottlenecks in the current development of the KSI in Taiwan is the lack of talent and capital, so there is clearly an urgent need for the training of professionals to meet the demands of the KSI and the corresponding provision of development funding for firms.

Recruitment and professional training
The amount of talent available for recruitment in e-commerce, environmental protection, logistics management, financing and insurance is still very limited; therefore, the Ministry of Education should urge higher education institutions to set up additional departments related to these domains and strive to develop the necessary talent for knowledge-based

services, especially those capable of integrating both manufacturing and services. In addition, it would be extremely helpful if the government were to reinforce the interaction between industry and academia with the common aim of KSI development. Since it may take a considerable period of time to train an appropriate workforce in universities and colleges, the government should follow the examples of Singapore and Denmark, revising the relevant laws and lifting the restrictions on overseas research working permits in Taiwan. By so doing, the recruitment of overseas technical professionals will help with the development of Taiwan's KSI and, to some extent, help to solve the problem of the manpower shortage. Training programmes for personnel involved in the KSI should be reorganised according to changes in the industrial structure so as to deliver better professional training and ultimately provide a better KSI workforce.

Funding through simplified stock listing in the TAIEX and OTC

Technology-based firms tend to require capital at the very start of their business operations; therefore, shortening the preparatory period for stock listing would undoubtedly help them to raise funds from the market for further development. Although the venture capital industry in Taiwan has already reached a certain scale, in contrast to US venture capital funds, which provide high-tech and KSI firms with considerable support, most of the investment in Taiwan is made right at the end of the preparatory period. There should be a more flexible stock market in Taiwan (e.g. an SME stock exchange or a newly developed technology stock exchange) similar to the case in Hong Kong, where venture capital investors are able to sell their stocks for profit during the early stages, in a less restricted market, instead of waiting for the stocks to be listed on the board. This will help them to obtain profits earlier, reducing their risk and modifying their investment arrangements at the beginning of their business operations.

In order to promote the development of its domestic knowledge economy, the government in Singapore established its own investment firms to manage large amounts of government funds. Apart from directly investing in the entrepreneurial investment industry so as to direct its future development, the government used this co-investment approach to participate in investment projects, both regional and overseas, in order to strengthen the interconnecting relationship between Singapore and overseas investment. The Singaporean government can also use this reciprocal investment model to attract overseas entrepreneurship investment funds or entrepreneurship management firms to invest in investment projects related to Singapore. Germany also has a similar scheme aimed at promoting start-up companies in the technology sector. The experiences of these two countries can clearly serve as good examples for Taiwan.

Privatisation of government research institutions

A number of government research institutions, such as the Industrial Technology Research Institute (ITRI) and the Institute for Information Industry (III), serve as the government's main R&D force, as well as a medium for technical transfer between the government and the private sector; in a broader sense, they can be regarded as part of the KSI. Hence it would be beneficial to the development and improvement of Taiwan's domestic KSI if these institutions were able to become private enterprises and release their R&D capacity to the private sector. There should also be greater interaction between business and academia in order to help to promote the KSI with the support of the highly skilled research staff that these institutions possess.

Demand Side Measures

Our overall analysis ends with an examination of policy focus in the government's function of providing stable market demand, such as procurement and contract research for the promotion of industries, and looks at two main demand policy factors, subcontracting and procurement, along with the improvement of information application capacity and the creation of business opportunities.

Expansion through government procurement and subcontracting

In the early stages, KSI development in Taiwan will tend to be limited by the island's small domestic market and the lack of economies of scale. The subcontracting of business by the government (in those areas not related to security or confidentiality) will facilitate the emergence of the necessary economies of scale in this area.

Improvements in information to create more business opportunities

Despite having become one of the major suppliers of information products, as compared to the US, Japan and Singapore, Taiwan lacks competence in the application of information technologies. This also deters the development of a number of areas of the KSI, such as software, information services and e-commerce. New strategies need to be implemented to improve the capacity for information technology application and the development of those areas of the KSI relating to the information industry and the Internet. The government should, for example, embrace more IT procurement cases, fostering cross-departmental cooperation, providing Internet window access, improving IT education in elementary and high schools, digitising teaching materials for mandatory education (and putting their resources online), sponsoring online teaching and Internet access in poor areas, providing support to export-based businesses, and finally, improving overall Internet marketing capabilities.

CONCLUSIONS

Taiwan's traditional industries have been in the doldrums in recent years, a time when its high technology industry has also seen significantly slower growth. During the current period of structural transformation, the successful implementation of the island's KSI will serve to combine Taiwan's manufacturing strength and related services, not only adding value to its currently declining manufacturing industry, but also providing integrated services with the ability of distinguishing Taiwanese products from the current pure 'manufacturing' competition coming from the developing economies. The KSI can therefore serve as the driving force for the next stage of Taiwan's economic development.

As regards the necessary support for the development of its KSI, Taiwan can rely upon the strength of its solid manufacturing bases, an abundant supply of qualified engineers, the ongoing, and relatively successful, development of a sound venture capital system, as well as popular use of the Internet, and so on. Notwithstanding the current drawbacks within the Taiwanese economy, the emerging potential market of mainland China, which is a market of huge proportions, provides Taiwan with considerable opportunities for the successful development of its KSI, since Taiwan has already demonstrated its ability to integrate various resources in its established market operations in the Chinese-speaking regions. However, insufficient R&D investment, an out-of-date financial system and unsatisfactory infrastructure, are just some of the barriers opposing the successful development of Taiwan's KSI.

Under such circumstances, it seems clear that the government should now be providing the necessary support, in terms of environmental, supply and demand policy measures, in an effort to promote its KSI; however, the government can, of course, only play a supportive role. Firms, as well as the public sector in general, must assume the greatest share of the responsibility for making the KSI a reality. With the necessary effort from all parties, it is expected that Taiwan's KSI can flourish, and that it will facilitate the island's economic transformation, playing a major role in Taiwan's continuing economic development.

NOTE

In addition to comparative advantages, indicators such as high market potential and uncertainty should be considered in order to facilitate more objective decision-making, thus avoiding the influence of interest groups and avoiding the selection of the wrong businesses due to asymmetric information.

REFERENCES

CEPD (2000), *Project for the Development of Knowledge-Based Economies*, Taipei: Council for Economic Planning and Development, Executive Yuan.

Hsueh, L.-M., A.-L. Lin and S.-W. Wang (2003), 'The Growth and Potential of Taiwan's Foreign Trade in Services' in I. Takatoshi and A.O. Krueger (eds.), *Trade in Services in the Asia-Pacific Region*, NBER - East Asia Seminars on Economics, Chicago, Ill: University of Chicago Press, Vol. II, pp.137-98.

Nomura Research Institute (2000), *Economic Structure Reformation Action Plans*, Tokyo: Nomura Research Institute.

OECD (2000), *Science and Engineering Indicators*, Paris: OECD.

Rothwell, R. and W. Zegveld (1981), *Industrial Innovation and Public Policy*, London: Frances Pinter Ltd.

Wang, J.-C. and H.-H. Chen (2000), *The Strategy for Industrial Upgrading in the Knowledge-Based Economy*, Taipei: Chung-Hua Institution for Economic Research.

Wang, J.-C. and K.-N. Sun (2000), 'A Study of Assisting Industrial Upgrading, Transformation and Government Policy Measures', Mimeo.

Wang, J.-C. and K.-H. Tsai (2000), *The Continued Study of the Effects of the Asian Financial Crisis on Taiwan's Industrial Competitiveness*, Taipei: Chung-Hua Institution for Economic Research.

Wang, J.-C. and Y.-Y. Tu (2000), *Analysis of the Trend Towards a Knowledge-based Service Industry and the Role of the Government*, Taipei: Chung-Hua Institution for Economic Research.

Wu, S.-H. and C.-T. Wen (1999), *Industrial Innovation in a Knowledge-based Century.* Taipei: Graduate School of Technology and Innovation Management, National Chengchi University.

9 US Semiconductor Patents Granted to Taiwan, South Korea and Japan

Chin Chung, Pwu Tsai and Sze-Yueh Wang

INTRODUCTION

The semiconductor industry emerged in the 1960s, and irrespective of whether its position is measured in terms of technology, product applications, production or marketing, the US was clearly the dominant player at that time. The US was also the first country to undertake research and development (R&D) work on semiconductor technologies such as 'complementary metal oxide semiconductor' (CMOS), IC (integrated circuit) production processes, microcontrollers, 'charge coupled devices' (CCDs), and 'dynamic random access memory' (DRAM). However, with the emergence, in the 1980s, of standardised DRAM products from Japan, things began to change; that particular decade also saw burgeoning development of semiconductor industries in other Asian countries. Under such circumstances, the US gradually lost its dominant position in the global market, and was subsequently overtaken, in 1986, by Japan. At around the same time, the economies of South Korea, Taiwan and Singapore were also striving to develop their own domestic semiconductor industries. In the mid-1980s, South Korea imitated the Japanese paradigm which involved dedicating all of its resources to the development of the DRAM industry. As a direct consequence, in 1993, Samsung, the leading South Korean manufacturer, became the largest supplier in the global DRAM market.

The semiconductor industry in Taiwan was also highly competitive; since beginning to take off in the mid-1980s, it has made impressive progress in product specifications, mass production capability, cost control, supply chain management and global logistics. Taiwanese companies established close partnerships with brand-name product vendors in the US, Japan and Europe which led to enhanced cooperation in manufacturing, investment, marketing and R&D, along with the formation of a transnational division of labour. These achievements made Taiwan one of the leading manufacturers in the global semiconductor industry and led to Taiwan's success in building up its own domestic industry.

Generally speaking, generation shifts in the global semiconductor industry are very significant, particularly since the industry is subject to dramatic ups and downs in the business cycle. The companies which led the industry in the early days, such as National Semiconductor (NS), Texas Instruments (TI), Philips Electronics and International Business Machines (IBM), fell back into the secondary ranks of manufacturers as they found themselves unable to compete effectively against new entrants such as Intel, Motorola, AMD and Micron. The investment strategies and global deployment adopted by different semiconductor companies have contributed to the changes in the relative strength of the semiconductor industries of the various economies; the most pronounced industry cluster effect has been in the Asia-Pacific region (South Korea and Taiwan), whilst semiconductor industry supply capacity between North America, Japan, Europe and the Asia-Pacific region (mainly South Korea, Taiwan and Singapore) has shifted from their former respective shares of 70 per cent, 18 per cent, 10 per cent and 2 per cent, to significantly adjusted shares of 55 per cent, 24 per cent, 9 per cent and 12 per cent in 2001.

As Table 9.1 shows, in 2001, Japan achieved output value of US$33.34 billion, accounting for 24 per cent of total global output. South Korea's output value reached US$9.58 billion, representing a 6.89 per cent share, whilst Taiwan's output value was US$6.51 billion, accounting for a 4.69 per cent share.

Table 9.1   Regional semiconductor output as a proportion of total global output

Unit: %

	1975	1980	1985	1990	1995	1999	2001
North America	70.0	63.0	46.0	36.0	42.0	54.5	55.0
Japan	18.0	27.0	43.0	50.4	35.2	25.0	24.0
Europe	10.0	8.0	9.0	10.0	7.0	9.5	9.0
South Korea	-	-	1.0	4.0	10.7	7.25	6.89
Taiwan	-	-	-	<1.0	3.12*	5.11*	4.69*
Other	2.0	2.0	2.0	6.0	15.0	14.0	12.0
Total Global Output (US$ billion)	-	-	-	49.5	144.4	173.0	138.9

Note: * There may be some overlap between output from the foundry paradigm/ model and the output of products from integrated device manufacturers (IDMs).

Source: ICE, Dataquest. The data used in this chapter were revised in accordance with the 'Chart Showing Semiconductor Industry Trends', Digitimes, (September 2000), p.243.

There were also huge changes in the geographical structure of demand in the global semiconductor market. This is because the demand for semiconductors in countries such as mainland China and India has increased dramatically due to the rapid economic development of the Asia-Pacific area. In consequence, by 2001, the Asia-Pacific area had replaced the US as the largest semiconductor market in the world. Table 9.2 presents the changes in the relative size of the world's semiconductor markets, and according to a forecast produced by WSTS, it is extremely unlikely that the trend shown in the table will change in the foreseeable future; indeed, greater expansion of the gap between the US market and the Asia-Pacific market can be expected in the future. Given the fierce competition in the semiconductor industry, R&D is without question a vital method for establishing competitive advantage, with the securing of patents for key technologies being one of the best possible ways of establishing a dominant position in the market. Patent output is therefore an important index in the overall evaluation of industrial R&D and market competitiveness. For companies in those countries that are falling behind in the competition, there are two major advantages in establishing an independent R&D capability and securing patents. First of all, it can be the key to success in negotiations; and secondly, it lays the foundations for building up the company's intellectual property and elevating the company's technical profile.

Given that the US is the largest market in the world, the number of successful patent applications in the US is regarded as an important indicator of a country's competitiveness in the area of technology and innovation. The total number of US patents obtained by the US, Taiwan, South Korea and Japan, between 1981 and 2001, is presented in Table 9.3, which shows that Japan has remained in second place ever since the start of that period, whilst the US itself obtained the most patents. Both Taiwan and South Korea have thus far secured only a very limited number of patents; however, this number is growing rapidly for both of these economies.

Table 9.4 provides a league table of successful US patent applications by Taiwan, South Korea and Japan, between 1981 and 2001, based on data released by the US Patent and Trademark Office (USPTO). As the table shows, Taiwan has climbed from twentieth place to third place, still behind Japan and Germany, but nevertheless ahead of the likes of France, Britain and Canada, which clearly represents an impressive achievement. South Korea, on the other hand, also has great potential, having at one point risen from twenty-sixth place to fifth place, ahead of Taiwan. Closer analysis of the total number of patents secured by South Korea shows that although it secured fewer than Taiwan, it nevertheless has similar breadth of industry coverage and patent quality; indeed, it is even superior to Taiwan in some areas, with the South Korean semiconductor industry constantly forging ahead.

Table 9.2 Changes in demand in regional semiconductor markets, 1995-2001

Year	Asia Pacific *		Japan		Europe		US		Total
	US$ bn	Share (%)	US$ bn	Share (%)	US$ bn	Share (%)	US$ bn	Share (%)	US$ bn
1990	7.5	13.7	20.5	37.4	9.9	18.1	16.8	30.8	54.7
1997	29.9	22.0	31.8	23.4	28.8	21.2	45.4	33.4	136.0
1998	28.9	23.0	25.9	20.6	29.4	23.4	41.4	33.0	125.6
1999	37.2	24.9	32.9	22.0	31.8	21.3	47.5	31.8	149.4
2000	51.33	25.1	46.83	22.9	42.33	20.7	64.00	31.3	204.4
2001	40.28	29.0	40.67	24.0	30.56	22.0	36.11	26.0	138.9
Average Growth (1990-2001) (%)	39.7		8.9		19.0		10.4		14.0
Average Growth (1997-2001) (%)	8.7		7.0		1.5		-3.0		0.5

Note: * The 'Asia-Pacific' region does not include Japan or the United States.

Source: ITU Internet Reports (2002).

Table 9.3 Comparison of the total number of patents granted to the US, Japan, Taiwan and South Korea

Year	US		Japan		Taiwan		South Korea		Total USPTO Patents
	Total No.	Share (%)	Total No.	Share (%)	Total No.	Share (%)	Total No.	Share (%)	
1981	39,224	59.64	8,388	12.75	80	0.12	17	0.03	65,771
1982	33,895	58.55	8,149	14.08	88	0.15	14	0.02	57,888
1983	32,871	57.81	8,793	15.46	65	0.11	26	0.05	56,860
1984	38,367	57.09	11,110	16.53	99	0.15	30	0.04	67,200
1985	39,556	55.20	12,746	17.79	174	0.24	41	0.06	71,661
1986	38,126	53.80	13,209	18.64	208	0.29	46	0.06	70,860
1987	43,520	52.46	16,557	19.96	343	0.41	84	0.10	82,952
1988	40,497	51.97	16,158	20.74	457	0.59	97	0.12	77,924
1989	50,185	52.53	20,168	21.11	591	0.62	159	0.17	95,537
1990	47,391	52.44	19,525	21.61	732	0.81	225	0.25	90,365
1991	51,178	53.03	21,026	21.79	906	0.94	405	0.42	96,513
1992	52,253	53.62	21,925	22.50	1,001	1.03	538	0.55	97,444
1993	53,231	54.13	22,293	22.67	1,189	1.21	779	0.79	98,342
1994	56,066	55.14	22,384	22.02	1,443	1.42	943	0.93	101,676
1995	55,739	54.96	21,764	21.46	1,620	1.60	1,161	1.14	101,419
1996	61,104	55.73	23,053	21.03	1,897	1.73	1,493	1.36	109,645
1997	61,707	55.10	23,179	20.70	2,057	1.84	1,891	1.69	111,983
1998	80,292	54.43	30,840	20.91	3,100	2.10	3,259	2.21	147,521
1999	83,905	54.67	31,104	20.27	3,693	2.41	3,562	2.32	153,485
2000	85,070	54.01	31,296	19.87	4,667	2.96	3,314	2.10	157,495
2001	87,610	52.76	33,224	20.01	5,371	3.23	3,538	2.13	166,045

Source: USPTO (http://www.uspto.gov).

192

Table 9.4   League table of patents awarded to Taiwan, South Korea and Japan, 1981-2001

Year	Taiwan	South Korea	Japan
1981	20	32	1
1982	18	31	1
1983	20	26	1
1984	17	26	1
1985	16	23	1
1986	14	23	1
1987	12	22	1
1988	10	20	1
1989	10	18	1
1990	10	16	1
1991	9	12	1
1992	8	11	1
1993	6	10	1
1994	6	9	1
1995	6	8	1
1996	6	7	1
1997	6	7	1
1998	6	5	1
1999	4	6	1
2000	3	7	1
2001	3	6	1

Source: USPTO (http://www.uspto.gov).

This chapter sets out with the aim of discussing a number of questions which relate to the area of US patents granted to Japan, Taiwan and South Korea. First of all, does the increasing number of US patents obtained by the Taiwanese semiconductor industry suggest that some companies have moved away from pure-play foundry operations towards 'integrated competition'? Alternatively, is the industry moving towards a specialist division of labour, with foundry operations continuing to be the basis of the business model but with efforts being made to achieve deepening in the area of technology? With respect to technological capabilities, where do the strengths and weaknesses of Taiwan's semiconductor industry lie in comparison with its major competitors such as South Korea and Japan? And finally, in the long term, how can Taiwan's semiconductor industry build up appropriate international competitiveness?

In its attempt to answer these questions, this chapter focuses on two main areas, namely the status of patent applications in the US and the development of the semiconductor industry in Taiwan, South Korea and Japan. Discussion of the first aspect will be based upon comparison between the R&D strategies and patents of semiconductor companies, followed by analysis of the patent performances of these three economies and the potential implications of their long-term business strategies. As regards the second aspect, this chapter goes on to discuss the relationship between industrial and technical competitiveness in order to undertake an in-depth exploration of the interaction between technical competitiveness and industrial development.

CHANGES IN TECHNOLOGY, BUSINESS MODELS AND COMPETENCES

The semiconductor industry is a classic example of a technology-intensive and capital-intensive industry. As in the case of most high-tech industries, the initial stage of the semiconductor industry was characterised by vertical integration. Later on, opportunities emerged for new manufacturers to enter the industry, along with the possibility of the emergence of a technology-based division of labour focusing upon expanding market scope, technical development and the driving forces of ongoing product innovation and short product life cycles. Gradually, the operation of the market mechanism led to the formation of a relatively stable division of labour.

There have been three major technical revolutions in the semiconductor industry since the 1960s, each of which occurred when the players involved found that they could not independently complete system design or IC design as a result of financial or technical concerns. As a result, the industry value chain produced new opportunities for new players to secure their position in the market, which subsequently led to fundamental changes in the structure of the industry.

The first transition was led by 'device standardisation'. Between 1960 and 1970, systems companies had produced all of the software and hardware for computers, with a tendency to design their hardware by embedding the small or medium IC which they had developed independently onto PC motherboards. However, the extremely time-consuming process of systems design made the workload increasingly unaffordable for the major systems companies. By around 1970, microprocessors, memory and other small IC devices were all becoming standardised, allowing companies to achieve considerable labour savings, since their systems could be designed to incorporate these standardised devices. From then on, the semiconductor industry was divided into two types of businesses, 'systems manufacturers' and 'IC companies'; the latter were also referred to as 'integrated device manufacturers' (IDMs) because they had their own IC fabrication plants (fabs) and were involved in every process from product design and manufacturing through to marketing.

The second transformation took place between 1980 and 1990. Although some IC products had already become standardised, there were many other non-integrated IC products that were still available on the market. The less than satisfactory performance of systems, due to the large numbers of non-integrated ICs being used, led to the emergence of the concept of 'application-specific integrated circuits' (ASIC). Since ASIC involved extensive use of 'gate array' and 'standard cell' technology, engineers could use logic gate component databases directly in IC design without the need to understand the minutiae of circuit design. This approach soon became a dominant force in the market as it boosted design performance to a considerable extent, with the conceptual transition leading to the emergence of fabless companies which integrated some independent IC into 'application-specific standard products' (ASSP) or ASIC for systems companies. This in turn led to the emergence of the 'foundry model' to fill the void in production capacity created by the growth of the fabless firms.

The third revolution came with the emergence of 'silicon intellectual property' (SIP) in the 1990s. As production process technology became ever finer, the density of individual chips increased, which made it very difficult for manufacturers to deliver new products by means of ASIC to satisfy the market demand. In order to solve this problem, the idea emerged of a 'SIP module'. SIP requires the modulation of certain functions so that a designer can recycle the original design, and the development of SIP led to the emergence of professional IP and design service providers; this was a major step forward when compared with the simple IC design companies that emerged after the second transformation.

Although the three revolutions obviously created revolutionary changes, even after some thirty years, the most traditional of all IC businesses, namely IDMs, continue to dominate the semiconductor industry. The first transformation had divided semiconductor manufacturers into downstream systems manufacturers and specialist semiconductor firms; the second transformation had added IDMs, fabless companies and the specialist foundries serving the fabless companies; and the third revolution led to the emergence of SIP and design service providers. Nevertheless, despite these changes, IDMs still continue to account for around 90 per cent of the total operating revenue for the whole of the semiconductor industry. However, IDMs generally have lower revenue growth than the fabless companies, which is leading to a shift in the dominance of the two businesses in the industry; indeed, it is anticipated that by the end of 2003, the share of total revenue held by IDMs will fall below 90 per cent.

After forty years of transformation and development, the semiconductor industry has developed a specific industrial ecology, characterised by three main features, the first of which is the rapid pace of change in industrial technology. It can be very difficult for players in the industry to sustain superiority with only one technique, since the life cycle of a new product or technology is now very short. In consequence, those companies whose technology represents their core capability must constantly invest in R&D and seek to exercise control over industry specifications. Other strategies such as making effective use of patents and legal action to counter violations of rights can also be adopted as an effective means of blocking or delaying competitors.

Secondly, strategic alliances and mergers are very common within the industry. It is almost impossible for a company to survive the ever-changing market, the need for considerable R&D investment and the inevitable economic cycles, by struggling on in isolation; thus, strategic alliances and mergers are of great importance, and making effective use of industry network resources to enhance a company's competitiveness has become an important strategy.

The third feature is globalisation. The development of the semiconductor industry has accelerated the process of economic globalisation; this in turn has significantly reduced the time needed for growth in the market for a given product. As a result, the life cycle of semiconductor products is gradually getting shorter, which presents a major challenge to those market leaders whose technical innovation is their core competency. With the rapid growth of the market, new entrants will be attracted and competition will come to be based mainly on cost at a much earlier point than would otherwise have been the case. Product life cycles will be further shortened, forcing companies to withdraw from the market and to begin focusing on other products. South Korean manufacturers, for example, have moved into the DRAM market in a big way over the past five or six years, forcing the leading Japanese companies such as NEC, Hitachi and Toshiba to totally withdraw from DRAM production.

From the point of view of the foundries, which, in terms of technology, have to follow the lead set by the IDMs, the compressed product life cycle and early arrival of competition based on lower cost will similarly test their ability to shorten the learning curve and improve the yield rate. The requirements, in terms of production, materials and logistics management, will also become more rigorous. More importantly, new foundries will replace their seniors, driving them out of the market, once they obtain similar or more advanced technical licensing and production capacity. In other words, the demand-based economies of scale in a globalised market, like diverse technical development, will push market players towards higher standards. Those who fail to follow the trend will become marginalised, and will be forced to withdraw from the market.

The most important factor in business development in the semiconductor industry is thus the development of superior core competences. For those companies operating as IDMs, these core competences include having control over one's own technology, R&D, brand marketing, relationships with consumers and customer services. The core competences of foundries include mass production capability, technology-following capability, production management and cost control. Under the current semiconductor market environment, these two types of company either implement a division of labour to complement each other's capabilities, or else they engage in agent-based competition for market share.

The key to success for foundries within the semiconductor industry, where new products replace existing products with great frequency, lies in their ability to achieve rapid technology following. In other words, a foundry can only win the race in the market, and thereby obtain 'original design manufacturer' (ODM) or 'original equipment manufacturer' (OEM) orders for new products, by means of its technology foundation based on past experience, efficiency in delivering the design of compatible products, improving its yield rate and entering the mass production stage with the shortest learning curve. A foundry without such technical experience and technology-following capability is unlikely to survive the fierce competition within the semiconductor industry. This is why the foundries in the semiconductor industry need to possess much higher technological capabilities than companies in traditional industries in which technical transitions take place at a much slower pace.

In addition to core competence, both systems companies and foundries need other supplementary capabilities to be able to stand out in harsh market competition. These capabilities include economies of scale in business operation, economies of scope (diversified operation), organisational flexibility, value chain management, network coordination (or intra-industry collaboration) and resource management. These supplementary capabilities can be the deciding factor in the competition between two foundries with similar core competences.

Table 9.5 provides a list of the core competences possessed by systems label companies and foundries. The table does not show the supplementary capabilities, referred to above, which add to a company's competitiveness; this is because rather than belonging to any specific type of company, these supplementary capabilities are applicable to all kinds of (strategy-oriented) semiconductor companies. Companies with such competences will be more competitive in the market, while those that lack them will be relatively less competitive.

Table 9.5   Comparison between the business models and core competences of semiconductor firms

	Core Competences	Business Model		Foundry	
		Vertical Integration	Market-based Disintegration	ODM	OEM
1	Systems Integration	✓	✓	*	-
2	Technical Innovation	✓	✓	*	-
3	Marketing Channels	✓	✓	-	-
4	Consumer Contact	✓	✓	-	-
5	Customer Services	✓	✓	✓	✓
6	Technology Following	-	-	✓	✓
7	Mass Production	✓	-	✓	✓
8	Production Management	✓	-	✓	✓
9	Cost Control	-	-	✓	✓

Note: * Indicates insignificant core competence.

THE STATUS OF THE SEMICONDUCTOR INDUSTRIES IN TAIWAN, SOUTH KOREA AND JAPAN

As discussed in the previous section, Japan, South Korea and Taiwan have all emerged as leading semiconductor manufacturers, following in the wake of the US, with their respective semiconductor industries having each achieved rapid growth, so much so that they are now flourishing. In terms of their size, semiconductor firms in Japan, South Korea and Taiwan now rival the major semiconductor companies in Europe and the US.

Table 9.6 presents a comprehensive league table of the world's top twenty semiconductor manufacturers (by operating revenue) covering the period from 1990 to 2001. The table shows that Samsung (South Korea) rose from tenth place in 1990 to fourth place in 1995, and although the company subsequently experienced some ups and downs, it nevertheless remained in the number four spot in 2001.

In 1995, the other two South Korean semiconductor companies, Hyundai and LG, were respectively, tenth and twelfth; however, following the outbreak of the Asian financial crisis, in 1998 the two companies merged their semiconductor divisions together into Hynix to retain their overall competitiveness. Hynix nevertheless fell to nineteenth position in 2001. As for the Japanese companies, NEC had held the number one slot in 1990, but had fallen to sixth place by 2001.

Table 9.6 Top twenty global semiconductor manufacturers, by operating revenue, 1990-2001*

Unit: US$ millions

Rank	1990	1995	1997	1998	1999	2000	2001
1	NEC (4,145)	Intel (13,172)	Intel (21,660)	Intel (22,784)	Intel (26,806)	Intel (30,298)	Intel (24,927)
2	Toshiba (3,570)	NEC (10,151)	NEC (8,554)	NEC (6,868)	NEC (8,838)	Toshiba (10,864)	Toshiba (6,783)
3	Hitachi (3,205)	Hitachi (8,025)	TI (7,450)	Motorola (5,941)	Toshiba (7,623)	NEC (10,643)	STMicro (6,360)
4	Intel (2,915)	Samsung (8,011)	Motorola (6,270)	TI (5,773)	Samsung (7,125)	Samsung (10,585)	Samsung (6,303)
5	Fujitsu (2,765)	Toshiba (7,951)	Toshiba (5,752)	Samsung (4,481)	TI (7,120)	TI (9,202)	TI (6,060)
6	Motorola (2,750)	TI (7,772)	IBM (5,410)	Toshiba (4,293)	Motorola (6,394)	STMicro (7,890)	NEC (5,389)
7	TI (2,715)	Motorola (7,022)	Samsung (5,100)	Hitachi (3,803)	Hitachi (5,560)	Motorola (7,678)	Motorola (4,828)
8	Mitsubishi (2,035)	Fujitsu (4,935)	Hitachi (5,009)	STMicro (3,638)	Infineon (5,223)	Hitachi (7,286)	Hitachi (4,724)
9	NS (1,611)	Mitsubishi (4,446)	Fujitsu (4,240)	Fujitsu (3,462)	STMicro (5,077)	Infineon (6,732)	Infineon (4,512)
10	Samsung (1,335)	Hyundai (4,132)	Mitsubishi (3,781)	Philips (3,449)	Philips (5,074)	Micron (6,341)	Philips (4,402)
11	-	IBM (3,522)	Philips (3,280)	IBM (3,234)	Hynix (4,830)	Hynix (6,287)	IBM (3,892)
12	-	LG Simicon (2,863)	Siemens (2,610)	Mitsubishi (3,099)	Fujitsu (4,671)	Philips (6,275)	Mitsubishi (3,876)

Table 9.6 (contd.)

Rank	1990	1995	1997	1998	1999	2000	2001
13	-	SGS-Thomson (2,087)	Hyundai (2,550)	Infineon (2,838)	Mitsubishi (4,474)	Mitsubishi (6,270)	Fujitsu (3,786)
14	-	Philips (2,798)	Lucent (2,487)	Lucent (2,778)	Lucent (3,780)	Fujitsu (5,925)	AMD (3,701)
15	-	Matsushita (2,347)	NS (2,365)	AMD (2,543)	IBM (3,520)	Lucent (5,104)	Agere (2,975)
16	-	AMD (2,337)	AMD (2,356)	NS (2,147)	Micron (3,410)	AMD (4,361)	Matsushita (2,804)
17	-	Siemens (2,314)	Matsushita (2,231)	Micron (1,858)	Matsushita (3,220)	IBM (4,328)	Sony (2,570)
18	-	NS (2,236)	LG (2,000)	Hyundai (1,799)	AMD (2,871)	Matsushita (3,992)	Sharp (2,519)
19	-	Sanyo (22) (1,866)	Micron (1,840)	Matsushita (1,709)	Sharp (2,688)	Sony (3,641)	Hynix (2,426)
20	-	Lucent (24) (1,534)		Sanyo (1,629)		Sharp (3,602)	Micron (2,410)
*	Taiwan (558)	Taiwan (4,502)	Taiwan (5,292)	Taiwan (6,146)	Taiwan (8,838)	Taiwan (9,146)	Taiwan (6,512)
	(-)	(9)	(8)	(4)	(2)	(6)	(3)

Note: * The combined operating revenue of all Taiwanese semiconductor companies is provided at the foot of this table for reference (figures in parentheses are the ranking which the Taiwanese semiconductor industry would have if it constituted a single company).

Source: The data in this table were gathered from several editions of the *Yearbook of the Semiconductor Industry.* In cases of conflicting data, the data given in the later edition are used.

With operating revenue far higher than any of its competitors, the US semiconductor company, Intel, became the outright leader in the 1990s, enabling the US to maintain its position as world leader within the semiconductor industry. It should be noted, however, that despite the fact that Taiwanese semiconductor companies tend to be much smaller than the major IDM companies, these firms are doing well. In 1995, in terms of operating revenue, Taiwan's semiconductor industry was ranked ninth in the world, with overall output from the industry reaching approximately US$6.512 billion by 2001, hoisting Taiwan up to the number three position of the world's top twenty semiconductor industries, ahead of European company STMicro (US$6.36 billion) and Samsung (US$6.303 billion).

Looking at the operating revenues of individual companies, in 1997, Taiwan's TSMC achieved operating revenue of US$1.53 billion, placing it twenty-third in the list of global semiconductor companies; however, by 2001, this company's operating revenue had increased to US$3.61 billion, hoisting it into the number fifteen spot in the world.

Unlike South Korea and Japan, where most companies have adopted the IDM business model, in Taiwan, the main emphasis has been on the development of specialist foundries, with TSMC and UMC being the leading players, although there are some (generally small) IDMs. Since the number of different products manufactured by the semiconductor industry is so large, simply adding together the production value of design, IC manufacturing, assembly and testing companies tends to result in the same data being counted twice. The following analysis focuses on the major product segments in order to gain a more accurate picture of the changes which have taken place in recent years in the semiconductor industries of Taiwan, South Korea and Japan.

DRAM

The leaders in the DRAM market in 2001 were Samsung, the US-based Micro (its production capacity increasing dramatically after a merger with the semiconductor division of TI), the South Korean firm Hynix (created as a result of a merger between Hyundai and LG Semiconductor), Infineon (the company created by the spinning off of Siemens' DRAM division) and Elpida, a new company founded as a joint venture by NEC and Hitachi (see Table 9.7).

Four out of the five largest semiconductor companies in the world were involved in major mergers or business reengineering over recent years, thus demonstrating how fierce the competition in the semiconductor industry can be; it also demonstrates the importance of economies of scale, with the leading companies tending to get even bigger. Since DRAM is a standardised product, the lead which a company is able to establish in terms of production capacity and production process technology is crucial with regard to its profitability.

Table 9.7 *Top fifteen global DRAM companies, by sales figures, 1998–2001*

Unit: US$ millions

Company	1998		1999		2000		2001	
	Sales	Ranking	Sales	Ranking	Sales	Ranking	Sales	Ranking
Samsung (South Korea)	2,854	1	4,750	1	6,500	1	3,200	1
Micron (USA)	1,244	4	3,319	3	5,260	3	2,260	2
Hyundai/Hynix (South Korea)[a]	2,627	2	4,212	2	6,000	2	1,716	3
Infineon (Germany)	966	5	1,665	5	2,570	4	1,154	4
NEC/Elpida (Japan)[b]	1,263	3	1,716	4	2,120	5	1,011	5
Nanya (Taiwan)	164	14	320	13	149.7	-	117.4	-
Hitachi (Japan)[b]	894	7	1,080	6	-	-	-	-
Toshiba (Japan)	655	8	933	7	-	-	-	-
Mitsubishi (Japan)	961	6	681	8	-	-	-	-
Fujitsu (Japan)	545	9	551	9	-	-	-	-
Mosel Vitelic (Taiwan)	344	11	495	10	-	-	-	-
TSMC (Taiwan)	272	12	380	11	-	-	-	-
IBM (USA)	385	10	375	12	-	-	-	-
OKI (Japan)	215	13	95	14	-	-	-	-
Alliance (USA)	26	15	40	15	-	-	-	-
PSC (Taiwan)	-	-	-	-	190.4	-	111.6	-
Winbond (Taiwan)	-	-	-	-	238.9	-	480.2	-
Total Sales	14,011	-	20,714	-	-	-	-	-

Notes:
a Hyundai's semiconductor division merged with LG Semiconductor in October 1998 to form a new company, Hynix. The production capacity of the two companies is combined from 1999.
b In December 2000, NEC and Hitachi established Elpida, a joint venture company specialising in DRAM manufacturing; thereafter, the two parent companies gradually withdrew from the DRAM market.

Source: The table is based on a modification of the data provided in Liu (2000) and figures from the *Yearbook of the Semiconductor Industry* (2001; 2002).

Japan emerged, in the 1980s, as a competitive manufacturer of DRAM products and, although it subsequently became the leading player in the global semiconductor industry in 1986, it was nevertheless forced to cede dominance to the US in the 1990s because of changes in the domestic and international environments. Given the rapid fall in the price of DRAM over the two-year period from 1996 to 1997, as well as the difficulties that companies were finding in reducing their production costs, semiconductor firms began to take more aggressive measures to modify their product mix, resulting in investment projects either being scaled down or postponed. Even the Japanese companies, which, in the past, had always insisted on undertaking in-house production, eventually learned their lesson and gradually began to accept the need for outsourcing. NEC held out for some time, but by 1999, even this major company had been forced to start outsourcing DRAM production, and in 2000, the company established a specialist DRAM manufacturer, Elpida, in a joint venture with Hitachi. In 1997, the other four leading Japanese companies (Mitsubishi, Fujitsu, Toshiba and Hitachi) began looking for foundries to take on the role of strategic partners. Most of these partners were Taiwanese companies, although South Korea's LG was also chosen.

Since establishing its dominance in the memory business in 1993, Samsung maintained consistently outstanding performance until 2001, with a global market share in excess of 20 per cent. Even during the Asian financial crisis, and the severe slump in the semiconductor market which followed, Samsung continued to invest in and to develop its R&D capability. These efforts made Samsung the biggest winner when the upturn began, as the price of DRAM began to climb rapidly in 1999. Samsung's strategy in the memory business was based on maintaining technical superiority, delivering new products ahead of schedule, and securing 'first mover' advantage.

The other two leading South Korean semiconductor firms, Hyundai and LG, merged their semiconductor businesses in 1999; prior to this, the two companies had been placed second and fifth, respectively, with a combined market share of over 20 per cent. If one adds in LG's OEM production for Hitachi, the combined market share is actually 22.7 per cent, higher than Samsung's market share of 20 per cent. Adding together the production capacity of Samsung, Hyundai and LG, South Korea's overall share of the global DRAM market was in excess of 42 per cent in the late 1990s.

The visibility of Taiwanese semiconductor companies in the global DRAM market remains low. The leading players in Taiwan, namely TSMC and UMC, are both foundries. Other companies, such as Mosel Vitelic, Nanya and Winbond, positioned themselves mainly as IDMs, developing own-brand (mostly DRAM) products, although they also undertake some contract manufacturing work. These companies were deficient in both economies of scale and economies of scope (narrow technological background and limited R&D competence). As a result, few of them made it into the global top ten in terms of sales.

SRAM

The market leaders in the global SRAM market include Samsung, NEC, IBM, Hyundai, Motorola, Mitsubishi, Hitachi, Toshiba and Fujitsu. However, Samsung remained the world's largest SRAM supplier in 1998, with an operating revenue growth rate of 13.3 per cent and a market share of 15.7 per cent. Two other leading players, NEC and IBM, achieved operating revenue growth rates of 15.5 per cent and 6.1 per cent respectively, putting them in second and third place. Hitachi has begun to focus on microcontroller and 'system on a chip' (SoC) products, gradually withdrawing from the memory market, and thereby causing it to fall back in the rankings. Other leading Japanese and US manufacturers, such as Mitsubishi and Motorola, also experienced a decline in revenue as they became confronted with fierce competition in the telecommunications and DRAM industries. Taiwanese companies producing Flash memory include Winbond and Macronix, the latter being particularly competitive in Flash and Mask ROM, having achieved a global market share of more than 50 per cent in Mask ROM in 2001, and thus making it the worldwide leader in this field.

Microcontrollers

The current market leader in microcontrollers is Intel, which has maintained a market share in excess of 80 per cent for many years. Other US companies that have been in the industry for a long time, which include IBM, NS, TI and Motorola, have also maintained steady output. IBM focuses on workstations whilst Motorola has been concentrating on Power PC chips for iMac. New entrants include AMD (IDM) and VIA Technologies (fabless). There are very few Japanese and Korean companies in this industry segment for two reasons. Firstly, this is a highly competitive industry requiring very high (cutting-edge) technology. Secondly and most importantly, the right environment is needed for the development of an appropriate division of labour.

Only VIA Technologies has entered this market in Taiwan, having acquired Cyrix X86 microprocessor division from NS in June 1999 at a cost of NT$5.5 billion (US$167 million). Two months later, VIA announced that it had purchased Centaur, IDT's microprocessor division, and had thus acquired all of IDT's Winchip CPU patents and the X86 design team. In the latter half of the 1990s, Cyrix and IDT were behind only Intel and AMD, as the third largest players in the global CPU industry; thus, having obtained CPU-related technologies from Cyrix and IDT through these takeovers, VIA had acquired the necessary tools to compete with Intel in terms of product performance. At the very least, VIA is now confident of being able to penetrate the market for CPUs for low-price PCs, as it is now outsourcing production to low-cost foundries. The company will, in all likelihood, be able to maintain high growth if it can secure the share of the market formerly held by Cyrix and IDT.

IC fabrication

The leaders in the Taiwanese semiconductor industry are, without doubt, TSMC and UMC, both of which are pure-play foundries. These two companies have benefited from many contract manufacturing opportunities created by the competition between leading players in the US, Japan and South Korea. The sales figures for both TSMC and UMC grew rapidly in the 1990s, and the two companies have maintained an excellent track record in terms of operating revenue and profit margins for many years. TSMC and UMC combined currently hold a foundry market share in excess of 70 per cent. Chartered Semiconductor Manufacturing Pte. Ltd. of Singapore, and Anam Semiconductor of South Korea, are currently in third and fourth place, followed by the German company X-Fab (see Table 9.8).

Table 9.8   Top five global IC foundries, by output value

Unit: US$ million

Rank	Company Name	Output Value 2001	Output Value 2002 *	Growth Rate (%)
1	TSMC (Taiwan)	3,705	4,900	24.4
2	UMC (Taiwan)	1,898	2,185	13.1
3	Chartered Semiconductor (Singapore)	490	463	6.0
4	Anam Semiconductor (South Korea)	181	225	19.6
5	X-Fab Semiconductor Foundries (Germany)	93	125	25.60

Note: * Figures here are estimated.

Source: IC Insights (2002).

Initially, foundry players relied mainly on fabless firms for their orders, for two reasons. Firstly, the technical competence of the foundries had not achieved a level high enough to meet the exacting requirements of the IDMs. Secondly, at that time the IDMs could still afford to invest in fab construction; thus, if they needed to increase their production capacity, they could do so by simply expanding their own fabs. However, as the IDMs found it difficult to afford investment in fabs due to increasing costs, the need to outsource production capacity emerged. Another factor was that the foundries' production process technology had gradually caught up with the IDMs' and SIAs' roadmap timetable. Sometimes the foundries even moved ahead of these companies' schedules. For example, when the foundries established a lead over the IDMs in the 0.18 μm production process in 1999, this created a situation whereby the foundries could undertake OEM production on behalf of the IDMs. It is thus anticipated that more and more IDMs will start to outsource IC fabrication due to the emergence of a specialist division of labour and the frequent generation shifts in semiconductor products. Under such conditions, foundries will become the major owners of manufacturing production capacity in the semiconductor industry.

IC design

Specialist IC design houses began to emerge in the early 1990s. At that time the key to success lay in innovative capability. The barriers to entry were low, and most of the IC design firms' products focused on niche markets in which the range of applications is extremely broad. In order to survive, the IC design houses had to keep their finger on the pulse of changes in demand; they had to be able to design products that the market would accept, using their own technology, as rapidly as possible. As Table 9.9 shows, the leaders in this business over the past ten years have been the US (with 11 out of 15) and Canadian (with 2 out of 15) design houses. It should be noted that the rankings of Taiwanese companies such as VIA and Mediatek rose rapidly in 2000. VIA went from thirteenth place in 1998 to fourth place in 2001, whilst Mediatek rose from thirteenth place in 2000 to eighth place in 2001. More growth is expected for these two companies since their revenue growth has been far higher than that of other design houses.

There are several reasons for the rise of Taiwanese IC design houses. Taiwanese firms have been very successful at spotting new trends in product design, whilst another key factor is Taiwan's position as the world's largest IC foundry industry. The IC foundry industry supported the IC design houses, at least in the early stage of development, with an adequate supply of production capacity. Japanese and South Korean players, on the other hand, have tended to focus on IDM, so their local IC design industry is not as highly developed as the industry in Taiwan.

The foregoing analysis of the state of competition between the semiconductor industries of Taiwan, South Korea and Japan provides a number of very clear characteristics, as follows: (i) The semiconductor companies in South Korea and Japan have stuck with the IDM business model, whereas IC foundry is the dominant business model in Taiwan, although Taiwan does have a few IDMs. (ii) Within the DRAM market, South Korea has become the dominant force, overtaking Japan, and this situation is unlikely to change in the near future. Whilst the Japanese players

Table 9.9 *Top fifteen IC design houses, by operating revenue, 1998–2001*

Company	1998 US$bn	Rank	1999 US$bn	Rank	2000 US$bn	Rank	2001 US$bn	Rank	Growth rate (%)
Qualcomm (US)	639	2	774	3	1,080	4	1,240	1	14
Nvidia (US)	147	-	374	7	699	7	1,210	2	73
Xilinx (US)	630	3	899	1	1,560	1	1,150	3	-26
VIA (Taiwan)	179	13	371	8	909	5	1,010	4	11
Broadcom (US)	203	10	512	6	1,100	3	962	5	-12
Alterra (US)	653	1	836	2	1,380	2	839	6	-39
Cirrus Logic (US)	511	4	531	4	729	6	534	7	-27
ATI Technologies (Canada)	447	5	527	5	630	11	520	8	-8
MediaTek (Taiwan)	-	-	-	-	411	13	447	9	9
Qlogic (US)	-	-	-	-	362	14	357	10	-1
PMC-Sierra (Canada)	161	14	211	12	695	8	323	11	-54
SanDisk (US)	-	-	-	-	602	9	317	12	-47
Lattice (US)	206	9	323	10	568	10	295	13	-48
ESS Technology (US)	239	6	310	11	303	16	271	14	-11
GlobeSpan (US)	-	-	-	-	348	15	270	15	-22
fabless Total	8,850		11,900		16,930		12,890		-24

Source: IC Insights (2002).

have gradually begun to withdraw from the market, the Taiwanese DRAM manufacturers should be able to stay in business, albeit on a relatively small scale, thanks to technology licensing from major European and US IDMs. (iii) The major IDM companies in Europe, the US and Japan have started to show more and more interest in outsourcing production to the Taiwanese foundries. Under pressure to reduce production costs, and unwilling to shoulder the huge financial burden of investing in new production facilities, the trend for these companies to outsource IC fabrication to the Taiwanese foundries will continue; therefore, the supremacy of the Taiwanese foundries is unlikely to be challenged in the near future. (iv) For the most part, the microcontroller business is still dominated by US firms; Taiwanese, South Korean and Japanese players have found it difficult to penetrate this market. Taiwan's VIA recently attempted to move into this market by way of acquisitions, but it remains to be seen whether VIA will be able to exploit, to maximum effect, the technologies and the market obtained through these acquisitions. (v) Taiwanese IC design houses have established a strong position in the global market thanks to the support provided by the local IC foundry industry. By contrast, South Korea and Japan have yet to develop world-class IC design houses owing to the absence of a developed foundry sector in these two countries.

The above analysis is based mainly on observations of the changes which have taken place in the semiconductor industry. The next section will consider the future development of the semiconductor industry in Taiwan, South Korea and Japan through analysis of the patent output of these economies, in terms of both quantity and quality.

US SEMICONDUCTOR-RELATED PATENTS GRANTED TO TAIWAN, SOUTH KOREA AND JAPAN

Patent analysis, which comprises of two parts, namely quantitative and qualitative analysis, is often used as an index of industrial or corporate technical competence. Quantitative analysis is based on the quantity of patents, and is used to evaluate the status of technology-based activities in an individual business, industry or country, whilst qualitative analysis focuses on whether a patent is important (or a key element) in the field in question. The higher the number of citations which a patent receives, the more likely it is that the patent is a key patent in that industry.

The quantitative statistics in this chapter are taken from data provided by the USPTO, whilst the qualitative analysis is based on data from the 'patent citations data files' from the National Bureau of Economic Research (NBER). The database covers US patents granted between 1963 and 1999, with three million data entries having been recorded, dated between 1975 and 1999, and sixteen million citations being recorded on this database. Here, we provide an in-depth analysis of the contents of semiconductor patents obtained by Taiwan, South Korea and Japan.

The technological orientation and patent mapping of the semiconductor industries within these economies are also compared and discussed to analyse the differences in techniques within these different semiconductor industries. Thus, the aim here is to discuss three main issues, country-based quantitative patent analysis, country-based patent citation analysis and country- based technical orientation analysis. By exploring these issues, we seek to examine the patent mapping of semiconductor-related technologies in Taiwan, South Korea and Japan.

USPTO Classification for the Semiconductor Industry

All patents from the USPTO are classified into six category codes within the NBER. These codes are as follows:

1. Chemical;
2. Computers and communications;
3. Drugs and medical;
4. Electrical and electronic;
5. Mechanical; and
6. Others.

Each category code is further subdivided, providing between four and nine subcategories. Eight technology-based classes relating to the semiconductor industry were selected for analysis in accordance with the NBER category codes and USPTO classification.

As shown in Table 9.10, these categories comprise of two NBER subcategory codes. The first of these is subcategory code number 46 'Semiconductor Devices', which comprises of 'Semiconductor Device Manufacturing: Processes' (USPTO Class 438), 'Active Solid-State Devices' (USPTO Class 257), 'Electronic Digital Logic Circuitry' (USPTO Class 326) and 'Superconductor Technology: Apparatus, Materials and Process' (USPTO Class 505).

The second main NBER subcategory code is number 24 'Information Storage', which includes 'Dynamic Magnetic Information Storage or Retrieval' (USPTO Class 360), 'Static Information Storage or Retrieval' (USPTO Class 365), 'Dynamic Information Storage or Retrieval' (USPTO Class 369) and 'Electrical Computers and Digital Process Systems: Memory' (USPTO Class 711).

Table 9.10   Semiconductor-related category codes and US patent classification

NBER Category Code and Title	NBER Sub-category Code and Title	USPTO Class. No.	US Patent Title
		360	Dynamic Magnetic Information Storage or Retrieval
2	24	365	Static Information Storage or Retrieval
Computers and Communications	Information Storage	369	Dynamic Information Storage or Retrieval
		711	Electrical Computers and Digital Processing Systems: Memory
		257	Active Solid-State Devices (e.g. transistors, solid-state diodes)
4	46	326	Electronic Digital Logic Circuitry
Electrical and Electronic	Semiconductor Devices	438	Semiconductor Device Manufacturing: Processes
		505	Superconductor Technology: Apparatus, Materials and Processes

Source: USPTO (http://www.uspto.gov).

Although the eight categories do not fully cover all important businesses throughout the upstream, midstream and downstream segments of the semiconductor industry, the analysis here should at least provide useful information regarding key issues in the semiconductor industry, namely manufacturing processes, devices, circuitry and memory.

Country-based Quantitative Patent Analysis and Comparison

Table 9.11 reproduces the USPTO's official statistics on the total number of US patents obtained between 1997 and 2000 by Taiwan, South Korea, Japan and the US itself. As the table shows, Taiwan performed extremely well in the category of 'Semiconductor Device Manufacturing: Processes' (Class 438), with 3,343 US patent applications from Taiwan having been successful between 1997 and 2001. This amounted to 19.05 per cent of the total number of successful patent applications approved by the USPTO during that period. Over the same period, Japan succeeded in obtaining a total of 3,874 US patents (22.08 per cent), whilst South Korea obtained only 1,512 (8.62 per cent). The US itself achieved an enormous number of successful patent applications, a total of 7,604 (43.34 per cent).

Table 9.11 Semiconductor and IT patents granted to the US, Japan, Taiwan and South Korea, 1997-2001

NBER Category Code	USPTO Class No.	Contents	US	Japan	Taiwan	South Korea	Total
	257	Active Solid-State Devices (transistors and solid-state diodes)	4,919 (39.91)	4,932 (40.06)	756 (6.14)	672 (5.46)	12,313 (100.00)
46 Semiconductor Devices	326	Electronic Digital Logic Circuitry	1,402 (66.73)	395 (18.80)	40 (1.90)	72 (3.43)	2,101 (100.00)
	438	Semiconductor Device Manufacturing: Processes	7,604 (43.34)	3,874 (22.08)	3,343 (19.05)	1,512 (8.62)	17,544 (100.00)
	505	Superconductor Technology: Apparatus, Material, Processes	203 (48.68)	145 (34.77)	- (0.00)	6 (1.44)	417 (100.00)
Subtotal			14,123 (43.62)	9,346 (28.87)	4,139 (12.78)	2,262 (6.99)	32,375 (100.00)
	360	Dynamic Magnetic Information Storage or Retrieval	2,558 (47.91)	2,194 (41.09)	8 (0.15)	316 (5.92)	5,339 (100.00)
24 Information Storage and Retrieval	365	Static Information Storage or Retrieval	3,444 (41.63)	2,922 (35.32)	245 (2.96)	968 (11.70)	8,237 (100.00)
	369	Dynamic Information Storage or Retrieval	693 (14.84)	3,302 (70.69)	56 (1.20)	361 (7.73)	4,671 (100.00)
	711	Electrical Computers and Digital Processing Systems: Memory	3,040 (72.90)	731 (17.53)	43 (1.03)	54 (1.29)	4,170 (100.00)
Subtotal			9,735 (43.36)	9,149 (40.75)	352 (1.57)	1,699 (7.57)	22,453 (100.00)
Total			23,858	18,495	4,491	3,961	54,828

Note: Figures in parentheses are the percentage of total US patents.

Source: Adapted from information from the USPTO website (http://www.uspto.gov).

211

In recent years, Taiwan has actually achieved the most impressive performance in patent applications under the category of 'Semiconductor Device Manufacturing: Processes'. Taiwan also showed itself to be slightly more competent than South Korea in the area of 'Active Solid-State Devices' (Class 257), a technology closely related to IC design. In this area, Taiwan obtained 756 US patents (6.14 per cent) whilst South Korea achieved 672 patents (5.46 per cent). However, they were well behind both Japan (4,932 patents) and the US (4,919 patents); generally speaking, Japan and the US have dominated almost all the eight areas of semiconductor core and peripheral technologies; indeed, Taiwan and South Korea are only just starting to make their mark in the area of semiconductor patents. It can be seen from Table 9.11 that Taiwan's performance in patent applications has not been very impressive, except in the areas of 'Semiconductor Device Manufacturing: Process' and 'Active Solid-State Devices'. Taiwan has actually achieved very few patents in memory, dynamic and static information storage or retrieval, and electronic digital logic circuitry. As a result, the patents filed by Taiwan have achieved only around 2.0 per cent of the total patents approved by the USPTO.

By contrast, South Korea has displayed much more impressive performance in these peripheral technologies. For example, South Korea achieved 7.57 per cent of the total US patents relating to memory, 11.7 per cent of patents relating to 'Static Information Storage or Retrieval' (365), and 7.73 per cent of patents relating to 'Dynamic Information Storage or Retrieval' (369). Indeed, it seems that in terms of the breadth of its independently-developed semiconductor technology, South Korea has now succeeded in surpassing Taiwan.

Country-based Citation Analysis and Comparison

In addition to the number of patents, in this chapter we also wish to place significant emphasis on the quality of the patents. We therefore use 'citations received' as a basic index of patent quality. A patent's theoretical or practical value is generally recognised as coming under one of two situations. The first possibility is that the players in the industry start to pay attention to the patent soon after it is obtained. The second is that the patent is cited in the followers' R&D process, either as an intriguing factor in their R&D, or as a footnote in their results. The number of citations received also indicates whether the patent belongs to the growth-type technologies attracting the most R&D attention within the industry.

Table 9.12 provides comprehensive details of the citations received by Taiwan, South Korea and Japan in the eight semiconductor-related categories, including core and peripheral technologies.

*Table 9.12   Country-based analysis of citations received in the eight
categories relating to semiconductors*

Country	USPTO Class. No.	Total No. of Patents Approved [1]	Total No. of Patents Obtained [2]	Total No. of Citations of Obtained Patents [2]	Average No. of Citations per Patent Obtained
Japan	257	4,932	5,788	12,799	2.211
	326	395	584	1,074	1.839
	438	3,874	2,885	5,935	2.057
	505	145	-	-	-
	360	2,194	2,567	3,664	1.427
	365	2,922	2,934	6,499	2.208
	369	3,302	3,254	6,067	1.864
	711	731	553	1,016	1.837
Total		18,495	18,565	37,054	1.995
Taiwan	257	756	1,008	1,802	1.788
	326	40	71	96	1.352
	438	3,343	2,751	7,269	2.642
	505	-	-	-	-
	360	8	14	14	1.000
	365	245	271	404	1.491
	369	56	55	62	1.127
	711	43	39	49	1.256
Total		4,491	4,209	9,696	2.304
South Korea	257	672	356	1,467	4.121
	326	72	132	248	1.879
	438	1,512	1,183	2,468	2.086
	505	6	-	-	-
	360	316	386	422	1.093
	365	968	923	1,755	1.901
	369	361	369	560	1.518
	711	54	46	56	1.217
Total		3,961	3,395	6,976	2.055

Sources: Data adapted from (1) USPTO datasheet; and (2) NBER database.

As Table 9.12 shows, within Class 438, 'Semiconductor Device Manufacturing: Process', Taiwan received the highest citation rate, at 2.642, whilst South Korea achieved 2.086, similar to Japan's citation rate of 2.057. This may indicate that Taiwan's semiconductor manufacturing processes have reached world-class standard and that they are also starting to attract considerable attention from companies in other countries; hence researchers in other countries are now often citing these patents when releasing their own R&D results.

However, apart from Class 438, Taiwan obtained very few patents in other semiconductor peripheral technologies and also had very low citation rates (mostly <1.5). As for the citation rates achieved in the same fields by Japan and South Korea, Japan had a higher citation rate in Class 257 'Active Solid-State Devices' (2.211) and Class 365 'Static Magnetic Information Storage and Retrieval' (2.208), whilst South Korea received more citations in Class 257 'Active Solid-State Devices' (4.121), as well as in Class 438 'Semiconductor Device Manufacturing: Processes' (2.086).

Country-based Technical Orientation Analysis

Observation of the technical development of the world's semiconductor industry shows that product applications always lead the development of industrial technology. For example, the increasing demand in recent years for high frequency, high-speed or mixed-signal chips (telecommunications chips, multimedia, and so on) has not only contributed to the emphasis on 'bipolar complementary metal oxide semiconductor' (Bi-CMOS), but also to the renewed emphasis on 'gallium arsenide' (GaAs) semiconductors, which had long been neglected. The future technical development of the semiconductor industry will thus continue to depend on the trends in commercial microelectronic applications with respect to density, speed, power and cost. The CMOS application product market, for example, which accounts for at least 75 per cent of the output value of global semiconductor design and manufacturing, demands continuous improvements in chip performance, including faster computing, higher density, and the need to integrate analogue and digital signals on a signal chip with SoC products. In CMOS technology the main emphasis is currently on the following aspects: (i) developing high-k materials for the gate insulating layer; (ii) the need to effectively reduce the resistance of metallic gate contact materials; (iii) ways of controlling the yield rate, stability and reliability of the products in the copper conductor manufacturing process; and (iv) seeking lower k materials for the insulating layers between the metal conductors. Since these four aspects constitute the main agenda in the development of CMOS process technology, we therefore treat these areas as key issues for exploration when comparing the patented process technologies within the semiconductor industries of Taiwan, South Korea and Japan.

In line with these principles, a keyword-based approach is used to represent the latest trends in technical development in the semiconductor industry. These keywords include: (i) basic IC manufacturing processes, including steps such as 'oxide formation', 'diffusion ion implantation', 'deposition', 'etching' and 'photolithography'; (ii) cutting-edge technologies, including 'low-k substrates', 'high-k substrates', 'copper', 'nano technology',

'Bi-CMOS', 'GaAs', 'system on insulator' (SOI), 'strained silicon' and 'SoC'; and (iii) product applications, including 'DRAM', 'high-density DRAM', 'SRAM', 'flash memory', 'erasable programmable read-only memory' (EPROM), 'electrically-erasable programmable read-only memory' (EEPROM), 'cache memory', 'thin-film transistor' (TFT), 'digital signal processing' (DSP) devices, 'micro-processing units' (MPUs), 'detectors' and 'microcontrollers'. These three groups of keywords, which represent the major areas of focus for R&D in the semiconductor industries in Taiwan, South Korea and Japan, are used in this section for a convergence search (this also requires human reading of the abstract of each patent found). The purpose of this approach is to gain an understanding of the actual contents of the US patented technologies obtained by the three economies.

Tables 9.13 to 9.15 list the collated results of the computer search as well as the human correction. The search results for Group 1, 'Semiconductor Device Manufacturing: Process', show that Taiwan outperformed Japan and South Korea to a significant extent in Class 438 'Semiconductor Device Manufacturing: Process'. Although it fell behind Japan in Class 257, relating to semiconductor material and design, Taiwan did do better than South Korea in this category. In Group 2, 'Cutting-Edge Technologies', Taiwan took the lead in the quantity of patents relating to 'next generation processes' such as low-k substrates and copper; however, Taiwan was behind both Japan and South Korea in terms of technologies relating to DRAM, such as high-k substrates.

Another significant point is that Japan and South Korea were dominant in those patents relating to the use of GaAS in high-frequency communication because hardly any Taiwanese companies have undertaken research into this area. In SOI (relating to deep submicron), Japan was the dominant force, surpassing both Taiwan and South Korea by quite a considerable margin. Finally in product applications, Japan has been striving to develop DRAM, SRAM, flash memory, EEPROM, TFT, detectors and microcontroller technology, whilst Taiwan's efforts have centred on DRAM, SRAM and flash memory. South Korea was strong in research on DRAM, TFT, flash memory, detectors and microcontroller technology.

The findings of the analysis of patents obtained by Taiwan, South Korea and Japan can be summarised as follows. With regard to the quantity of patents obtained relating to semiconductor device manufacturing, Taiwan could only keep up with Japan in 'Semiconductor Device Manufacturing: Process' (Class 438); indeed, it lagged behind Japan, by a considerable margin, in all other categories. The second largest group of patents obtained by Taiwan was in the active solid-state devices category (Class 257), although the number of patents was about the same as the number obtained by South Korea. Taiwan was beaten by South Korea in the remaining six categories.

Table 9.13 US 'semiconductor device manufacturing: process' patents obtained by Japan, Taiwan and South Korea, 1997-2001

Class No.		Semiconductor Device Manufacturing: Process					
		Oxide	Diffusion	Ion Implantation	Deposition	Etching	Photolithography
257	Japan	361	235	39	28	95	12
	Taiwan	202	28	2	19	25	4
	South Korea	65	23	2	5	14	1
326	Japan	12	2	3	-	-	-
	Taiwan	8	-	1	-	-	-
	South Korea	1	-	-	-	-	-
438	Japan	403	136	9	70	199	11
	Taiwan	826	65	4	138	293	24
	South Korea	183	47	2	62	95	4
360	Japan	17	6	-	4	18	-
	Taiwan	-	-	-	1	-	-
	South Korea	-	-	-	-	-	-
365	Japan	27	18	-	-	7	-
	Taiwan	20	1	3	-	2	2
	South Korea	11	1	3	2	2	-
369	Japan	3	5	-	-	-	-
	Taiwan	-	-	-	-	-	2
	South Korea	-	-	-	-	-	-
711	Japan	-	-	-	-	9	-
	Taiwan	-	-	-	-	1	2
	South Korea	-	-	-	-	-	-
Totals	Japan	823	402	57	104	328	23
	Taiwan	1,056	94	8	157	321	28
	South Korea	260	71	7	68	113	7

Table 9.14 US 'technical features' patents obtained by Japan, Taiwan and South Korea, 1997–2001

Class No.		Technical Features								
		Low-k substrates	High-k substrates	Copper	Nano	BiCMOS	GaAs	SOI	Strained Silicon	SoC
257	Japan	13	28	15	9	43	97	37	22	11
	Taiwan	6	2	12	–	38	19	11	2	2
	South Korea	3	12	11	1	21	4	7	–	6
326	Japan	–	2	–	–	64	1	6	–	–
	Taiwan	–	–	–	–	22	–	–	–	1
	South Korea	–	–	–	–	17	–	–	–	–
438	Japan	7	25	29	3	51	20	68	2	1
	Taiwan	29	18	65	3	88	1	17	2	8
	South Korea	7	24	9	4	24	8	12	1	1
360	Japan	–	–	4	–	–	–	–	4	–
	Taiwan	–	–	–	–	–	–	–	1	1
	South Korea	–	–	1	–	–	–	–	–	–
365	Japan	–	–	–	–	33	1	5	2	1
	Taiwan	–	–	–	–	3	–	–	–	4
	South Korea	–	–	–	2	3	–	–	–	12
369	Japan	–	–	–	1	–	20	–	1	–
	Taiwan	–	–	–	–	–	–	–	–	–
	South Korea	–	–	–	–	–	–	–	–	–
711	Japan	–	–	–	–	–	–	–	–	–
	Taiwan	–	–	–	–	–	–	–	–	2
	South Korea	–	–	–	–	–	–	–	–	2
Totals	Japan	20	55	48	13	191	139	116	31	13
	Taiwan	35	20	77	3	151	20	28	4	17
	South Korea	10	36	21	7	65	12	19	2	22

217

Table 9.15 US 'product application' patents obtained by Japan, Taiwan and South Korea, 1997-2001

Class No.		DRAM	High Density DRAM	SRAM	Flash Memory	EPROM	EEPROM	Cache Memory	TFT	DSP device	MPU	Detector	Micro controller
257	Japan	69	-	51	19	-	5	-	244	20	-	52	6
	Taiwan	92	2	34	51	3	19	-	19	-	-	5	-
	South Korea	24	-	23	19	-	13	-	110	-	-	10	-
326	Japan	9	-	-	3	-	-	-	3	-	-	4	-
	Taiwan	2	-	2	-	-	-	-	-	-	-	3	-
	South Korea	1	-	-	-	-	-	-	-	-	-	7	-
438	Japan	55	1	18	12	7	10	-	143	-	-	9	-
	Taiwan	439	25	50	119	14	36	-	29	-	-	3	-
	South Korea	176	-	19	17	-	17	-	71	-	-	1	-
360	Japan	-	-	-	2	1	5	6	-	1	2	69	93
	Taiwan	-	-	-	-	-	-	-	-	-	-	1	-
	South Korea	-	-	-	-	-	-	-	-	1	4	26	27
365	Japan	288	-	70	117	4	78	50	4	-	1	29	120
	Taiwan	19	-	19	38	11	25	4	-	-	-	3	6
	South Korea	77	-	18	71	3	19	6	-	-	-	31	86
369	Japan	-	-	-	-	-	-	2	-	1	-	83	57
	Taiwan	-	-	-	-	-	-	-	-	-	-	3	7
	South Korea	-	-	-	-	-	-	-	-	1	-	79	28
711	Japan	19	-	3	-	-	-	151	-	1	3	-	85
	Taiwan	1	-	1	-	-	-	-	-	-	-	-	10
	South Korea	3	-	-	-	-	-	36	-	-	-	-	6
Totals	Japan	440	1	142	153	12	98	209	394	23	6	246	361
	Taiwan	553	27	106	208	28	80	4	48	-	-	18	23
	South Korea	281	-	60	107	3	49	42	181	2	4	154	147

218

The quantitative analysis thus implies that Taiwan has reached a world-class standard only in those technologies relating to semiconductor manufacturing processes, whilst remaining below world-class standard in all other categories.

Taiwanese players were almost invisible in the NBER subcategory 24, whilst South Korea achieved a considerable number of patents in this field. This indicates that South Korea has significant technical strength in the field of semiconductor storage, such as DRAM. Looking at the number of citations, Taiwan received more than either Japan or South Korea in the area of 'Semiconductor Device Manufacturing: Process' (Class 438), which indicates that in terms of both the quantity and quality of patents, individual Taiwanese companies, and the Taiwanese semiconductor industry as a whole, have achieved impressive performance in this area; this is clearly a field in which Taiwan possesses world-class technology.

In 'Active Solid-State Devices' (Class 257), even though the quantity of patents granted to Taiwan was more or less the same as that for South Korea, Taiwan had a much lower citation rate than South Korea, 1.79 as opposed to 4.12. One interpretation of this could be that, in terms of their technical value, the patents obtained by the Taiwanese companies were less important than those obtained by South Korean firms. In the other categories, the patents granted to Taiwanese companies were rather unsatisfactory.

Regarding technical orientation by country, it is clear that in terms of next generation manufacturing-related technologies such as low-k substrates and copper, Taiwan has obtained a much larger number of patents than its Japanese and South Korean competitors; however, both Japan and South Korea surpassed Taiwan in high-k substrates and DRAM manufacturing processes. There is almost no Taiwan-based research on the use of GaAs in high frequency communications; indeed, this field continues to be dominated by Japanese and Korean companies. In SOI, which is related to deep submicron production, Japan was the leader with far more expertise than either Taiwan or South Korea. In addition, both Japan and South Korea have been engaged in a considerable amount of work in areas such as cache memory, TFT, detectors and microcontrollers, areas in which Taiwan lags well behind.

The above analysis shows that Taiwan's processing technology is superior to that of the other countries examined, both in quantitative and qualitative terms; Taiwan is thus a world leader in semiconductor production process technology. However, although Taiwan led the field in 'Semiconductor Device Manufacturing: Process', it was well behind both Japan and South Korea in terms of IC design, DRAM, communication IC and deep submicron, thus revealing the somewhat limited scope of Taiwan's semiconductor industry.

THE CORE COMPETENCES AND COMPETITIVENESS OF THE SEMICONDUCTOR INDUSTRIES

This section compares industrial development and technical intensity in Taiwan, South Korea and Japan based on the development status of their respective semiconductor industries, as well as the number and quality of US patents obtained by them (see Table 9.16). It then goes on to provide a forecast of the future development of the semiconductor industries under examination here. The findings are summarised below.

With regard to the process of industrial development, the main business model in both Japan and South Korea is IDM, whereas in Taiwan, IC foundry is the dominant business model. This situation is reflected in the classes of patents granted to the respective semiconductor industries of the three economies. The patents obtained by Japanese and South Korean companies covered a wide range of technologies, including cache memory, TFT, detectors and microcontrollers. By contrast, Taiwan's competence lay only in 'Semiconductor Device Manufacturing: Process' (Class 438) and 'Active Solid-State Devices' (Class 257); Taiwan remained at the lower levels in all other classes.

As regards the level of development achieved by the semiconductor industry, Taiwan's IC foundries have a 70 per cent share of the global market, with the patents obtained by Taiwanese companies also reflecting this dominance in the foundry business where Taiwan achieved roughly the same number of production process patents as Japan, but far more than South Korea. Taiwan also had a much higher citation rate than the other two countries, suggesting that Taiwan's semiconductor processing technology has surpassed that of both Japan and South Korea, thus making Taiwan a world leader in this field. We can therefore say with some confidence that Taiwan's IC foundry industry will be able to maintain its dominance for many years to come. Nevertheless, despite Taiwan's superior performance, the patent analysis also shows that Japanese and South Korean players have paid special attention to process design and materials selection, a field in which Taiwan has fallen slightly behind these two competitors.

Japan and South Korea are still the dominant forces in the SRAM industry. As compared with these two countries, Taiwan has a much lower SRAM output value. This finding is in keeping with the data relating to the number of patents granted to the three economies; in other words, both Japan and South Korea had a much greater number of SRAM-related patents than Taiwan. US companies continue to enjoy near-total dominance of the microcontroller industry, although Taiwanese company, VIA, has attempted to penetrate the market by way of a merger. As might be expected, Taiwan has secured few patents in this particular field.

Table 9.16 Comparison of industry development and patent performance in the semiconductor industries of Taiwan, South Korea and Japan

Results of Patent Analysis	Observation of Industry Development					
	IDMs	IC Foundry	DRAM	SRAM	Microcontroller	IC Design
	Japan and S. Korea focus on IDM, with similar product development and product selection. IC foundry operation is the dominant business model in Taiwan.	Taiwan's IC foundry industry has a global market share of over 70%.	S. Korea is the dominant player in DRAM. Japan has withdrawn from the market, and Taiwanese firms are finding it difficult to stay in business.	Japan and S. Korea dominate the SRAM industry.	US players hold the lion's share of the Microcontroller market; Taiwan has tried to develop this market through merger.	Taiwan has achieved a certain degree of visibility in IC design. Japan and S. Korea have not established the necessary industry environment.
Japan's and S. Korea's patent applications covered a wide range of disciplines. Taiwan was competent in only 'Semiconductor Device Manufacturing: Processes' (Class 438) and 'Active Solid-State Devices' (Class 257).	Very consistent	Very consistent	(Irrelevant)	Very consistent	(Irrelevant)	The result suggests that Taiwan's IC design industry was supported by local IC fabrication; patented technology is not of great significance.
In 'Semiconductor Device Manufacturing: Processes' (Class 438), Taiwan had a similar number of patents to Japan. Taiwan had far more patents than S. Korea.	Very consistent	Very consistent. This shows that Taiwan is a world leader in IC fabrication, outperforming Japan and S. Korea.	(Irrelevant)	(Irrelevant)		

Table 9.16 (contd.)

Results of Patent Analysis	Observation of Industry Development					
	IDMs	IC Foundry	DRAM	SRAM	Microcontroller	IC Design
Japan achieved far more patents for Active Solid-State Devices relating to semiconductor material and design (Class 257) than either S. Korea or Taiwan. Patent quality in Class 257 was much higher for S. Korea than Taiwan.	Very consistent; showing that Taiwan's focus is on IC fabrication whilst Japan and S. Korea have focused on design and materials development.	Consistent. However, Taiwan has focused only on production process technology, and is less competent than either Japan or S. Korea in new materials selection.	Not consistent. Although Japan obtained a substantial number of DRAM patents, it has failed to perform well in terms of output value.	Very consistent	(Irrelevant)	-
Taiwan obtained more patents than Japan or South Korea in DRAM, Flash Memory and EEPROM.	Consistent; indicating that there is a high level of concentration in Taiwan's product mix.	Not very consistent, showing that, although Taiwan put more effort into DRAM and Flash Memory than Japan or S. Korea, its output value in these areas was less than the other two countries.	Not very consistent, showing that, although Taiwan has put considerable effort into DRAM technology, it failed to perform well in output value.	(Irrelevant)	Consistent; reflecting Taiwan's attempts to develop the Microcontroller market through acquisitions rather than technical competence.	-
Japan and South Korea have put a great deal of effort into Cache Memory, Detector, Microcontroller and TFT technology; Taiwan lags behind in these areas.	Very consistent	Very consistent	(Irrelevant)	(Irrelevant)	Not consistent. Despite the large number of patents obtained by Japan and S. Korea, they have failed to secure a niche in this area.	-

All three of the economies examined had very few patents in IC design. The poor showing in this area by both Japan and South Korea is easy to understand because neither country has any IC design industry to speak of; however, Taiwan has also failed to secure many patents in this area, despite the relatively high global visibility of Taiwan's IC design industry. This may indicate that the IC design industry in Taiwan is a 'sub-industry' supported by the highly-developed IC foundry industry.

Whilst the above discussion demonstrates considerable consistency in many aspects of the findings, there are still some inconsistencies. First of all, although Taiwan has secured far more DRAM patents than either Japan or South Korea, the island's DRAM output value is much lower than that of South Korea. Secondly, despite having put considerable effort into R&D in the field of DRAM, and having secured more patents than South Korea, Japan has nevertheless now withdrawn from the DRAM market; this may indicate that technology does not determine the outcome of competition in this market; i.e., technology is no longer a major determinant. Furthermore, although Japan and South Korea have both conducted a great deal of research into microcontroller technology (as implied by the number of patents granted), no Japanese or South Korean player has achieved high visibility within this industry. This could indicate one of two things; either that the two countries' cumulative number of patents (or technical energy) may have been too low to stimulate the take-off of the industry, or that there may have been other obstacles in the microcontroller industry that have prevented the Japanese and South Korean players from achieving market penetration.

CONCLUSIONS

The comparisons and analysis undertaken in this chapter may be interpreted as demonstrating a strong positive correlation between patent performance (including the quantity and quality of patents) and industrial development.

As regards overall trends, business strategies in the semiconductor industry in Taiwan, South Korea and Japan vary depending on the local industrial environments. The Japanese and Korean players have displayed a similar pattern of development, namely vertical integration, large business groups and diversification. Given the vertically-integrated production model which is dominant in these two countries, a company's core competence incorporates systems and brand marketing, with a business model based on vertical integration. By contrast, Taiwanese companies tend to develop the market through a specialist division of labour. Another important point is that so far, no vertically-integrated systems companies or brand-name product vendors have emerged in Taiwan (see Table 9.17).

Table 9.17   Comparative business models and competitive strategies of Taiwanese, South Korean and Japanese ICTs

	Business Models/ Competitive Strategies	Japan	South Korea	Taiwan
Brand-name Product Vendor	Vertical integration	a	a	-
	Division of labour	✓	✓	b
OEM/OBM	Vertical integration	-	-	-
	Division of labour	-	-	✓

Notes:
[a] Indicates that the strategies or business models are still developing.
[b] Indicates the requirement for enhancement to core competences.

Although there are some 'system brands', in most cases these operate through a division of labour, with the parts and key components being assembled by the systems company. As regards the competitiveness of the semiconductor industry as a whole, amongst Japanese companies, both mass production capability and production management capability have been falling off; this is particularly evident in the DRAM industry. By contrast, South Korea has developed the core competences needed by systems or specialist brands, despite inadequate systems integration capability. In addition, South Korea is continuing to improve its competence in mass production, production management and cost control, whereas, for Taiwan, mass production, production management and technology following continue to be the core competences.

As regards autonomous technology innovation capability, although Taiwan already has world-class production processes, it remains weak in other areas. As regards competence in peripheral capabilities, most of the Japanese and South Korean companies are very competitive in terms of their business scope, diversification, value chain management and resource management, whilst Taiwanese companies display competence in organisational flexibility, value chain management, network cooperation and resource management. Table 9.18 provides a comparison of the competences of the semiconductor companies in the three economies examined in this chapter.

In summary, it seems that IC fabrication will continue to be the most important segment in Taiwan's semiconductor industry; this is an area in which Taiwan has already achieved world-class performance. The IC design industry in Taiwan can be viewed as a sub-industry of IC fabrication, since Taiwan has secured very few patents relating to IC design; however, Taiwan still has the opportunity to develop a strong IC design industry since the industrial environment in both Japan and South Korea is not suited to IC design development, an industry which relies heavily upon the division of labour.

Table 9.18   Comparison of the competences of semiconductor companies in Taiwan, South Korea and Japan

	Core and Peripheral Competences	Japan	South Korea	Taiwan
1	Systems integration	*	*	-
2	Technical innovation	✓	✓	✓
3	Marketing channels	✓	✓	*
4	Consumer contact	✓	✓	-
5	Customer services	✓	✓	✓
6	Technology following	-	✓	✓
7	Mass production	-	✓	✓
8	Production management	-	✓	✓
9	Cost control	-	✓	✓
10	Business scope	✓	✓	✓
11	Diversification	✓	✓	-
12	Flexible organisation	-	-	✓
13	Value chain management	✓	✓	✓
14	Network cooperation	-	-	✓
15	Resource management	✓	✓	✓

Note: * Indicates that the system is still under development.

As regards technical capability and industry development, a high degree of similarity exists between Japan and South Korea in these areas. The only difference is that Japan is basically the leader whilst South Korea is striving to catch up. The future development of the semiconductor industry will therefore follow a pattern of Japanese players making money from innovation and South Korean players profiting from efficient production. Eventually, however, the South Korean companies will push their Japanese competitors out of the market.

REFERENCES

Albert, G.Z.H. and B.J. Adam (2001), 'Patent Citations and International Knowledge Flow: The Cases of Korea and Taiwan', *National Bureau of Economic Research, Working Paper No.8528*.

Albert, M.B., D. Avery, F. Narin and P. McAllister (1991), 'Direct Validation of Citation Counts as Indicators of Industrially Important Patents', *Research Policy*, **20**: 251-9.

Archibugi, D. and M. Pianta (1996), 'Measuring Technological Change through Patents and Innovation Surveys', *Technovation*, **16**(9): 451-68.

Buckley, P.J., C.L. Pass and K. Prescott (1988), 'Measures of International Competitiveness: A Critical Survey', *Journal of Marketing Management*, **4**(2): 175-200.

Chiu, C.-M. and C.-K. Yuan (2000), 'Patent Maps in Lithography and Photo-masks', *Industrial Materials*, **168**: 154-60 (in Chinese).

DigiTimes (2000), *Trends in the Semiconductor Industry*, Taipei: DigiTimes Publication Inc. (in Chinese).

Ernst, H. (1998a), 'Industrial Research as a Source of Important Patents', *Research Policy*, **27**: 1-15.

Ernst, H. (1998b), 'Patent Portfolios for Strategic R&D Planning', *Journal of Engineering and Technology Management*, **15**: 278-308.

Griliches, Z. (1990), 'Patent Statistics as Economic Indicators: A Survey', *Journal of Economic Literature*, **28**(4): 1661-707.

Hall, B.H., A.B. Jaffe and M. Tratjenberg (2001), 'The NBER Patent Citation Data File: Lessons, Insights and Methodological Tools', *NBER Working Paper No.8498*.

IC Insights (2002), at website: http://www.icinsights.com/news.html.

ITRI (2000), *Semiconductor Industry Yearbook*, Taipei: Industrial Technology Research Institute ITRI, (in Chinese).

Ku, Y.-H., D.-N. Liu, M.-C. Liu and T.-J. Chen (2000), *A Study of the Semiconductor Industries in Japan and Korea*, unpublished project report, Taipei: Chung-Hua Institution for Economic Research (in Chinese).

Lee, P.-Y. and W.-Y. Hong (2002), *Silicon Island Power - Trends in the Semiconductor and Electronic Components Industries*, Taipei: DigiTimes Publications Inc., pp.9-17 (in Chinese).

Lin, H.-Y. (1997), 'A Study of Patent Index and Global Technological Competitiveness', *Taiwan Economic Research Monthly*, **20**(9): 78-84 (in Chinese).

Lin, H.-W and H.-Y. Lin (2002), 'Dynamism of Taiwan's Innovations and Comparative Advantage - A Study Based on Patent Data', paper presented at the Conference on Industrial Technology Innovations and Location Advantages held in Taipei, (15-16 August) (in Chinese).

Liu, S.-J. (2000), 'Industry Competition and Patenting Strategy: The Case of VIA vs. Intel', *Technology Development and Policy Report*, Taipei: National Science Council, Science and Technology Information Center (STIC), pp.1085-98 (in Chinese).

Meng, H.-C. (2000), 'Index of Innovations: Patent Citation Analysis and Patent Index', *Journal of Technology Management*, **5**(1): 31-49, (in Chinese).

Narin, F., E. Noma and R. Perry (1987), 'Patents as Indicators of Corporate Technological Strength', *Research Policy*, **16**: 143-55.

Porter, M.E. and S. Stern (2000), 'Measuring the 'Ideas' Production Function: Evidence from International Patent Output', *NBER Working Paper, No.7891*.

Praest, M., (1998), 'Changing Technological Capabilities in High-tech Firms: A Study of the Telecommunications Industry', *Journal of High Technology Management Research*, **9**(2): 175-93.

Sedra, A.S. and K. Smith (1982), *Microelectronic Circuits* (4th edn.), Oxford: Oxford University Press.

Soet, L. and S. Wyatt (1983), 'The Use of Foreign Patenting as an Internationally Comparable Science and Technology Output Indicator', *Scientometrics*, **5**: 31-54.

Sood, J. and F. DuBois (1995), 'The Use of Patent Statistics to Measure and Predict International Competitiveness', *International Trade Journal* (Fall): 363-79.

Stern, S., M.E. Porter and J.L. Furman (2000), 'The Determinants of National Innovative Capacity', *NBER Working Paper No.7876*.

Topology Research (1998), 'An Essay on the Semiconductor Industry', Taipei: Topology Research, Inc. (in Chinese).

US Patent and Trademark Office (1999), Technology Assessment and Forecast Database, USPTO.

Wang, S.-J. and Y.-W. Su (2000), *Mega-trends in Silicons*, Taipei: DigiTimes Publications Inc., pp.10-22 (in Chinese).

10 Knowledge Intensification in Taiwan's IT Industry

Shin-Horng Chen

INTRODUCTION

The evolution of the information and communications technology (ICT) paradigm is rapidly shifting the basis of economic activity from material and labour inputs to knowledge and intangible inputs, spawning the knowledge-based economy (KBE). The OECD (1996) defined a KBE as an economy in which the production, distribution and use of knowledge are the main drivers of growth, wealth creation and employment across all industries. We can of course argue that all economic activities have something to do with knowledge, although differing in degree; however, if we consider that knowledge, as an economic good, outweighs all other goods, then there may be a requirement for fundamental structural changes to the economic system.

Against this backdrop, this chapter sets out to examine the features of the evolving KBE in Taiwan with special focus on the area of information technology (IT), approaching the topic more from a perspective of industrial organisation, as opposed to a policy standpoint. Based on the author's work over the past few years, this chapter represents an attempt to take stock and reflect on the qualitative changes that have taken place in Taiwan's IT industry, changes which are arguably in line with the shift towards a KBE, and attempts to go beyond the conventional wisdom regarding the strength of Taiwan's IT sector based upon pure manufacturing muscle and local clustering. In specific terms, the aim is to demonstrate the knowledge intensification in Taiwan's IT industry from three different aspects.

First of all, Taiwanese IT firms have traditionally entered a particular product market as 'fast followers' during the growth stage, with a key success factor being their capacity to combine low-cost production in Taiwan with rapid response to changes in both markets and technology (Ernst, 2000); however, it is equally true that a trend has emerged within this sector which is shifting the focus from foreign technology to indigenous innovation. Secondly, in response

228

to the trend towards globalisation, IT manufacturers in Taiwan have also 'gone global' in deploying their production and logistics networks so as to maintain cost efficiency and better serve their customers. As a result, they have evolved from pure manufacturers towards 'integrated service providers', shouldering many other functions such as supply chain management, logistics operations, and after-sales services, particularly through the medium of e-commerce. Thirdly, there is an additional trend emerging in Taiwan which seems to indicate that the IT sector is becoming increasingly involved in two-way R&D internationalisation to facilitate the leveraging of international R&D networks.

Conceptualisation of a Knowledge-based Economy

The term 'knowledge-based economy' has drawn considerable attention in both academic and political circles, yet its exact meaning is still not entirely clear. Since knowledge is an intangible good, in its most basic form a KBE should be qualitatively different from an economy based on either materials or manufacturing. Elsewhere, we have related the characteristics of a KBE to the unique features of knowledge (Chen and Liu, 2000); our earlier conceptualisation is summarised as follows.

First of all, with knowledge having become increasingly important as an economic good, the distance between knowledge and economic activities has shrunk considerably. Secondly, knowledge, as an input, generates scale and scope economies, but the magnitude of these economies depends on the speed at which knowledge depreciates and becomes obsolete, as well as on market size. Therefore, speed and 'first mover' advantage are central aspects of industrial competition in the KBE era. Thirdly, as knowledge is increasingly integrated into economic output, giving rise to the dematerialisation of final products, the boundaries between manufacturing and services and between hardware and software are becoming increasingly blurred. Wise and Baumgartner (1999), for example, described several cases in which US manufacturers had moved downstream to integrate the service functions, thereby becoming more profitable; at the extreme, therefore, some aspects of industrial and economic activities may become weightless. Fourthly, information technology and networks, which are central to the creation, distribution and utilisation of knowledge, will become necessary conditions for industrial development in the era of the KBE because IT is an enabling technology for collaborative commerce between firms, involving not only inter-organisational coordination of the supply chain, but also cooperation in product definition, design and R&D (Berryman and Heck, 2001). Finally, a KBE is characterised by the globalisation of a wide range of value-added corporate activities. Globalisation has been driven by the outreach of capital and production by multinational corporations (MNCs), (Michalet, 1991) and, more recently, by the spread of technology (Sigurdson 1990; Patel and Pavitt 2000). In addition, the IT network, which is by nature global and real-time, will enable firms to synchronise their supply chains and to organise cross-border corporate activities more efficiently. As a result, globalisation clearly means more than just the international division of labour in the production process.

For the purposes of this chapter, it will be necessary to elaborate a little more on three aspects, the first of which is the emergence of the KBE which is placing greater emphasis on knowledge accumulation; from a Taiwanese perspective, this comes particularly in the form of technological innovation. This is not to reduce the term 'knowledge' merely to a technological context, but to argue that if economies such as Taiwan are to evolve towards a KBE, based on their industrialisation heritage, their strength in technological innovation will be indispensable. Within a KBE, a firm is a producer, repository and user of knowledge, producing or acquiring knowledge and putting it to the most efficient use. Each firm's competitive advantage lies in its stock of knowledge, and because firms possess idiosyncratic knowledge they are likely to be heterogeneous. In particular, R&D as an essential element of technological innovation has two facets, namely innovation and learning (Cohen and Levinthal, 1989). One additional outcome of globalisation over the past few decades has been the increasing disintegration of capabilities in production, and even innovation, across nations (Feenstra, 1998). Driven by such disintegration, the outreach of MNCs not only takes the form of direct investment, but also the outsourcing of production, and even knowledge. Of equal importance is the fact that the further this disintegration goes, the more competitive the bidding becomes for the subcontracting work on behalf of these MNCs. To offset this, strength in technological innovation based on intangible knowledge outweighs the manufacturing muscle built up on the basis of tangible inputs. This is particularly significant if we take into account the fact that nowadays, subcontracting work for MNCs often involves wafer-thin profit margins.

The second aspect is the organisational separation of innovation from production, which may become the norm within a KBE. Although the knowledge used to invent a product can be useful in the manufacture of that product, and vice versa, it does not pay an innovator to invest in the manufacturing function unless it is unable to realise the value of the innovation through outsourcing. In fact, contract manufacturers invariably perform the production function at a lower cost than innovators because, by sharing their manufacturing capacity with more than one client, they can exploit economies of scale. In order to make a perfect product, the innovator usually needs to share some knowledge with manufacturers, and conversely some of the manufacturer's knowledge can aid in product innovation. The sharing of knowledge works best in cooperative relationships because knowledge is intangible and sharing entails organisational learning. In a KBE, therefore, alliances are an important form of business organisation and an important source of learning and innovation. Sharing knowledge outside the organisation may be more efficient than accumulating knowledge internally because of the 'non-rival' nature of knowledge, which allows the one who partakes of the knowledge to pay only a small marginal cost to compensate the owner. Acquiring knowledge through exchanges or alliances may also be more efficient than acquiring the firm that owns the knowledge because the latter solution also entails acquiring non-essential assets along with the knowledge. In sum, a KBE is characterised by alliance capitalism.

Product innovation involves an assortment of knowledge related to various stages of the value chain. Knowledge applied to manufacturing, marketing, and customer services is complementary to the knowledge used in product innovation. Vertical integration of the innovation function in the value chain is only justified, however, if internalisation is the best way to acquire the relevant knowledge, and this is not often the case. Since product innovations address the needs of customers, the knowledge most valuable to product innovation is that obtained from interacting with customers, in other words, marketing. Therefore, product innovation combined with marketing may be the optimal mix of services offered by a firm. Nike, Reebok and Calvin Klein are typical examples of this innovator-marketer combination in the traditional industries of footwear and apparel. What's more, this trend towards innovation and marketing becoming the core functions of the firm is even taking place in the high-technology industries. In the IT industry, for example, integrated device manufacturers (IDMs) including Apple, Compaq, Dell and Motorola have partitioned themselves from manufacturing, which they now delegate to their subcontractors. Indeed, the driving force of innovation in the semiconductor industry has been the so-called 'fabless' designers which rely on foundry service providers to actually produce the chips. Meanwhile, contract manufacturers are being required to perform customer service functions in addition to producing and delivering products. So-called 'global logistics' has prevailed mainly because knowledge of supply-chain management is as important to the manufacturer's success as knowledge of the production process. Therefore, the division of labour in a KBE tends to reflect the distribution of knowledge. Firms perform production activities in line with their heterogeneous endowments of knowledge and the knowledge content of production, and country-specific advantages based on material inputs are secondary factors in determining the distribution of global production.

This discussion suggests that the emergence of a KBE may undermine the formation of traditional oligopolies and give rise to a situation of rival industrial networks, each comprising of multiple firms with different knowledge bases. In many cases, innovations inherently comprise of a 'technical system', a set of interdependent products that are consumed jointly. Given network externalities and product compatibility, successful innovations for technical systems generally entail intensive interfacing between actors with different knowledge and skills bases in an 'innovation network' (Windrum, 1999). Consequently, such innovations will often result from the collective efforts of interrelated firms; moreover, the value chain need not be completely internalised within any individual firm. At the same time, as argued above, the division of labour in a KBE is determined more and more by knowledge rather than by material-based inputs. As a result, technology sourcing has been driving firms to internationalise their R&D (Cantwell and Santangelo, 1999; Gerybadze and Reger, 1999; Niosi, 1999; Zander, 1999) and to form inter-firm partnerships (Delapierre and Mytelka, 1998). Firms can build sustainable competitive advantage based on knowledge by leveraging and aligning both their internal and external networks on an international scale.

The third aspect for elaboration is the importance of the application of IT to global networking where the functioning of a KBE needs to be acknowledged. IT can be considered as an innovation of 'transaction' technology, which can facilitate intra- and inter-organisational value chain management in a real-time and cost-effective manner (Economist Intelligence Unit, 2000). The use of IT, in conjunction with the reshuffling of business models, can help firms to achieve speed and flexibility in an industry where time is crucial (Kraemer et al., 2000). In this regard, IT is more than a transaction facilitator, and in fact, is promoted to the role of an enabling technology for collaborative commerce amongst firms, involving not only inter-organisational coordination of the supply chain but also cooperation in product definition, design and R&D (Berryman and Heck, 2001). In this way, production networks in the 'bricks and mortar' world may be transformed into virtual supply networks and collaborative communities. This is not to suggest that industrial advantages derived from the physical world will become dispensable, but rather, as will be shown in due course, that they can go hand in hand with IT applications to bolster the prospects of the firms involved.

The Current Status of Taiwan's IT Industry

Ever since the 1980s, the IT industry has increasingly become the primary engine for economic growth in Taiwan. On a global scale, Taiwan currently ranks as the fourth largest producer of information hardware, the fourth largest producer of IC products, and the third largest in the area of optoelectronics; furthermore, Taiwan has recently experienced an explosive growth in mobile communications, despite its less impressive global ranking in that particular sector (see Table 10.1).

Table 10.1   Taiwan's global rankings in the 3C industries

Industry	Sales (US$ millions)				CAGR (%)	Ranking (2000)
	1997	1998	1999	2000*		
Information (hardware)	18,889	19,252	21,023	23,081	6.9	4
Communications	2,676	2,898	3,654	4,322	17.3	17
Consumer Products	2,161	2,699	3,334	5,303	34.8	6
Optoelectronics	5,132	5,800	8,328	14,000	39.7	3
IC	10,114	9,822	13,234	22,434	30.4	4

Note: * The exchange rate for 2000 was US$1.00 = NT$32.00 (excluding overseas output, for example, to mainland China).

Sources: Industrial Technology Information Service database; Wu et al. (2002).

With particular regard to the information hardware industry, a number of Taiwanese-made products, such as LCD monitors, motherboards, scanners, keyboards and notebook PCs have continued to enjoy a significant global market share. The factors underlying this are the highly-regarded production and design capabilities of Taiwanese IT producers which, in turn, have resulted in Taiwan becoming a major source of contract work for prominent international IT companies. The international significance of Taiwan's IT industry can also be further seen in a wider context.

First of all, as Taiwan-based IT product manufacturers have gone global, their volume of offshore production has largely outstripped that of domestic production, particularly in certain products such as CD ROMs, desktop PCs, monitors, digital cameras and motherboards. As a result, Taiwanese IT firms have successfully evolved from pure manufacturers towards integrated service providers, a point on which we shall elaborate further in the later sections of this chapter. Secondly, within the IC sector, Taiwan has performed particularly well in foundry, capturing a massive 72.9 per cent of the global market share in 2001; indeed, in terms of IC design, Taiwan is second only to the US. Underlying this are intensive international and domestic linkages that sustain Taiwan's IC industry and the broadly-defined IT sector as a whole. Thirdly, Taiwan also has an impressive ranking, at number four in the world, in terms of the total number of US patents granted (see Table 10.2). In this regard, electrical and electronic machinery, equipment and supplies, as a product field, outnumber all other fields, having registered an enormous increase from 2,013 to 7,644 over the second half of the 1990s. This implies that Taiwan's IT sector has moved from a focus on foreign technology to indigenous innovation (Wu et al., 2002). On top of this, there emerges the international aspect of Taiwan's innovation system, particularly within the IT sector, a point to which we shall also return later.

Table 10.2   Patents granted in the USPTO [a]

Rank	Country [b]	Total No.		Share (%)		Growth	CAGR
		1990	2001	1990	2001	Rate 2001	1990-2001
All Patents							
1	USA	52,977	98,663	53.39	53.61	1.70	5.82
2	Japan	20,743	34,890	20.91	18.96	5.97	4.84
3	Germany	7,862	11,894	7.92	6.46	9.91	3.84
4	Taiwan	861	6,545	0.87	3.56	12.73	20.25
5	France	3,093	4,456	3.12	2.42	6.78	3.37
6	UK	3,017	4,356	3.04	2.37	6.50	3.40
7	Canada	2,087	4,063	2.10	2.21	3.52	6.24
8	Korea	290	3,763	0.29	2.04	8.38	26.24
9	Italy	1,498	1,978	1.51	1.07	0.56	2.56
10	Sweden	885	1,935	0.89	1.05	11.33	7.37
14	Israel	311	1,031	0.31	0.56	23.33	11.51
18	Hong Kong	151	620	0.15	0.34	9.23	13.70
21	Singapore	16	304	0.02	0.17	6.02	30.69
23	China	48	266	0.05	0.14	6.92	16.84
Utility Patents							
1	USA	47,391	87,607	52.44	52.76	2.98	5.74
2	Japan	19,525	33,223	21.61	20.01	6.16	4.95
3	Germany	7614	11,260	8.43	6.78	10.03	3.62
4	Taiwan	732	5,371	0.81	3.23	15.08	19.86
5	France	2,866	4,041	3.17	2.43	5.81	3.17
6	UK	2,789	3,965	3.09	2.39	8.13	3.25
7	Canada	1,859	3,606	2.06	2.17	5.47	6.21
8	Korea	225	3,538	0.25	2.13	6.76	28.46
9	Sweden	768	1,743	0.85	1.05	10.53	7.74
10	Italy	1,259	1,709	1.39	1.03	-0.29	2.82
13	Israel	299	970	0.31	0.56	0.33	0.58
19	Hong Kong	12	296	0.15	0.34	0.01	0.18
22	Singapore	52	237	0.02	0.17	0.06	0.14
24	China	47	195	0.05	0.14	0.05	0.12

Notes:
[a]   Figures refer to patent counts of all types, and utility patent grants, as at the calendar year of the granting of the patent.
[b]   The country of the patent is determined by the country of residence of the first inventor.

Sources: USPTO Patent Full Text CD-ROM, TIER; Wu et al. (2002).

INFORMATION INDUSTRY UPGRADING

Beyond Manufacturing Muscle to Global Presence

Although the development of Taiwan's information industry was initially driven by foreign direct investment (FDI), the momentum has steadily shifted towards local firms, which has led to local industrial clustering having become well documented as a characteristic feature of Taiwan's information industry (Hobday, 1995; Kraemer et al., 1996; Kim and Tunzelmann, 1998). Recent developments, however, have called into question the extent to which local agglomeration adequately encapsulates the dynamics of Taiwan's information industry. Under the pressure of globalisation, global production networks have thus come to the fore in Taiwan's industrial strategy. In this regard, an important milestone in the development of Taiwan's PC industry was the outreach achieved by local firms starting from the late 1980s. Their outward investment had initially been directed towards Southeast Asia, but has more recently been directed towards mainland China and elsewhere in the world; indeed, the offshore production of Taiwan-based PC firms now outweighs their domestic production, with mainland China having accounted for 46.9 per cent of total production in 2002.

Along with the PC industry's determined drive to reduce production costs, lead-time to market and inventory costs, came a profound change in the manufacturing system and inter-firm competition within the industry. It became commonplace for components to be sourced from a global network of suppliers and for final assembly to be undertaken within the end market (Angel and Engstrom, 1995; Borrus and Borrus, 1997). Specifically, major brand marketers moved to adopt outsourcing and order-based production, which greatly rationalised their global supply chain, and hence altered their contractual relationships with the Taiwanese firms. Compaq, for example, pioneered the so-called 'optimised distribution model', which, in essence, aimed to allow customers to choose what they wanted, when and how, at the lowest prices. There are three salient features to this operational model. Firstly, in order to narrow the gap between supply and demand, production must aim to meet orders, i.e. 'build-to-order' rather than some unrelated compliance with forecasts. Secondly, in order to meet the wide variety of consumer demands, producers must not only build-to-order but also configure-to-order, making customised products in specific quantities. Thirdly, vendors must undertake final assembly, bringing together a set of subassemblies produced and delivered by the subcontractors.

Such contractual arrangements with global leaders in the PC industry prompted Taiwanese IT firms to upgrade their position within the global production system; as a result, they began to shoulder the essential functions of coordinating the global supply chain for their OEM customers. For example, under its new business model, Compaq outsourced every element of the value chain, with the exception of marketing, to Taiwanese subcontractors, imposing a '98-3' operational formula on its subcontractors, which required them to collect 98 per cent of the components and parts needed for production within three days of the order and to ship the product within six days of receipt of the order. By so doing, Compaq completely handed over its inventory costs to its subcontractors, who were also required to produce and deliver subsystem products on tight schedules and in tune with the vagaries of market demand. The Taiwanese firms had to ensure that everything was synchronised up and down the supply chain, and in order to do this, they had to participate in cross-border supply-chain management, logistics operations and after-sales services. In order to coordinate all of these functions, they had to form a fast-response global production and logistics network, or 'global logistics' (Schive, 2000).

It should also be noted that these new forms of contractual arrangements entail the progressive deployment of e-commerce links between Taiwanese PC producers and their vertical and horizontal counterparts. Indeed, it was Compaq's requirement, which stated 'no electronic data interchange (EDI), no order', which prompted some firms in Taiwan to embark on the application of e-commerce. Moreover, a government initiative, which was aimed at promoting e-commerce links between Taiwanese firms and their international customers ranging from online logistics management to online joint R&D, succeeded in facilitating the electronic links between leading brand marketers and their Taiwanese partners, migrating, in part, from an EDI-base to an Internet-base (see Table 10.3).

The author has documented elsewhere the role of e-commerce in the global logistics network operated by a leading Taiwanese PC manufacturing service company, Mitac (Chen, 2002). Although driven by brand-name marketers (such as Compaq), Mitac has now electronically linked both its inter-firm and intra-firm value-chain activities. Over the electronics network, multilateral and timely information flows and sharing have, on balance, been greatly enhanced, facilitating effective synchronisation both up and down the inter-organisational and international supply chain. Mitac and its partners are now involved in design collaboration, commodity management, supplier rationalisation and supply collaboration, all of which strengthen not only their transaction efficiency, but also their learning and innovation capabilities. A significant change brought about by such global logistics practices, or more specifically, BTO, has been the substantial increase in the frequency of ordering, and a corresponding acceleration in the pace of delivery.

Table 10.3 Taiwan's network information management initiatives

Component	Scope	Participants	Remarks
A	Automated transactions between global OEMs and their suppliers in Taiwan in the areas of order and inventory management, and logistics services	IBM, Compaq, HP and thirty-one domestic firms	International procurement function
B	Automated transactions between Taiwanese PC companies and their suppliers in the areas of order and inventory management, and logistics services	Fifteen domestic system manufacturers and their component and parts suppliers	Virtual integration of Taiwan-based firms' global supply chain
C	Supply chain cash-flow system between Taiwanese PC companies and domestic banks	Eleven production systems involving 2,700 IT suppliers	Including account aggregation, e-financing, and e-factoring functions
D	Vendor Managed Inventory (VMI) and Third Party Logistics (3PLs)	Eleven production systems involving 1,338 IT suppliers, 308 logistics service providers, 34 warehouse service providers, 280 international purchasers, and five international logistics service providers	Full integration of domestic and international logistics with their counterparts in the supply chain
E	Online cross-border and inter-firm joint R&D	Will involve six production systems	Collaborative commerce

Whereas in the past, it took 40 to 60 days for PC firms to complete the transaction process, from order to delivery, under BTO, subcontractors, such as Mitac, now have to meet much tighter schedules. In addition, patchy production, rather than mass production, has become the dominant practice for Mitac; thus modular manufacturing and IT networking are now indispensable to the company's formation of a rapid response global production and logistics network. From a Taiwanese perspective, the essence of this development is that local IT firms, such as Mitac, are now transforming themselves from stand-alone OEM manufacturers into providers of integrated service packages encompassing a wide range of value-chain activities. This development is particularly significant in terms of a frequently neglected aspect of high-technology manufacturing industries (such as the PC industry), since they are widely regarded as high value-added; however, the fact is, that as a direct result of the rapid changes in technology, these industries tend to be vulnerable to accelerating competition and narrowing profit margins even before they reach the mature stage of the product life cycle. Thus firms, and indeed nations, that tend to place significant reliance on high-technology hardware manufacturing can easily find themselves caught up in deteriorating terms of trade. Furthermore, most of the IT firms in Taiwan are engaged in OEM/ODM contract work, with no real ability to control, or even gain direct access to, the final market. In their case, outreach – moving elements of their manufacturing and/or assembly functions overseas – involves the need to generate additional profits through the widening of their value chains. In the case of global logistics, they have begun to shoulder service functions, such as the coordination of cross-border supply chains and logistics, in addition to their initial manufacturing function. It is therefore arguable that they have looked beyond manufacturing profits to seek profits from the services they provide to brand-name marketers.

Central to global logistics is the ability of subcontractors to weave together the cross-national elements of the value chain into an effectively competitive and rapidly responsive production and logistics system. As such, they are now subject to the new rules of the game that industrial competition in the PC industry relies not merely on cheaper costs, but more on flexibility and rapid response capabilities. However, whilst Taiwanese IT firms are by no means in the driving seat, they have, nevertheless, proved themselves capable of taking part in setting up the new rules of the game; therefore, with a global production and logistics network at their disposal capable of satisfactorily meeting the needs of their customers, Taiwan-based IT firms may well have preempted the entry of many of their foreign counterparts into the established networks. As a result, from a Taiwanese point of view, it could well be said that many of the owners of world-class PC brand names, which are core firms in the industry on an international scale, may now have been 'anchored' to Taiwan's economy (Chen and Liu, 2000).

TAIWAN'S IC INDUSTRY

Vertical Integration and Disintegration

Taiwan's IC industry is currently the fourth largest in the world, behind only the US, Japan and Korea. In a sense, Taiwan's IC industry is organised as an industrial network system with a strong connection to Silicon Valley, the global centre of the IC market and IC technology. The development of Taiwan's IC industry has clearly been driven by organisational innovation, with foundry services having been created as a market niche to specialise in production for external customers. This was a choice taken deliberately by local entrepreneurs as a way of avoiding the risks associated with the market volatility of DRAM. Although Taiwan does have some brand-name producers, local IC production is centred mainly on foundry services which accounted for 67 per cent of all IC production in 2001. By disintegrating the IC value chain in Taiwan, the emergence of foundry services facilitated the proliferation of small- and medium-sized firms engaged in other market segments, such as IC design, testing and packaging, which gave rise to a balanced and vertically-disintegrated industrial structure.

In essence, the development of Taiwan's IC industry has, to a large extent, come to resemble the scenario of the flexible specialisation thesis (Piore and Sable, 1984). The emergence of fabless IC design houses in Taiwan was, in part, the result of access to external fabrication capacity lowering the barriers to entry in the IC design market; however, the concentration of IC and computer-related firms in the Hsinchu Science-based Industrial Park (HSIP) also generated agglomeration effects that allowed those firms to exploit the benefits of proximity and outsourcing. Therefore, even though they specialise in one segment or another of the value chain, IC firms in Taiwan are networked by their social and business connections.

Taiwan's IC industry is also closely connected to the industrial heartland of Silicon Valley. Although the US ranks first amongst the world's four largest IC-producing economies (the US, Japan, Korea and Taiwan) with regard to R&D intensity, when it comes to capital expenditure intensity, Taiwan ranks in first place, whilst the US is only in fourth (Table 10.4); this points to an interesting pattern emerging in the international division of labour in the IC industry. Taiwan's strength lies in its foundry services, which depend on substantial investment in fabrication capacity; the IC firms in the US, on the other hand, tend to concentrate on R&D, design and marketing functions, which are backed up by access to Taiwan's foundry service capacity. In fact, most of the top ten fabless manufacturers in the US are, or have been, clients of Taiwanese foundries.

Table 10.4 R&D and capital expenditure intensity within the IC industries of the US, Japan, South Korea and Taiwan, 1995-1999 [a]

Unit: %

	1995	1996	1997	1998	1999
R&D intensity [b]					
US	9.7	11.6	12.1	13.9	–
Japan	6.6	6.5	6.6	6.5	–
Korea	–	7.9	11.6	12.9	–
Taiwan	7.0	6.9	8.8	9.1	–
Capital expenditure intensity [c]					
US	20.7	22.8	17.5	18.0	14.0
Japan	16.1	20.8	20.2	18.0	16.0
Korea	25.7	40.1	51.0	26.0	26.0
Taiwan	31.9	63.4	63.4	73.0	68.0

Notes:
[a] Data refer to fiscal year.
[b] R&D intensity is the ratio of R&D expenditure to sales, in percentage terms.
[c] Capital expenditure intensity is the ratio of capital expenditure to sales, in percentage terms.

Source: Industrial Technology Information Service database.

Taiwan Semiconductor Manufacturing Corporation (TSMC), the world's largest foundry service provider, shares its resources and information with its customers considering them as partners. Each year, TSMC informs its customers of the foundry's plans for the development of process technology over the next five years. The provision of such information helps TSMC's customers to ensure that the proposed process technologies can support their proposed future development of products. Sharing resources and information in this way not only facilitates the development of much closer long-term relationships with customers, but also helps to reduce the uncertainties over technology development on both sides.

Another facet of the connection between the IC industry in Taiwan and in the US is the intensive interchange between specialists in both countries. Underlying this exchange are Taiwanese and Chinese expatriates, who have played important roles in establishing the trans-Pacific social and business networks that have proved crucial in connecting Taiwan's production system with advanced market knowledge and technology (Saxenian, 1997; Kim and Tunzelmann, 1998). Apart from the ethnic social network, the fact that the IC industrial systems in both Taiwan and Silicon Valley are decentralised and network-based has helped to facilitate this interchange. This type of industrial system encourages the pursuit of multiple technical opportunities, heavy reliance on outsourcing and inter-organisational knowledge flows (Saxenian, 1997). Such similarities, in terms of their industrial structure, makes networking between Silicon Valley and the HSIP, the centre of Taiwan's IC industry, much easier and much more intensive.

The sort of industrial networking that exists in Taiwan's IC industry has benefited from recent innovations in IT; first of all, by reducing the uncertainty and transaction costs involved in purchasing from the best outsiders, IT reduces the advantages of large firms' centralised purchasing and in-house supply. Secondly, technological changes have resulted in smaller production runs, increasing the feasibility of product changes and allowing small, specialised firms to exploit fragmented product markets on the basis of their flexible response. In addition, the IC industry is following the lead of the PC industry by moving rapidly towards order-based production. The leading IC firms in Taiwan are championing the concept of the 'virtual factory' by deploying the Internet and Extranet to electronically link with their customers and suppliers.

In order to illustrate these points, we can refer back to the case of TSMC; whilst starting out as a stand-alone OEM foundry, TSMC has come to resemble a provider of integrated service packages covering a wide range of value-chain management activities thanks to its extensive application of e-commerce (Chen, 2002). Basically, through its arm's-length relationship with its customers, TSMC is not just a pure manufacturer; instead, it has become the natural place to verify the manufacturability of its customers' designs and to ensure the quality and timely delivery of their finished wafers. The ability of the electronic Internet and e-commerce links to accelerate and broaden the transfer of information between TSMC and its customers not only helps to simplify the tasks of knowledge management and exchange, but also induces TSMC to widen the scope of its extended supply chain management activities.

In a sense, the method of e-commerce employed by TSMC, or more specifically, 'TSMC-Online', acts as a portal to provide comprehensive support for its customers' major operational tasks, ranging from prototyping and design, to engineering and logistics. In terms of design, aided by its business-to-business (B2B) Internet applications, TSMC has drawn on a portfolio of design solutions from third parties to help its customers to achieve better designs, more reliable design reuse and faster time-to-market, leading to virtual integration of a network of firms.

In TSMC's B2B e-commerce model, goods and cash flows are secondary to information flows. As a pure-play foundry, its inventory costs for finished products are not an important issue, whereas in contrast, customer relationship management is regarded as central to its operations since it is regarded as representing the means of securing its capacity utilisation rates and profitability. Indeed, from TSMC's own viewpoint, B2B e-commerce is essential if foundries are to come to terms with the trend towards 'system-on-a-chip' (SOC) technology. Therefore, TSMC's e-commerce initiatives are targeted to meet the across-the-board needs of its customers, in order to enhance customer loyalty.

It is possible to identify the operational impact of TSMC's e-commerce, but its strategic significance has to be interpreted in a wider context of inter-firm relationships. In operational terms, TSMC was able to deliver 'work in progress' (WIP) reports three times a day in 1998, whilst a Korean counterpart at that time managed to do this only once a week. Nowadays, TSMC's WIP reporting is real-time. In addition, thanks to e-commerce, order confirmation in TSMC can now be completed in two seconds, as compared to the two days of the past. TSMC's e-commerce applications enable it to provide tailored packages for its customer that include design support, cell library, IP, quality/reliability as well as process technology and wafer capacity. As a result, its customers can 'virtually' own a foundry, providing a total solution, by leveraging TSMC's internal and external resources. In such a way, TSMC has set the rules of the game for the industry, which dictate that foundry must go beyond manufacturing muscle to become an essential platform for its customers to gain access to across-the-board competencies. TSMC's case proves that e-commerce applications can be a fertile ground for building up such new comparative advantage.

OFFSHORE R&D BY TAIWANESE MULTINATIONALS

Although it is well-documented that FDI has played an important role in Taiwan's economic development, it is seldom realised that, to a certain extent, there has also been some investment in R&D by MNCs in Taiwan. Panel data for 1999, collated by the Investment Commission at the Ministry of Economic Affairs, show estimated R&D intensity of 1.94 per cent for foreign-owned subsidiaries over the period 1996-1998, whilst the electronics and electrical appliances industry achieved an intensity level of 2.36 per cent over the same period (Chen and Liu, 2002b). Taking advantage of this panel data, elsewhere we have conducted statistical analyses to explore the factors determining local R&D by MNCs' subsidiaries in the electronics industry. We find, amongst other things, that foreign-owned subsidiaries with higher R&D intensity are characterised by higher average wages and a higher degree of localisation, as regards the sourcing of both production materials and capital goods. To interpret this finding, we can refer to a well-established argument that MNCs' offshore R&D units are given higher hierarchical mandates if their ties with the local scientific and technological community are growing in strength, and probably therefore, also in R&D intensity (Westney, 1990). To put this another way, for countries such as Taiwan, 'first-tier supplier advantage' can be regarded as a locational advantage capable of attracting the offshore R&D units of MNCs, which may imply that foreign-owned subsidiaries with a higher degree of localisation may need to devote more effort to R&D in order to effectively interact with their local suppliers.

We also find that in Taiwan, foreign-owned electronics firms with higher export propensity tend to be more R&D intensive. As is widely known, the electronics industry in Taiwan is internationally competitive and export-oriented, with local players in many of the sub-sectors enjoying first-tier supplier status. By analogy, their MNC counterparts in Taiwan may have to act in the same way in order to exploit Taiwan's advantages. In a questionnaire survey conducted by the authors on the R&D activities of MNCs, R&D performers were asked to identify their highest level R&D activities in Taiwan (Liu et al., 2002). The predominant level appeared to be the modification and development of products for the international market. In stark contrast, only a small proportion of the respondents reported that their subsidiaries were mandated to conduct joint R&D with their sister subsidiaries elsewhere, to conduct contract R&D and/or technology exports for the parents (Figure 10.1).

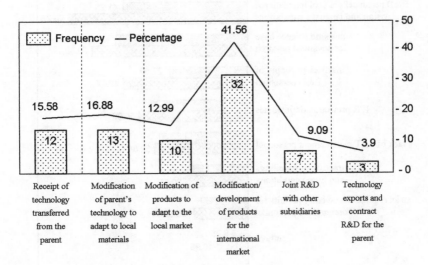

Source: Liu et al. (2002).

Figure 10.1 Highest level of MNCs' R&D activities in Taiwan

When examined in terms of Westney's (1990) categorisation of MNCs' offshore R&D units – namely technology transfer units, indigenous technology units, global technology units and corporate technology units – our findings may imply that quite a number of MNCs' subsidiaries in Taiwan are given a regional, or even international, R&D mandate. This is indeed consistent with the evidence, presented above, that foreign-owned electronics firms in Taiwan with a greater propensity for exports tend to be more R&D intensive. In addition, the firms surveyed were required to highlight the factors characterising Taiwan's strengths and weaknesses in R&D operations.

From the standpoint of R&D performers, there are generally considered to be three major factors that bring about local R&D: (i) accumulated managerial skills and production experience; (ii) high-quality and relatively low-cost R&D personnel; and (iii) a comprehensive satellite and supporting industrial system. Government provision of financial support for R&D and for R&D linkages between industry, universities and public research institutions appears to be of less significance in bringing about local R&D (Figure 10.2).

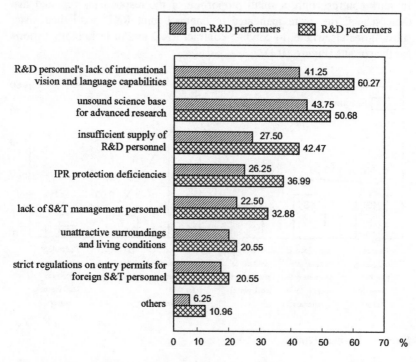

Figure 10.2   Taiwan's strengths in R&D operations

Non-R&D performers collectively placed much greater emphasis on accumulated production experience, managerial skills and relatively low-cost but high-quality R&D personnel as Taiwan's strengths in R&D operations, whilst tending to downplay the remaining specified factors and indeed, were somewhat indifferent towards them. It is fair to say that the factors specified as Taiwan's strengths in R&D operations in our questionnaire related mainly to the supply side, as well as being network-related. The reason for this was that in terms of domestic market and government procurements, in our opinion, Taiwan is small in scale. In addition, as Reddy (2000: 36) argued, amongst other motives, those that were technology-related were observed to have become more important than market-related motives for R&D globalisation. Indeed, both groups of respondents were greatly aware of Taiwan's advantages of accumulated production experience and managerial skills, and relatively low-cost but high-quality R&D personnel. Of some interest is the finding that R&D performers appear to be more appreciative than non-R&D performers of the comprehensive industrial satellite and supporting system. This may be because some, if not a great many, of the industrial sectors in Taiwan have comprehensive industrial satellite and supporting systems which enable major MNCs in the same sectors to exploit Taiwan's 'first-tier' supplier advantage, as discussed above.

In terms of Taiwan's weaknesses in R&D operations, both R&D performers and non-R&D performers shared the same views, in order of importance (as summarised in Figure 10.3).

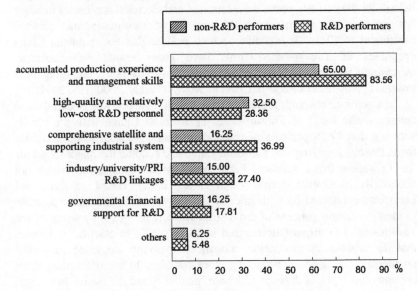

Figure 10.3   Taiwan's weaknesses in R&D operations

It was abundantly clear that the lack of international vision and language capabilities amongst R&D personnel stood out as Taiwan's first and foremost weaknesses, whilst the insufficient supply of R&D personnel in Taiwan and the unsound science base for advanced research were both regarded as secondary weaknesses. These three factors are all supply side-related; however, the lack of international vision and language capabilities of R&D personnel, and the unsound science base for advanced research, may have a significantly negative influence on the R&D operations undertaken in Taiwan. Furthermore, given that foreign-owned subsidiaries considered Taiwan's science base insufficiently sound for advanced research, it was not at all surprising that they downplayed Taiwan's R&D linkages between industry, universities and public research institutions. Conversely, factors such as intellectual property rights (IPR) protection, and the lack of science and technology (S&T) management personnel scored relatively low, whilst a few respondents pointed to the lack of systems integration capabilities as a major constraint for R&D in Taiwan.

TAIWANESE IT FIRMS' OFFSHORE R&D IN CHINA

Recent years have witnessed a new phase of cross-strait industrial interaction, with the newly-emerging geographical concentration of investment in the Long River Delta by Taiwan-based firms suggesting that Taiwanese outward investment to China is becoming more technology- and capital-intensive; indeed, for the past few years, the electronics and electrical appliances industry has accounted for approximately 40 per cent of Taiwan's annual outward investment to China. It has also become evident that the mainland China operations of Taiwan-based firms have gone beyond manufacturing, increasingly moving into R&D, which is in line with the newly emerging trend towards deployment of R&D in China by MNCs (Reddy, 2000; UN, 2001).

In a separate research project, a questionnaire survey was undertaken to determine the R&D of Taiwan-based IT firms in China, with the results showing that 47.56 per cent of respondents had conducted R&D activities there, thereby implying that mainland China had become the major target for the Taiwanese firms' offshore R&D, certainly in quantitative, though not necessarily qualitative, terms (Chen et al., 2002). Based on firm-level interviews conducted on both sides of the Taiwan strait, it became possible to identify certain patterns of cross-strait R&D deployment by some of the Taiwan-based IT firms (summarised in Table 10.5). In essence, it appears that the cross-strait production network is evolving alongside its global counterpart and hence is becoming more complex. In manufacturing, there are now new types of division of labour, going beyond the former horizontal and vertical dividing lines.

Table 10.5   Cross-strait R&D deployment by Taiwan-based firms

		Product		R&D or Technology Attributes	
	Type	Market	Life Cycle	Software/ hardware	R&D Process
Taiwan	Peripherals	International market	Development stage	Hardware	Product and process R&D
China	Systems-related	Domestic market	Mature stage	Software	Basic research, verification and fine-tuning of process

Elsewhere, we have identified five types of R&D portfolio across the Taiwan strait (Chen et al., 2002). First of all, where Taiwan-based firms' production lines are concentrated not only in mainland China, but also in other countries, product development is undertaken in Taiwan, whilst manufacturing-related R&D and engineering support is performed in China. This often entails the de-linking of R&D and manufacturing. Secondly, some Taiwanese firms outsource their software development services to China partly because of the leapfrogging potential of software.

The third type of portfolio involves a tendency for some Taiwanese firms to perform basic research in China, which often entails collaboration with local universities and/or research institutes. The fourth type has some Taiwanese firms performing their upstream (core) R&D (or R&D for products at the development stage) within Taiwan, whilst their subsidiaries in mainland China carry out downstream (non-core) R&D (or R&D for products at the mature stage). Finally, there are also those cases where Taiwanese firms perform R&D in China for system-related products, which are often modular products, such as motherboards for communications systems, whilst performing R&D for peripherals, such as handset motherboards.

Part of the survey for this chapter enlisted information on firms' R&D activities in China, with the respondents being asked to identify the major technology sources of their subsidiaries in mainland China. Figure 10.4 presents the distribution of the answers to this question. 'Support from the parent' stood out as the predominant technology source of Taiwan-based firms' subsidiaries in China, with almost 80 per cent of all respondents ranking it as being very important. The secondary source of support came from the 'R&D efforts of local subsidiaries'. These two were followed, by quite a substantial margin, by other sources such as 'joint efforts with local research institutes' and 'joint efforts with local firms'. It is therefore arguable that although heavily technologically reliant on their parent companies, the subsidiaries of Taiwan-based firms are also engaged in local R&D which cannot be regarded as negligible.

The respondents were further asked to assess the relative significance of certain elements of their R&D activities on both sides of the Taiwan strait; the responses to this question are summarised in Figure 10.5. Basically, Taiwan significantly outweighs mainland China in each type of R&D activity, and by counting the proportion of respondents who ranked Taiwan as 'very important' or of 'secondary importance', we can argue that Taiwan remains the major focus in these firms' cross-strait R&D operations, particularly in terms of the development of new products, modification of products, and new process technology.

Of equal importance was the finding that quite a large proportion of respondents expressed indifference towards both Taiwan and China with regard to machinery design, duplication of machinery and environment-related R&D. Part of the finding was consistent with the results gathered from the firm-level interviews (which are presented in Table 10.5). Indeed, as some of the Taiwanese IT firms have scaled down significantly, or even totally hollowed out their manufacturing operations in Taiwan and shifted them instead to mainland China (and elsewhere), it may well become necessary for them to rely increasingly upon their Chinese subsidiaries to undertake their manufacturing-related R&D. This seems more likely in the case where the de-linking of R&D and manufacturing is feasible (Reddy, 2000).

The global production networks in the IT industry have come to resemble a 'just-in-time' (JIT) system on a global scale entailing the modularisation of production across different sites and borders (Chen and Liu, 2002a). As a result, with regard to the introduction of new products into the marketplace, concurrent development may well become the norm within the industry, and this will necessarily be facilitated by the application of information and communication technologies. For example, referring back to our example of Mitac, one of the leading PC producers based in Taiwan; the company has now established a 'collaborative product commerce' (CPC) mechanism for online joint product design which incorporates an intra-link that enables its subsidiaries and partners to use the same design tools for joint product design and development, ranging from product definition to product R&D and product modularisation. This system not only helps to reduce the R&D cycle time for Mitac and its partners, but is also an essential precursor to the coordination of the overall production, assembly, delivery and repair and maintenance activities that follow (Chen, 2002). In light of this, it is not surprising to see that the Taiwan-based IT firms have, to a large extent, mandated their mainland Chinese subsidiaries to undertake certain elements of their R&D activities.

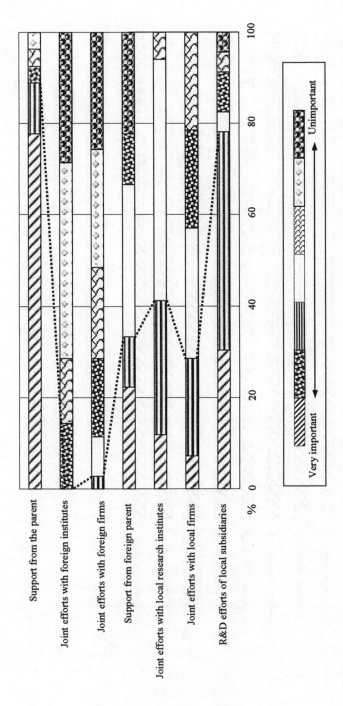

Figure 10.4 Technology sources of Taiwanese IT firms' subsidiaries in China

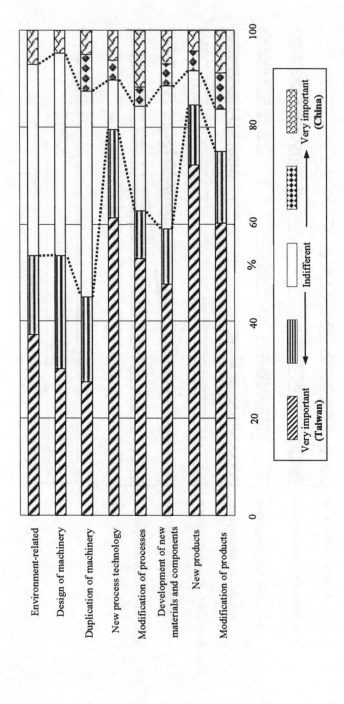

Figure 10.5 Relative significance of cross-strait R&D by Taiwan's electronics firms

CONCLUSIONS

Taiwanese IT firms have traditionally entered a particular product market as 'fast followers' during the growth stage, with a key success factor being the capacity to combine low-cost production in Taiwan with rapid response to changes in both markets and technology (Ernst, 2000). Nowadays, however, it is far too simplistic to state that Taiwan's success in the IT industry was attributable to manufacturing muscle alone; so too is the thesis on Taiwan's local industrial clustering.

Some sectors within the island's high-technology industry, notably the IT sector, are often considered to be the high value-added sectors; this can, however, be quite misleading, given that this sector in particular is extremely vulnerable to sharp declines in price, and consequently, significant narrowing of profit margins, and indeed, all of the constituent manufacturers may easily find themselves caught up in deteriorating terms of trade. This can be particularly significant if one takes into account the formation of global production networks, with the result that manufacturing muscle alone may no longer be deemed a sustainable comparative advantage. Such a perspective highlights the importance of intangible assets and their role in the knowledge intensification of industry. Taiwan's achievements in IT have something to do with its international linkages, to quite a considerable degree, and indeed, it has to be said that the nature of the international linkages at issue does matter, especially in the inter-firm context, giving rise to the question as to what these linkages mean to the parties involved. We need to determine to what extent these international linkages are footloose, and whether there are any 'lock-in' effects involved.

Basically, within an economy such as Taiwan's, industrial clusters evolve in tandem with the international industrial structure of the sectors concerned. In addition, whether or not such industrial clusters are sustainable depends heavily on the extent of localisation, which may depend on two issues; firstly, the presence of indigenous firms with substantial innovative capabilities, and secondly, the ability to 'anchor' the 'network flagships'. With regard to the latter, this refers to more than just the local operations or investments of the network flagships, because they can be as footloose as 'branch plants', as compared to 'performance plants'. Instead, it is meant to refer to something more along the lines of international linkages which are characterised by their enduring nature, and which enable the indigenous firms to leverage for industrial upgrading.

The current development of the Taiwanese PC and IC industries has shown that IT manufacturing involves much more than production of high-technology goods. In the underlying environment of globalisation, these industries in Taiwan are evolving from manufacturing-based subcontractors to providers of integrated service packages, and within this process, networking is important on two counts. First of all, the long-standing contractual relationships between the Taiwanese firms and the global brand marketers has facilitated reciprocal and concurrent knowledge flows between the two parties, which in turn, has helped to build up the capabilities of the former. This upgrading, together with the outreach of Taiwanese PC firms, has made it possible for them to take on the essential function of coordinating the global supply chains of their OEM customers. Secondly, it is clear that electronic networking is becoming increasingly important in bringing together PC and IC firms in Taiwan and linking them to the global supply chain, whilst also being of importance with regard to increasing their value-added. In indirect support of this argument, we have demonstrated elsewhere that it is possible to show empirically that the inputs for IT services have had a significant impact on industrial productivity in Taiwan, particularly in the manufacturing sector as a whole (Chen and Liu, 2003).

In addition, it is now abundantly clear that the days are long gone when the developed countries dominated manufacturing activities; so too are the days when R&D was a developed country-centric phenomenon. This does not arise within a historical vacuum, but has something to do with the increasingly obvious trend towards the disintegration of manufacturing and innovation capabilities on an international scale. The IT industry, and other areas in which economies such as Taiwan are substantially involved, illustrate these points vividly.

In summary, through conceptualisation and hard evidence, it can be determined that based on the heritage of industrialisation, Taiwan has been able to capitalise on its first-tier supplier advantage as a means of attracting MNCs to set up their offshore R&D facilities on the island. In particular, it is clear that foreign-owned subsidiaries with greater levels of R&D intensity are characterised by a higher propensity for exports and a higher degree of localisation, in terms of both the sourcing of production materials and capital goods. In addition, quite a number of MNCs' subsidiaries in Taiwan are indeed given a regional, or even international, R&D mandate.

Finally, it is also evident that quite a number of the Taiwan-based IT firms have given R&D mandates to their subsidiaries in China. As regards the patterns of their cross-strait R&D portfolios, R&D in Taiwan tends to focus more on product development and new process technologies, whilst in mainland China, the focus tends to be more on manufacturing-related R&D. What is clear, is that, driven by the emergence of the global production network, R&D services have now become an essential part of Taiwan's continuing economic development which, in essence, means much more than simply local R&D and innovation capabilities, and indeed, relies upon the ability to leverage international R&D networks.

REFERENCES

Angel, D.P. and J. Engstrom (1995), 'Manufacturing Systems and Technology Change: The US Personal Computer Industry', *Economic Geography*, **71**(1): 79-102.

Berryman, K. and S. Heck (2001), 'Is the Third Time the Charm for B2B?', *McKinsey Quarterly (Special Edition – 'Online Tactics'):* 18-22.

Borrus, M. and Z. Borrus (1997), 'Globalisation with Borders: The Rise of Wintelism and the Future of Global Competition', *Industry and Innovation*, 4(2): 141-66.

Cantwell, J. and G.D. Santangelo (1999), 'The Frontier of International Technology Networks: Sourcing Abroad the Most Highly Tacit Capabilities', *Information Economics and Policy*, **11**:101-23.

Chen, S.H. (2002), 'Global Production Networks and Information Technology: The Case of Taiwan', *Industry and Innovation*, 9(3): 249-65.

Chen, S.H. and D.-N. Liu (2000), 'Taiwan's Active Role in the Global Production Network', in P. Chow and B. Gill (eds.), *Weathering the Storm: Taiwan, Its Neighbours and the Asian Financial Crisis*, Washington, DC: Brookings Institute Press.

Chen, S.H. and M.C. Liu (2002a), 'The Knowledge-based Economy and Information Technology: The Taiwanese Experience', in C.S. Yue and J.J. Lim (eds.), *Information Technology in Asia: New Development Paradigms*, Singapore: Institute for Southeast Asian Studies.

Chen, S.H. and M.C. Liu (2002b) 'Technology Transfer and Networks between Local Firms and Foreign-owned Subsidiaries', Interim report for the National Science Council, Taipei: Chung-Hua Institution for Economic Research.

Chen, S.H. and M.C. Liu (2003), 'Taiwan's Transition from an Industrialising Economy to a Knowledge-based Economy', in S. Masuyama and D. Vandenbrink (eds.), *Towards a Knowledge-based Economy: East Asia's Changing Industrial Geography*, Tokyo: Nomura Research Institute and Singapore: Institute for Southeast Asian Studies.

Chen, S.H., M.C. Liu, and H.T. Shih (2003), 'R&D Services and Global Production Networks: A Taiwanese Perspective', *Working Paper Economics Series No.52*, Hawaii: East West Centre.

Chen S.H., H.T. Shih and C.H.C. Kao (2002), *The Trend of Taiwan-based Firms' R&D Activities in China and Its Impacts on Taiwan's Industrial Innovation*, final report for the Department of Industrial Technology, Ministry of Economic Affairs, Taipei: Chung-Hua Institution for Economic Research (in Chinese).

Cohen, W.M. and D. Levinthal (1989), 'Innovation and Learning: The Two Faces of R&D', *Economic Journal*, **99**: 569-96.

Delapierre, M. and L.K. Mytelka (1998), 'Blurring Boundaries: New Inter-firm Relationships and the Emergence of Networked Knowledge-based Oligopolies', in M.G. Colombo (ed.), *The Changing Boundaries of the Firm: Explaining Evolving Inter-firm Relations*, London and New York: Routledge.

Economist Intelligence Unit (2000), *The e-business Value Chain: Winning Strategies in Seven Global Industries*, New York: Economist Intelligence Unit.

Ernst, D. (2000), 'Global Production Networks and the Changing Geography of Innovation Systems: Implications for Developing Countries', *Working Paper No.9*, Hawaii: East-West Centre.

ERSO (2000), *Almanac of the Semiconductor Industry in Taiwan*, Hsinchu: Industrial Technology Research Institute.

Feenstra, R. (1998), 'Integration of Trade and Disintegration of Production in the Global Economy', *Journal of Economic Perspective*, **12**(4): 31-50.

Gerybadze, A. and G. Reger (1999), 'Globalisation of R&D: Recent Changes in the Management of Innovation in Transnational Corporations', *Research Policy*, **28**(2-3): 251-74.

Hobday, M. (1995), *Innovation in East Asia: The Challenge to Japan*, Aldershot: Edward Elgar.

Jovanovic, B. and R. Rob (1989), 'The Growth and Diffusion of Knowledge', *Review of Economic Studies*, **56**(4): 569-82.

Kawakami, M. (1996), 'The Development of Small- and Medium-sized Manufacturers in Taiwan's PC Industry', *CIER Discussion Paper Series 9606*, Taipei: Chung-Hua Institution for Economic Research.

Kim, S. and N. Tunzelmann (1998), *Aligning Internal and External Networks: Taiwan's Specialisation in IT*, Brighton: SPRU, University of Sussex.

Kojima, K. (1978), *Direct Foreign Investment: A Japanese Model of Multinationals*, London: Croom Helm.

Kraemer, K.L. and J. Dedrick (2000), 'Information Technology in Southeast Asia: Engine of Growth or Digital Divide', paper presented at the ASEAN Roundtable 2000, *New Development Paradigms in Southeast Asia: The Challenge of Information Technology* (12-13 October), Singapore: University of Singapore.

Kraemer, K.L., J. Dedrick and C. Huang (1996), 'Entrepreneurship, Flexibility and Policy Coordination: Taiwan's Computer Industry', *The Information Society*, **12**: 215-49.

Kraemer, K.L., J. Dedrick and S. Yamashiro (2000), 'Refining and Extending the Business Model with Information Society: Dell Computer Corporation', *Information Society*, **16**: 5-21.

Liu, M., S.H. Chen and Y.J. Lin (2002), *The Trend of R&D Internationalisation and Strategies for Attracting MNCs to Set up R&D Facilities in Taiwan*, final report for the Department of Industrial Technology, Ministry of Economic Affairs, Taipei: Chung-Hua Institution for Economic Research (in Chinese).

Michalet, C. (1991), 'Strategic Partnerships and the Changing Internationalisation Process', in L.K. Mytelka (ed.), *Strategic Partnerships: States, Firms and International Competition*, London: Pinter.

Niosi, J. (1999), 'The Internationalisation of Industrial R&D: From Technology Transfer to the Learning Organisation', *Research Policy*, **28**(2-3): 107-17.

OECD (1996), *The Knowledge-based Economy*, Paris: OECD.

Patel, P. and K. Pavitt (2000), 'Globalisation of Technology amongst the World's Largest Firms: Patterns and Trends', paper presented at the *Conference on the Measurement of Industrial Technological Competitiveness in the Knowledge-based Economy* (23-24 August), Taipei: Chung-Hua Institution for Economic Research.

Piore, M. and C. Sable (1984), *The Second Industrial Divide*, New York: Basic Books.

Quinn, J.B. (1988), 'Technology in Services: Past Myths and Future Challenges', in B. Guile and J.B. Quinn (eds.), *Technology in Services: Policies for Growth, Trade and Employment*, Washington, DC: National Academy Press.

Reddy, P. (2000), *Globalisation of Corporate R&D: Implications for Innovation Systems in Host Countries*, London: Routledge.

Saxenian, A. (1994), *Regional Advantage*, Cambridge, MA and London: Harvard University Press.

Saxenian, A. (1997), 'Transactional Entrepreneurs and Regional Industrialisation: The Silicon Valley-Hsinchu Connection', paper presented at the *Conference on Social Structure and Social Change: International Perspective on Business Firms and Economic Life*, Taipei: Academia Sinica.

Schive, C. (2000), 'Global Logistics: A New Way of Doing Business in Taiwan', paper presented at the *Conference on Global Entrepreneurship for the New Millennium* (20-23 August), New York: Syracuse University.

Sigurdson, J. (1990), 'The Internationalisation of R&D – An Interpretation of Forces and Responses', in J. Sigurdson (ed.), *Measuring the Dynamics of Technological Change*, London: Pinter.

Sturgeon, T. (2000), 'Turnkey Production Networks: A New American Model of Industrial Organisation', *Working Paper*, Cambridge, MA: MIT Industrial Performance Centre.

UN (2001), *World Investment Report: Promoting Linkages 2001*, New York and Geneva: United Nations.

Westney, E.D. (1990), 'Internal and External Linkages in the MNC: The Case of R&D Subsidiaries in Japan', in C. Bartlett, Y. Doz and G. Hedlund (eds.), *Managing the Global Firm*, London and New York: Routledge.

Windrum, P. (1999), *The MERIT Report on Innovation Networks in E-commerce*, prepared for the EU TSER Programme, SEIN Workpackage 4.

Wise, R. and P. Baumgartner (1999), 'Going Downstream: The New Profit Imperative in Manufacturing', *Harvard Business Review* (September-October): 133-41.

Wu, R.-I. (2000), 'Competitiveness Analysis of Taiwan's Industrial Technology', paper presented at the *Conference on the Measurement of Industrial Technology Competitiveness in the Knowledge-Based Economy* (23-24 August), Taipei: Chung-Hua Institution for Economic Research.

Wu, R.-I., X.W. Lin and H.Y. Lin (2002), 'Moving from Foreign Technology to Indigenous Innovation: The Case of Chinese Taipei', paper presented at the OECD-IPS Workshop on *Promoting Knowledge-based Economies in Asia* (21-22 November), Singapore.

Zander, I. (1999), 'How do you Mean Global: An Empirical Investigation of Innovation Networks in the Multinational Corporation', *Research Policy*, **28**(2-3): 195-213.

11 The Changing Economic Matrix between Taiwan and China

Charles H.C. Kao and Chu-Chia Steve Lin

INTRODUCTION

As a result of the significant advancements and continuing improvements in information technology (IT) over the past two decades, along with the overall reductions in transaction costs, there has been a steady increase in multilateral trade between various countries throughout the world. These two decades have also witnessed the simultaneous establishment of several important regional economic organisations, including the European Union (EU), the North American Free Trade Area (NAFTA) agreement, Asia Pacific Economic Cooperation (APEC) and the World Trade Organisation (WTO). Clearly, these developments have led to an exponential increase in the pace of economic globalisation, and consequently, given its significant position in the world with over 1 per cent of total global trade, Taiwan cannot avoid the impacts of this overall process of globalisation.

Although still politically sensitive, there has been some convergence in the existing economic ties between Taiwan and mainland China over the past twenty years, both in terms of trade and investment. These ties will inevitably have been further strengthened by the accession of these two economies into the WTO at the beginning of 2002, which now requires significant opening up of their domestic markets both to the rest of the world and to each other. Consequently, bilateral trade and mutual investment across the Taiwan strait will also be accelerated. Although the process of economic integration between Taiwan and the rest of the world will be influenced significantly by globalisation, integration across the Strait will undoubtedly prove to be even more rapid.

The pace of international integration will have significant impacts, not only on Taiwan's short-term economic performance, but also on its economic structure over the long term. Moreover, whilst Taiwan's own economy has gone through significant restructuring, shifting from a traditional economy to an increasingly advancing high-tech economy, it will be extremely difficult for the island to deal with the impacts of simultaneous integration with both mainland China and the rest of the world, particularly during this very early stage of its WTO accession.

This chapter sets out to describe the issues facing Taiwan in the forthcoming process of integration with the rest of the world, and particularly with mainland China, including the globalisation of Taiwanese firms and their global alliances. It provides a discussion of the current economic ties across the Taiwan strait along with the opening up of the markets of Taiwan and the mainland in order to satisfy their WTO accession commitments. Finally, this chapter analyses the opportunities and challenges for Taiwan, both for the government and for the island's industries, in light of the changing process of integration with the world and with mainland China.

GLOBALISATION AND GLOBAL ALLIANCES

A number of regional economic organisations such as the EU, NAFTA, APEC and the WTO have been established as a means of promoting multilateral trade and helping to realise the comparative advantages of individual countries. The major regional economic organisations are listed in Table 11.1 by their date of establishment. The rationale behind the establishment of such vehicles for economic cooperation is the effective elimination of trade barriers and the desire to expand multilateral trade between all member nations. Within some economic organisations, certain production factors, such as labour and capital, are allowed to move freely between member countries; indeed, the European Union (EU) even went as far as adopting a common currency.

An extremely important worldwide economic organisation, the General Agreement on Tariffs and Trade (GATT), was founded in 1947 with the main purposes of reducing trade barriers and providing a forum for negotiation between member countries. After three rounds of international negotiations, which have become widely referred to as the Kennedy, Tokyo and Uruguay rounds of talks, agreement was reached over significant reductions to trading barriers on a global scale, including tariffs, import quotas, agricultural products and intellectual property rights. By the time that the GATT had been restructured and subsequently launched as the World Trade Organisation in 1995, the national treaties clause had succeeded in drastically reducing a wide range of inequalities in the treatment of different member countries during the course of their multilateral trading.

Table 11.1   Regional economic organisations

Organisations		Date of Establishment
General Agreement on Tariffs and Trade	(GATT)	1947
Organisation of Petroleum Exporting Countries	(OPEC)	1960
Organisation for Economic Cooperation and Development	(OECD)	1961
Central American Common Market	(CACM)	1961
Pacific Basin Economic Council	(PBEC)	1967
Association of South East Asian Nations	(ASEAN)	1967
Pacific Economic Cooperation Committee	(PECC)	1980
Asia Pacific Economic Cooperation	(APEC)	1989
South American Economic Cooperation Zone Moving toward a Common Market	(MERCOSUR)	1991
European Union /European Commission	(EU/EC)	1993
Common Market for Eastern and Southern Africa	(COMESA)	1993
North American Free Trade Area	(NAFTA)	1994
West African Economic and Monetary Union	(WAEMU)	1994
World Trade Organisation	(WTO)	1995

258

With these international economic organisations having put significant effort into reducing trade barriers between countries and promoting inter-industry trade, there was a corresponding rapid increase in a new form of 'intra-industrial' international trade. Whilst inter-industry trade aims to realise the so-called comparative advantages of different industries within different countries, intra-industry trade aims to bring to fruition the comparative advantages of the same industry across different countries.

Within the exponential rise in the total amount of global intra-industry trade, improvements in modern technology generally stand out as a major factor. In the high-tech industry, for example, since the whole production process is now so specialised, each production step has now become clearly distinct; therefore, the outputs of each element of the production process, including the raw materials, parts, semi-finished products and final products, can be easily separated. A further crucial factor is the drastically reduced transaction costs involved in both information and transportation, since low transaction costs are a natural result of growth in intra-industry trade. Within the production of any given high-tech product, the raw materials may be produced in Country A, whilst the constituent parts and the semi-finished products could be produced in Country B, and the finished products finally assembled in Country C. This type of vertical integration of production, in conjunction with international strategic alliances, has become very commonplace in recent years and is especially common with regard to high-tech products since they are usually relatively small in size in comparison with their high value.

Given that the high-tech industries have become much more dominant over the past twenty years, Taiwan has been experiencing a deepening process of globalisation, with the island's firms having developed closer global alliances with a great many multinational corporations (MNCs) around the world.[1] Some of the global alliances that have been established with MNCs by selected Taiwanese IC firms are shown in Table 11.2. Each firm in this table has formed strategic alliances with at least two MNCs, whilst Taiwan Semiconductor Manufacturing Corporation (TSMC) and United Microelectronics Corporation (UMC) have built up cooperative alliances with more than four.

Lin (1998) provided several reasons for the formation of such strategic alliances as well as the international integration of production by high-tech firms in Taiwan. First of all, the processes involved in high-tech product manufacturing are so specialised that even small firms have the opportunity to participate in the various stages of production. Secondly, R&D investment in the high-tech industry is so high that firms prefer to form this type of strategic alliance in order to spread out the risks involved; for Taiwanese firms, given their relatively small size, as compared to their international competitors, risk sharing is a crucial issue. Thirdly, as already noted, the costs of both the information involved in the manufacture of high-tech products, and their subsequent transportation, are very low; therefore, it is relatively easy for these MNC alliances to engage in the international integration of production. Fourthly, in most countries around the world, the protection afforded by trade barriers is invariably greatest within its high-tech industry; therefore, MNCs will tend to form such strategic alliances as a means of circumventing these trade barriers. Finally, the high-tech industry usually has a higher growth rate, which essentially means that firms can look forward to better returns; this will, in turn, facilitate much easier international cooperation.

For these reasons, amongst others, Taiwan has enjoyed very high growth in both its inter-industry and intra-industry trade, and thus, it can clearly be more profitable for the island's high-tech firms to engage in production integration and to form strategic alliances with MNCs. Clearly, as Taiwan has now become one of the newest members of the WTO, there is no doubt that the island will now start to witness a dramatic acceleration of the process of globalisation.

Table 11.2   International strategic alliances in Taiwan's IC industries

Companies	Alliance Partners
United Microelectronics Corporation (UMC)	SGS-Thomson, Thesye, MIS, Meridian
UMAX	Mitsubishi
Macronix International Corporation (MXIC)	NKK, Sanyo, MIPS
Mosel Vitelic	Oki, Fujitsu
Hualon Microelectronics Corporation	Seeg, SGS-Thomson, Tech, AIPS, DHJ, Motorola, Burr-Brown
Taiwan Semiconductor Manufacturing Corporation (TSMC)	Cirrus Logic, ISSI, AMAD, AMD
Winbond Electronics Corporation	SMC, Philips, NCR, SGS-Thomson, HP, Opus, AT&T
Nanya Plastics Corporation	Oki

Source: Lin (1998).

ECONOMIC RELATIONS ACROSS THE TAIWAN STRAIT

Cross-strait Trade and Investment

Despite the fact that protracted political tension has endured on both sides of the Taiwan strait for a number of decades, bilateral trading nevertheless took off in 1979 when mainland China started to open its doors.[2] As Table

11.3 shows, total bilateral trade across the Strait amounted to only US$460 million in 1981; however, it has since experienced a spectacular growth rate.

Table 11.3   Bilateral trade across the Taiwan strait

Unit: US$100 million

Year	Exports	Imports	Total	Taiwan's Balance of Trade with mainland China	with the Rest of the World
1981	3.8	0.8	4.6	3.0	14.2
1982	1.9	0.8	2.7	1.2	33.2
1983	2.0	0.9	2.9	1.1	48.4
1984	4.3	1.3	5.6	3.0	85.0
1985	9.7	1.2	10.9	8.5	106.2
1986	8.1	1.4	9.5	6.7	156.8
1987	12.3	2.9	15.2	9.4	187.0
1988	22.4	4.8	27.2	17.6	110.0
1989	33.3	5.9	39.2	27.4	140.4
1990	43.9	7.7	51.6	36.2	125.0
1991	74.9	11.3	86.2	63.6	133.2
1992	105.5	11.2	116.7	94.3	94.6
1993	139.9	11.0	150.9	128.9	80.3
1994	160.2	18.6	178.8	141.6	77.0
1995	194.3	30.9	225.2	163.4	81.1
1996	207.3	30.6	237.9	176.7	135.7
1997	224.6	39.2	263.8	185.4	76.6
1998	198.4	41.1	239.5	157.3	59.2
1999	213.1	45.2	258.3	167.9	109.4
2000	250.0	62.2	312.3	188.0	83.1
2001	219.5	59.0	278.5	160.4	156.6
2002	319.4	79.5	398.9	236.7	180.7
Total	2,448.8	467.5	2,916.4	1,978.3	2,273.7

Source: MAC (2003).

By 2000, bilateral trade across the Strait had reached US$31.2 billion, with Taiwanese exports to the mainland accounting for US$25 billion, whilst Taiwanese imports from the mainland accounted for the remaining US$6.2 million. Clearly, therefore, Taiwan has enjoyed a trade surplus of US$18.8 billion from mainland China in a period of just two decades. Furthermore, this figure represents the largest contribution to Taiwan's current trade surplus.[3]

There are two reasons for such rapid development in trade. First of all, Taiwan's stage of development is totally distinct from that of the mainland. In 2000, whilst Taiwan's per capita income had grown to around US$13,000, per capita income in mainland China was only around US$800. Moreover, when starting to trade internationally, each of these economies set out with its own distinctive comparative advantages; thus, there are also very clear distinctions between the industrial structures on the two sides of the Strait. Secondly, once Taiwanese investment began pouring into the mainland, a significant trade expansion effect was generated. According to Kao et al. (1992; 1995), a high proportion of Taiwanese firms in mainland China brought with them substantial amounts of raw materials, parts and even machines from their parent firms or other firms in Taiwan; therefore, the rapid growth in the total output of Taiwanese firms was also accompanied by rapid growth in the total amount of imports from Taiwan.

Two very important factors help to explain why there has been such great enthusiasm for investing in mainland China by Taiwanese firms since such investment first began in 1988. The first of these is the fact that between 1986 and 1988, the Taiwan Dollar/US Dollar exchange rate had appreciated from NT$35.5:US$1.00 to NT$28.1:US$1.00, and as a result of such drastic appreciation of the local currency, exporting firms' profits were badly eroded; nevertheless, such appreciation also made investment in mainland China correspondingly cheaper. The second factor was the abolition of martial law in 1987, and the accompanying relaxation of restrictions on citizens' visits to their homeland, which provided new opportunities for Taiwanese businessmen to invest in the mainland. According to official records held by the Investment Commission in Taiwan, there were 22,974 cases of Taiwanese investment in mainland China between 1988 and 2000, totalling US$17.1 billion (see Table 11.4); however, official records kept by the Ministry of Foreign Trade and Economic Cooperation in China suggest that there were a total of 46,624 investment projects from Taiwan over the same period, amounting to US$49.4 billion, although the realised investment amount came to only US$26.2 billion.

It should be noted that there have been significant structural changes in Taiwanese investment in the mainland since 1992. Whilst the average amount of investment has grown steadily, the nature of the industries into which investment has flowed has also shifted from labour-intensive manufacturing of items such as textile goods, clothing and footwear, to technology- intensive areas, such as the computer industry (see Table 11.5). Furthermore, the location for investment has also shifted from the Pearl River Delta (mainly the Guangdong province) to the Yangzi River Delta (mainly Jiangsu province). The reason behind such a shift has clearly been to take advantage of China's domestic market.[4]

Table 11.4 Taiwanese investment in mainland China

Unit: US$ million

Year	Approved by MOEA in Taiwan [a]			Official Data from Mainland China				
	Cases	Amount	Average Amount	Projects	Contracted Amount	Average Amount	Realised Amount	Realisation Ratio (%)
1991	237	174.16	0.73	3,446	2,783	0.81	844	30.33
1992	264	246.99	0.94	6,430	5,543	0.86	1,050	18.94
1993	1,262	1,140.37	0.90	10,948	9,965	0.91	3,139	31.50
	(8,067)[b]	(2,028.05)[b]	(0.25)[b]					
1994	934	962.21	1.03	6,247	5,395	0.86	3,391	62.85
1995	490	1,092.71	2.23	4,778	5,777	1.21	3,162	54.73
1996	383	1,229.24	3.21	3,184	5,141	1.61	3,475	67.59
1997	728	1,614.54	2.22	3,014	2,814	0.93	3,289	116.88
	(7,997)[b]	(2,719.77)[b]	(0.34)[b]					
1998	641	1,519.21	2.37	2,970	2,982	1.00	2,915	97.75
	(643)[b]	(515.41)[b]	(0.80)[b]					
1999	488	1,252.78	2.57	2,499	3,374	1.35	2,599	77.01
2000	840	2,607.14	3.10	3,108	4,042	1.30	2,296	56.81
2001	1,186	2,784.15	2.35	4,214	6,914	1.64	2,980	43.10
2002 [c]	611	1,535.88	2.51	2,179	4,363	2.00	1,924	44.09
Total	24,771	21,422.61	0.86	53,017	59,093	1.11	31,064	52.57

Notes:
[a] Prior approval is required from the MOEA (Ministry of Economic Affairs) for all investment in mainland China.
[b] Figures in parentheses represent the totals for all registered firms.
[c] Figures for 2002 are for January to June.

Source: MAC (2003).

263

Table 11.5   Taiwanese investment in mainland China, by industries and regions

Unit: US$ million

Industry	Accumulation			Region	Accumulation		
	Cases	Amount	Share (%)		Cases	Amount	Share (%)
Electronic and Electrical Appliances	4,783	8,669.86	32.58	Guangdong	9,357	8,457.87	31.78
Chemicals	1,725	1,754.64	6.59	Jiangsu	7,133	10,484.25	39.40
Basic Metals and Metal Products	2,350	2,248.16	8.45	Zhejiang	1,407	1,443.53	5.42
Plastic Products	2,332	1,895.09	7.12	Fujian	3,672	2,539.98	9.55
Food and Beverage Processing	2,328	1,491.25	5.60	Hebei	1,850	1,373.36	5.16
Textiles	1,068	976.94	3.67	Sichuan	413	329.25	1.24
Non-metallic Minerals	1,068	976.94	3.67	Hubei	433	217.95	0.82
Transportation Equipment	836	999.963	3.76	Shandon	708	475.10	1.79
Machinery Equipment	1,006	875.79	3.29	Liaoning	441	290.34	1.09
Precision Instruments	2,506	1,416.08	5.32	Hunan	265	138.27	0.52
Others	7,075	5,010.20	18.83	Others	2,038	859.89	3.23
Total	27,276	26,609.79	100.00	Total	27,276	26,609.79	100.00

Source: MAC (2001).

Production Integration and Intra-industry Trade

Taiwanese investment in mainland China has contributed to a considerable trade expansion effect; indeed more than half of the raw materials used by Taiwanese firms in the mainland throughout the early-1990s were imported from Taiwan, along with over 70 per cent of their machines (Kao et al., 1992; 1995). Although, as a result of the continuing process of localisation, the degree of dependence on Taiwan has subsequently fallen, Chiu (1996) argued that in the mid-1990s, over 40 per cent of all the raw materials used by Taiwanese firms were still being imported from Taiwan.[5] Taiwanese firms in mainland China were, nevertheless, also exporting some parts and final goods back to Taiwan, either to their parent firms or to other firms in Taiwan. It becomes readily apparent, therefore, that intra-industry trade has always been of enormous significance across the Taiwan strait. As Table 11.6 shows, at the turn of the century, five of the top ten exported commodities from Taiwan to mainland China were related to the information industry (HS codes 8542, 8541, 8540, 8473 and 8471), and as Table 11.7 shows, seven of the top ten commodities reciprocally imported from mainland China to Taiwan were also related to the same industry (HS codes 8542, 8504, 8537, 8541, 8517, 8473 and 8471).

In addition to cross-strait intra-industry trade, there is a further indicator demonstrating the close economic relationship existing between Taiwan and mainland China. As can be seen from Table 11.6, the electronics and electrical industry accounts for 28.0 per cent of total investment from Taiwan into the mainland; the table also shows that Taiwanese investment is concentrated in the Guangdong and Jiangsu region, with the former accounting for 35.11 per cent of total investment and the latter accounting for 35.25 per cent. A combination of these two figures demonstrates that in terms of the production and exportation of electronic and electrical goods, Guangdong and Jiangsu are the two main sources in mainland China.[6]

The Impacts on Taiwan

Taiwan has been feeling the economic impact from bilateral trade across the strait for two decades although several of the indicators are positive. For example, the increase in exports to China has expanded the island's production, employment opportunities and income levels. The mainland China market not only provides Taiwan with a huge trade surplus, but also helps to explain why Taiwan was able to weather the storm of the Asian financial crisis in 1997. Without the support of this market, Taiwan may well have suffered devastating effects similar to those felt by most Asian countries during that turbulent period.

Table 11.6 Taiwan's top ten export commodities to mainland China

Units: US$ million

HS Code	Description of Goods	Amount			Ranking		
		2001	2000	1999	2001	2000	1999
8542	Other integrated circuits and micro assemblies	2,134.49	2,084.11	1,345.97	1	1	1
8473	Machine parts and accessories	816.14	821.32	709.96	2	2	2
3903	Polymers of styrene, in primary forms	479.24	558.62	376.62	3	3	6
5903	Other fabrics of cotton, impregnated, coated, covered or laminated with polyurethane	475.92	511.53	563.12	4	5	3
5407	Woven fabrics or synthetic textile materials	452.89	519.54	490.07	5	4	4
7219	Flat-rolled products of stainless steel, hot-rolled in coils	377.57	344.82	228.32	6	7	10
8471	Automatic data processing machines and other readers	316.43	319.38	230.73	7	8	9
8540	Parts of cathode-ray tubes and photo-cathode tubes	282.93	397.83	383.63	8	6	5
4104	Bovine leather, without hair on, vegetable pre-tanned	259.48	257.25	293.02	9	10	7
8541	Diodes, transistors and semiconductor devices	245.14	274.30	216.01	10	9	11

Source: BOIT (2001).

Table 11.7 Taiwan's top ten import commodities from mainland China

Units: US$ million

HS Code	Description of Goods	Amount			Ranking		
		2001	2000	1999	2001	2000	1999
8542	Other integrated circuits and micro assemblies	266.15	270.65	304.34	1	2	1
8504	Transformers and static converters	248.66	219.77	217.70	2	3	2
2701	Coal, briquettes, voids and similar solid fuels manufactured from coal	212.35	90.56	93.50	3	8	6
8473	Machine parts and accessories	196.59	164.03	180.49	4	5	3
8536	Switches and protective relays	159.71	164.43	115.23	5	4	4
8541	Diodes, transistors and semiconductor devices	147.16	160.63	110.26	6	6	5
7207	Semi-finished products of iron or non-alloy steel	127.89	275.11	87.14	7	1	7
8471	Automatic data processing machines and other readers	123.86	86.42	54.82	8	9	10
7108	Gold (including platinum plated gold)	71.39	122.72	61.98	9	7	9
8517	Line telephone sets and telegraphic apparatus	71.32	53.19	39.72	10	13	13

Source: BOIT (2001).

Furthermore, since most labour-intensive firms had already moved out of Taiwan to the mainland, Taiwan's economy was able to shift towards greater capital and technology intensity. Whilst those firms staying in Taiwan were more capital intensive, labour productivity became a much greater consideration than ever before. Moreover, the share of GDP provided by the service sector began to increase as soon as Taiwanese firms began investing in mainland China, since most of the departing firms were in the manufacturing sector. As the manufacturing sector declined, more workers were released, and although some of these managed to find jobs in other manufacturing firms (mainly capital-intensive and high-tech firms) most of them were able to find alternative employment in the service sector.[7]

The process of globalisation has also been hastened for parent firms in Taiwan. Not only does investment in mainland China represent direct investment outside of Taiwan, it also provides significant opportunities for these investing firms to grow into MNCs themselves. As the costs of both land and labour are much lower in China than in Taiwan, most Taiwanese firms have built much larger plants on the mainland than they had previously been able to establish in Taiwan, and some of these have grown so rapidly that they have already achieved MNC status. For instance, Po-Cheng has become a major footwear producer (mainly for Nike), Giant (Geu-Da) is a leading bicycle producer and President (Tong-Yi) has a strong foothold in the food products sector.

There are also, of course, consequences arising from cross-strait bilateral trade, the first of which is the fact that such investment in the mainland has increased the island's economic dependency upon the mainland Chinese market. In 2000, Taiwan's exports to the mainland market amounted to 16.9 per cent of the island's total exports, a point which gives rise to considerable concern amongst some commentators in Taiwan.[8] A further consequence is that as the manufacturing sector continues to shrink, greater numbers of unskilled workers will become unemployed. Whilst some of these unemployed workers will be able to find jobs in other capital-intensive firms, or within the service sector, there will still be a great many workers who will find themselves unemployed, or indeed, unemployable.

THE ACCESSION OF TAIWAN AND MAINLAND CHINA INTO THE WTO

In November 2001, Taiwan and mainland China were officially accepted as new members of the WTO but whilst they are both provided with greater trading opportunities than had previously been available, they also have to open up their domestic markets, and clearly, they are going to be faced with strong external competition. Moreover, there are also going to be drastic changes in the economic relationship across the Strait with the products of Taiwanese firms in mainland China facing heavy competition both in the global markets and in China's domestic market.

The governments of both sides have already made significant changes to their laws and trade policies to satisfy WTO regulations, and are required to make continuing adjustments in order to align themselves with all WTO regulations. Although Taiwan was admitted into the WTO as a developed economy, there will, nevertheless, be no significant impact from changes to its domestic laws and trade policies because Taiwan has been following the rules of the game as a world member for quite some time. On the other hand, mainland China's economy has been opened up for only twenty years and even though it has been admitted to the WTO as a developing economy, it is likely to struggle with the significant changes required to its laws and trade policies.

Concessions by Taiwan

In addition to the opening up of its domestic agricultural and service sectors, Taiwan has also agreed to reduce import tariffs on a wide range of products, affecting around 3,470 current import tariffs, with the average tariffs being reduced from the current 6.3 per cent, to a final target of 4.3 per cent. For certain products, such as iron and steel, medical equipment, timber, agricultural machinery and construction equipment, import tariffs will be reduced to zero, whilst the import duty on automobiles will be reduced to 17.5 per cent. An appropriate government apparatus will have to be established with all government procurement purchases being completely opened up to other WTO members. The government will simplify the examination procedure for imports and change its national standards in order to make them compatible with international standards.

Generally speaking, whilst the impact on the manufacturing sector should be relatively small, the agricultural sector has traditionally been less competitive and is therefore feeling the full brunt of external competition. The financial and 'other services' sectors are also facing stiff competition; indeed, there are some overall concerns as to how all of these sectors will respond to the new pressure.

Concessions by Mainland China

In order to be eligible for WTO membership, mainland China has made a great many promises and agreements to changes, although the requirements for mainland China are lower than those for Taiwan. In China's manufacturing sector, the average import tariff will be reduced from 24.6 per cent in 1997, to 9.4 per cent by 2005. The import tariffs on information products will be reduced to zero; for timber, paper products and chemical products to 5 per cent; and for automobiles and parts to 10 per cent. Furthermore, import inspection and national standards will be aligned with international standards, and rights to both domestic sales and exports will be open to foreign firms within three years.

In the service sector, the major agreements on the domestic market and distribution channels include: (i) US firms will retain all of their domestic sales rights; (ii) US firms can establish their own independent distribution channels; and (iii) the restrictions on distribution channel auxiliary services will gradually be removed.

In the telecommunications sector, the major agreements include: (i) foreign firms will be free to choose any form of technology in the provision of their telecommunications services; (ii) the limit on foreign investment holdings in telecommunications will be set at 49 per cent ownership in the beginning, rising eventually to a holding limit of 50 per cent; and (iii) selected cities will open up their telecommunications market to foreign firms in the first year with other cities following suit within three years.

In financial services, the major agreements include: (i) the life insurance and reinsurance sector will be opened up in the first year with other insurance services being opened up four years later; (ii) foreign banks will be able to set up branches in twenty-four cities during the first year; however, RMB-related services will not be permitted for two years; banking services will be opened up to foreign firms with no restrictions five years thereafter; and (iii) the transaction seat for B-type stocks will be opened up first, followed by the opening up of the transaction seat for A-type stocks within three years.

With its relatively low wage levels, mainland China's manufacturing goods are extremely competitive in the world market; therefore, the impact on the manufacturing sector may be of minor significance, or at least bearable. However, the service sector will be faced with stiff competition because of its level of inefficiency, resulting in potential rises in unemployment and bankruptcy levels. According to estimates by the US International Trade Commission, the impact on mainland China's economy as a direct result of WTO accession will be as follows: The country's economic growth rate will increase by 4.1 per cent, with exports increasing by 12.2 per cent and imports up by 14.3 per cent. Meanwhile, 9.6 million farmers will have to switch to other sectors, whilst 598,000 workers in the automobile industry and 582,000 workers in the machinery industry will become unemployed.[9]

Although the short-run impacts on the Chinese economy will be largely negative, average productivity levels within the service sector will grow rapidly in the long run, since foreign firms will no doubt bring in new managerial and information skills. Accession will also attract more foreign investment and through the required adjustments to its domestic laws to meet WTO requirements, a modernised sector will emerge in China.

The Impact on Taiwanese Firms in Mainland China

Taiwanese firms operating in mainland China will feel a number of positive impacts from the country's accession into the WTO. First of all, these firms will be able to expand their exports, simply because, as the world market will open up to mainland China, it will thus also be available to Taiwanese firms operating there. Moreover, since mainland China's domestic market will be opened up to foreign firms, it will, of course, also be open to Taiwanese firms whose operations may previously have been mainly export-oriented. As a result, we could expect to see more Taiwanese firms investing in mainland China in the future. However, since they are likely to face severe competition from MNCs, these firms may be reluctant to expand too soon. Secondly, Taiwanese businessmen could benefit greatly once legal reform takes place in mainland China, as they may no longer have to put significant effort into building up personal relationships with government officials. Thirdly, Taiwanese firms will enjoy better protections under WTO regulations, since no investment protection agreement currently exists between Taiwan and mainland China.

There are, on the other hand, two distinct disadvantages. First of all, under the new legal system, it will be more difficult for Taiwanese firms to gain benefits from rent-seeking behaviour, such as reliance on personal favours from government officials. Secondly, under the new clause of national treatment, certain special treatments, which had previously been provided for political reasons, will no longer be available to Taiwanese firms.

CONCLUSIONS

The Challenges and Responses in the Twenty-first Century

During the past two decades, Taiwan has experienced significant structural change, shifting from a labour-intensive economy towards a more capital- and technology-intensive economy. Consequently, in order to obtain more advanced technology and to share the investment risks, Taiwanese high-tech firms have been building up strong business alliances with foreign MNCs. At the same time, huge numbers of Taiwanese firms (estimated to be at least 40,000) have poured into mainland China, investing in almost every coastal city and in every industry imaginable. Such a move has turned out to be a very wise and crucial step towards becoming MNCs themselves.

WTO membership is an encouraging development for both Taiwan and mainland China with one of the immediate impacts being the requirement for the opening up of these two economies. Both are going to be faced with new opportunities as well as strong challenges. For Taiwanese firms, these opportunities and challenges are even greater since, in addition to competing with international MNCs, they will also have to deal with new policies on both sides of the Taiwan strait. Simply having secured a place in this important global trading body represents an enormous diplomatic success for Taiwan; however, whilst WTO membership will provide the island with a forum for settling international trade disputes, the opening up of its domestic market could well increase unemployment in the short run, a very undesirable situation for Taiwan at the present time.

Whether knowingly, or otherwise, mainland China has provided a considerable amount of assistance to Taiwan's economy; indeed, having accounted for more than US$140 billion in trade surplus over the past twenty years, it represents the single largest contributor to Taiwan's overall trade surplus. At the same time, the sheer magnitude of China's domestic market has also provided Taiwanese firms with an important stage in their operational enlargement, leading to increased efficiency, which has in turn resulted in Taiwanese firms becoming more competitive.

For Taiwan's government, the most appropriate and intelligent responses to these opportunities and challenges should be very clear. Since globalisation and openness are here to stay, the best way is to accept them unconditionally and to adapt to them accordingly. The economic matrix between Taiwan and mainland China will be an extremely perplexing issue for Taiwan in the years ahead, and the most productive response from the Taiwanese government would be to ponder how best to use mainland China's abundant labour resources to boost Taiwan's economy, and how best to use the mainland's domestic market in order to establish Taiwan as an operations centre or a logistics centre both for Taiwanese firms and for international MNCs. The strategy must be to utilise, not to ignore, mainland China's resources. In order to attract foreign MNCs and to get them to consider Taiwan as an operations or logistics centre, Taiwan must strive to make itself as accessible as possible, emphasising free trade and opening up its financial and transportation services market, both to the world and to mainland China. Such openness is the only feasible way of securing a win-win scenario for all parties concerned.

NOTES

[1] Intra-industry trade between Taiwan and mainland China is of even greater significance given the huge amount of investment moving from Taiwan into the mainland.

[2] At the same time that the US suspended diplomatic relations with Taiwan in 1979, it also established formal relations with mainland China.

[3] The total trade surplus for Taiwan for the year 2000 alone was US$8.3 billion.

[4] When Taiwanese firms first began investing in mainland China, in 1988, four Chinese cities, Shenzhen, Xiamen, Zuhia and Shentou, were selected as special economic zones (SEZs). In June 1990, when Pudong in Shanghai was also nominated as an SEZ, Taiwanese firms subsequently started to move into Shanghai, along with many MNCs. With China developing its great western regions from 2001 onwards, under its tenth five-year plan, we can expect to see Taiwanese firms increasing their investment in these areas.

[5] Some subsidiaries were still bringing in materials and machinery from their parent firms in Taiwan, whilst others were purchasing supplies from other firms on the island.

[6] The Electronics and Electrical Association of Taiwan has estimated that around 72 per cent of all electronic and electrical goods exported from mainland China to the rest of the world are in fact contributed by Taiwanese firms.

[7] Some of them, mainly the elderly and less well-educated workers, did lose their jobs and were unable to find alternative gainful employment. Further comment on this point is made later in this section.

[8] However, the share of imports from mainland China amounted to only 4.4 per cent of Taiwan's total imports. The total balance of trade with mainland China amounts to 10.8 per cent in favour of Taiwan.

[9] See Tsay (2000).

REFERENCES

BOIT (2001), *Quarterly Journal of International Trade Forecasting*, Vol.20, Taipei: Bureau of International Trade, Ministry of Economic Affairs, p.48.

Chen, L.I. (2000), *An Investigation of MNCs Investment and Production Integration across the Taiwan Strait*, Taipei: Chung-Hua Institution for Economic Research.

Chiu, S.C. (1996), 'A Study of the Interdependent Relationship across the Taiwan Strait', *Industry of Free China*, Council for Economic Planning and Development, pp.17-41.

Kao, C. (2000), 'Manufacturing Industry Investment in Mainland China and the Production Integration Strategy across the Taiwan Strait', paper presented at the CIER Conference on the Economic Development of Mainland China, Taipei: Chung-Hua Institution for Economic Research.

Kao, C.H.C., J.S. Lee and C.-C. Lin (1992), *An Empirical Study of Taiwan Investment in Mainland China*, Taipei: Commonwealth Publishing Co.

Kao, C.H.C., C.-C. Lin, C. Hsu and W. Lin (1995), *The Taiwanese Investment Experience in Mainland China: A First-hand Report*, Taipei: Commonwealth Publishing Co.

Lin, C.-C. (1996), 'Production Integration and Foreign Direct Investment: An Empirical Study across the Taiwan Strait', in J.S. Lee (ed.), *The Emergence of the South China Growth Triangle*, (chapter 7), pp.153-70, Taipei: Chung-Hua Institution for Economic Research.

Lin, C.-C. (1998), 'A Study of International Division of Labour of High-Tech Industry of Taiwan: The Case of the IC Industry', paper presented at the First International Conference on High-Tech Human Resource Management, held at the Graduate Institute of Human Resources, National Central University, Taiwan.

Lin, C.-C. (2001a), 'Globalisation and Economic Policies across the Taiwan Strait', Mimeo, National Policy Foundation.

Lin, C.-C. (2001b), 'WTO and Economic Perspective across the Taiwan Strait', Mimeo, National Policy Foundation.

MAC (2001) *Cross-Strait Economic Statistics Monthly*, No.105, Taipei: Mainland Affairs Council.

MAC (2003) *Cross-Strait Economic Statistics Monthly*, No.125, Taipei: Mainland Affairs Council.

Tsay, H.M. (2000), 'Mainland China's Economic Reform and Its Impact on Bilateral Trade across the Taiwan Strait', paper presented at the CIER Conference on the Economic Development of Mainland China, Taipei: Chung-Hua Institution for Economic Research.

Index

275